Superchefs

SIGNATURE RECIPES
FROM AMERICA'S
NEW ROYALTY

Superchefs

SIGNATURE RECIPES
FROM AMERICA'S
NEW ROYALTY

Karen Gantz Zahler

JOHN WILEY & SONS, INC.

NEW YORK   CHICHESTER   BRISBANE   TORONTO   SINGAPORE

PUBLISHER: Peggy Burns
SENIOR EDITOR: Claire Thompson
MANAGING EDITOR: Diana Cisek
EDITORIAL ASSISTANT AND PHOTOGRAPHY COORDINATOR: Maria Colletti
FOOD STYLING: Dwayne LiPuma and James Henderson
TEXT DESIGN AND COMPOSITION: Laura Ierardi, LCI Design

Photography by Susan Goldman
Photograph on page 119 by Rick Laakkonen and Gozen Koshida

Library of Congress Cataloging in Publication Data:
Zahler, Karen Gantz
        Superchefs: signature recipes from America's new royalty / Karen
    Gantz Zahler
            p. cm.
        Includes index.
        ISBN 0-471-14751-6 (alk. paper)
            1. Cookery, American.   2. Cooks—United States.   I. Title.
    TX715.Z2797   1996
    641.5973—dc20   96-1336

Printed in the United States of America

10   9   8   7   6   5   4   3   2   1

TO ERIC, BENJAMIN AND ARIEL—
THE GREATEST PASSIONS IN MY LIFE.

Contents

"The truth is one must be inspired to cook.
For you know, we always learn from others
and end up teaching ourselves."

JAMES BEARD

Karen Gantz Zahler and several of the Superchefs featured in this book.
Left to right, Rick Laakkonen, Jody Adams, Joyce Goldstein, Wayne Nish, Brad Steelman,
Gale Gand, and Anne Rosenzweig.

Preface

Today's American chefs have brought North America decisively into the global culinary arena. Their cross-cultural heritages enable them to use the best aspects of classic and ethnic cooking and blend them with American regional ingredients to create a distinctive cuisine.

This coming of age of American cuisine is greatly indebted to people from all corners of the world who have come to these shores over the years, bringing with them exotic, often indigenous approaches to cooking, not to mention ingredients that reward our palates and extend our culinary horizons. The U.S. Immigration Act of 1965, for example, has opened the floodgates for hundreds of thousands of Asian, Latin American, and Caribbean people to the United States. The Immigration Act of 1990 has brought an explosion of immigrants, particularly Chinese, Southeast Asian, Russian, South American, and Indian. In New York City alone, over 100,000 immigrants have been entering the marketplace annually. These waves of immigration explain why our relationship to tradition is different from that of other classic cuisines. Although many contemporary American chefs are trained in French culinary techniques, they depart from those Eurocentric models and borrow freely elsewhere to create distinctly American dishes that have won universal acceptance.

As a result, America's food today reflects our changing sense of cultural identity. Root vegetables were once déclassé, while the more carefully cultivated asparagus was considered aristocratic. Corn and grains, considered readily available peasant food, are venerated. Foods do not carry the social connotations they used to. The once humble roots and grains are now celebrated. Contemporary, ingredient-driven American cuisine stresses the intrinsic properties of food as in David Burke's Blini with Salmon and Horseradish Crème Fraîche at New York City's Park Avenue Cafe. Bite into the pancake and you taste the crunch of fresh kernels of corn that give the dish its special character. Chef Burke is particularly fond of corn, and many of his dishes feature this ancient grain.

Classical relationships between foods and sauces are no longer rigidly observed. There are new, different ways of combining foods. The great chefs in *Superchefs* excel at crossing those boundaries, while still respecting the integrity of the food. The genius of the contemporary superchefs is in knowing just how far to go with their experimentation. Innovative American chefs also present food in new, flavorful ways. Todd English at Boston's Olives constructs an Italian-inspired towering mushroom, tomato, and onion torte sandwiched with crêpes and mascarpone, and drizzled with a porcini essence. Herb- and vegetable-flavored oils, popularized by New York City's Jean-Georges Vongerichten, are being emulated and marketed widely, offering numerous varieties for discerning palates.

Douglas Rodriguez, formerly of Miami's Yuca and currently at Patria, in New York City, uses Caribbean and Latino ingredients such as plantain and boniato, and presents his dishes in a bold, architectural manner. He has forged a new Latin culture in American food with creations resplendent with color, shape, and taste.

California chefs, with relative proximity to Asia, were the first to experiment with Eastern flavors. They crusade for the freshness of food, and favor raw fish, crunchy vegetables, rice vinegars, and sesame oils. They highlight their foods with ginger, wasabi, or soy sauce. Barbara Tropp, of San Francisco's China Moon, brings California influences to Chinese cuisine. Her intriguing Strange Flavor Eggplant is a case in point. Because of its pungency, a stunning American aubergine is used instead of the Chinese or Japanese eggplant variety. The American eggplant combines with such Asian spices as ginger and scallions to forge a Californian-Asian delicacy.

The American chefs' approach is clearly global. The absence of boundaries and the blending of influences create fusion cooking at its best. Wayne Nish's cosmopolitan East-meets-West menu boasts of dazzling flavors. His Baby Clams in Light Broth with Sake produce a beguiling taste. His Beggar's Purses with Lobster and Black Truffles are, in Nish's words, "a fantasy for all the senses."

No longer do American kitchens rely solely on European, Asian, and South American products. While respecting the integrity of their products, American farmers cater to today's more discerning food market. The wild mushroom industry now racks up $50 million in annual sales. Chanterelles and white truffles are a boon for Oregon foragers. Washington State provides our woodsy conical morels. Lobsters are spawned in Maine. Kiwis, once imported from New Zealand, are bountiful in California, as is that beautiful Mediterranean thistle, the artichoke. Duck ranchers in New York's Catskill Mountains and Hudson Valley, as well as California's Sonoma Valley produce a rich yet tender foie gras. The preeminent supplier of game and foie gras reports proudly that of the 3,300 foie-gras-yielding ducks slaughtered each week for the American market, 75 percent come from New York State.

Another defining aspect of the contemporary American chef is the visual composition of culinary tableaux. Chefs are devoted to the artistic as well as the gustatory appeal of their creations. As a result, the spatial quality of food and three-dimensional architectural designs have become an additional asset of tables in fine restaurants. At Kaspar's in Seattle, Kaspar Donier highlights his Dungeness Crab Sushi with Sesame Dressing by presenting the crab roll slices wrapped in toasted seaweed with Belgian endive leaves standing upright on the plate. Adding to the plate's decor is a confetti of finely diced peppers, zucchini, and carrots. Dinnerware, too, is designed for visual appreciation. Chefs today bring a broad variety of background influences to their artistry. In fact, Anne Rosenzweig of New York City's Arcadia was an anthropology student. Wayne Nish of March studied architecture, and Mark Miller of Santa Fe's Coyote Cafe and Washington, D.C.'s Red Sage was an archaeology student.

Women restaurant operators and executive chefs have given this traditionally male-dominated field healthy competition. Women now represent 15 percent of chefs nationwide. For the first time in its 15-year history, the American Culinary Federation has elected a certified executive chef as its first female president. Not only have women helped improve working conditions of employment, they have also modified the grueling hours and are steadily challenging the hierarchy to promote genderless leadership roles in the field. As Executive Chef Elka Gilmore of Kokachin in New York, and formerly owner of Elka's and Liberté in San Francisco, reported in Nation's Restaurant News, "My entrepreneurial spirit has always been one of my strengths. It really is creative freedom. That's what I wanted all my life, that ultimate creative freedom to cook the way I like, to operate the business in the fashion that I like, to make it a place where I want to be." Emily Luchetti, former pastry chef at San Francisco's Stars, Chairman of the International Association of Women Chefs and Restaurateurs, explains the difference as one of management style and participation in the kitchen. Her organization has over 1,100 members.

Chefs of the nineties, long confined to behind-the-scenes roles, are increasingly escaping not only their profession's traditional mold but their kitchens as well. Many own and manage several restaurants, shuttling back and forth. They write cookbooks, demonstrate recipes on their own television programs, organize cooking schools, and promote products. Some even lecture at colleges and make celebrity appearances in television commercials. They have gone far beyond simply being chefs to being superchefs and superstars.

Twenty-five years ago, chefs' names were largely unknown. Relatively few prominent restaurateurs were celebrities. But chefs are now taking center stage. They are becoming increasingly newsworthy personalities. Alice Waters, of Chez Panisse in Berkeley, California, made the integrity of ingredients a *cause célèbre*. She wrote numerous articles and cookbooks, lectured extensively, and demonstrated her foods at celebrity benefits. Rozanne Gold gained recognition as chef to New York's Mayor Koch in the eighties and went on to become chef of The Rainbow Room and subsequently a restaurant consultant. Her signature Venetian wine cake is a favorite at specialty shops.

Wolfgang Puck owns five fine dining restaurants and 20 casual dining cafes. He lectures, write cookbooks, and appears in television commercials and on network programs. His renowned Spago restaurant has progeny from Los Angeles to Chicago, Las Vegas, Mexico, and Tokyo. His California pizzas studded with sun-dried tomatoes and basil and a wide variety of other pizzas and pastas sell in supermarkets nationwide. His culinary empire has expanded to include the packaging of salads and dressings.

David Burke, also a television personality, markets his trademark salmon pastrami to specialty food stores from coast to coast. Mark Miller owns four Southwestern restaurants in Washington, D.C., Las Vegas, and Austin, Texas, and three contemporary Asian cuisine bistros in Washington, D.C. and San Francisco. An innovator of contemporary Southwestern cuisine, Miller has educated people about the diversity and complexity of chilies. He rates chilies, has authored five cookbooks, and has a booming gourmet store business, marketing bottled Southwestern delicacies such as fire-roasted salsa and chipotle hot sauce, and his "Coyote Cucina" line of Southwestern specialties. Emeril Lagasse of New Orleans has a cooking show, "The Essence of Emeril," on the TV Food Network. He has written two cookbooks, has a namesake restaurant, Emeril's, and markets "Essence," his trademark seasoning salt, nationwide. All of these chefs participate regularly in fund-raising events and national organizations feeding the homeless, infirm, and elderly such as City Meals on Wheels and Share Our Strength. Moreover, the culinary arts are celebrated annually at their own "Oscar Award" evening of entertainment and presentations by the James Beard Foundation.

Several years ago, I wrote *Taste of New York*, to unlock the closely guarded secrets of New York's star chefs and share them with readers and culinary enthusiasts. I had the privilege of cooking with the great chefs who appeared in the book, and learned from them the special techniques that make their creations so extraordinary. Thus inspired, I decided to go national with my culinary adventure to share with you the techniques of North America's most renowned contemporary chefs.

Our American chefs are clearly superstars, contributing triumphantly, not only to our gastronomic legacy, but also to the richness of our culture. Their dedication to the integrity of their art adds a vital dimension both to our heritage and our quality of life. *Superchefs: Signature Dishes from America's New Royalty* is a tribute to their incomparable artistry.

Karen Gantz Zahler

Acknowledgments

Superchefs was written because *Taste of New York* had such a broad group of fans who wanted to recreate signature recipes in their homes. *Superchefs* is devoted to innovative American chefs on a national scale. I am indebted to my readers for their enthusiasm.

First, let me convey my deepest respect for the culinary artistry of superstar David Burke, who generously donated his talent and kitchen, enabling me to test the recipes for this book. Dan Budd, Jim Henderson and Dwayne LiPuma, not to mention Steve Purmail and Brad Steelman, challenged my culinary skills and were available at the crack of dawn, welcoming me with open arms. Dwayne and Jimmy exhibited rare culinary acumen and agility in food styling the dishes for the photo shoots. For giving my book panache, I wish to thank Nurit Kahane and Kenneth Alpert, who provided the more sumptuous settings and good taste to accessorize *Superchefs*.

I am deeply grateful to all the chefs represented in the book for their tireless efforts in working methodically with me so that I was able to present the best of contemporary American cuisine.

I am most thankful to the James Beard Foundation for allowing me to observe, interview, and assist guest chefs as they demonstrated their regional cuisines; I am no less indebted to Tim Zagat for his access to restaurant data.

On a personal note, for his illuminating insights and encouragement, I wish to thank my devoted husband Eric, who helped convince me that I could be a home entertainer, lawyer, literary agent, mother, community activist, and author.

My mother, Pat Gantz, was her punctilious self in her interest in every detail of the book and an anchor for all I do; for her editorial input and confidence and that of my father Manny, I am forever grateful.

The book reflects the invaluable literary insights of Steve Honigman, Bella Brodski and Laura Baddish. My gratitude to Lillibeth Miranda and Renee Yarzig for their typing agility.

As always, I am devoted to Michael Hall, publicist par excellence, for his acumen in discerning that superchefs today are indeed America's emerging royalty.

Special thanks to Leon Jacobson for his unwavering support and editorial input. He reminded me, as Shakespeare so aptly taught, that "brevity is the soul of wit."

I particularly want to thank my editor, Claire Thompson, at John Wiley & Sons, who championed my book and had the commitment and faith that *Superchefs* would enhance the culinary marketplace of ideas.

KAREN GANTZ ZAHLER

Superchefs and their Restaurants

JODY ADAMS
Rialto at the Charles Hotel
1 Bennett Street
Cambridge, MA 02138
(617) 661-5050

FRANCESCO
ANTONUCCI
Remi Restaurant
145 West 53rd Street
New York, NY 10019
(212) 581-4242

ED BROWN
Sea Grill
19 West 49th Streeet
New York, NY 10020
(212) 332-7610

JEFFREY BUBEN
Vidalia
1990 M. Street, N.W.
Washington, DC 20036
(202) 659-1990

DAN BUDD
Culinary Institute of America
433 Albany Post Road
Hyde Park, New York 12538
(914) 452-9600

DAVID BURKE
Park Avenue Cafe
100 East 63rd Street
New York, NY 10021
(212) 644-1900

PATRICK CLARK
Tavern on the Green
Central Park West
& 67th Street
New York, NY 10023
(212) 873-3200

JIM COHEN
The Phoenician Resort
6000 East Camelback Road
Scottsdale, AZ 85251
(602) 941-8200, ext. 2738

JIM COLEMAN
Treetops
210 West Rittenhouse Square
Philadelphia, PA 19103
(215) 546-9000

BRUCE COOPER
Jake's
24365 Main Street
Manayunk, PA 19127
(215) 483-0444

SANFORD D'AMATO
Sanford
1547 N. Jackson Street
Milwaukee, WI 53202
(414) 276-9608

ANDY D'AMICO
Sign of the Dove
1110 Third Avenue
New York, NY 10021
(212) 861-8080

KASPAR DONIER
Kaspar's
19 West Harrison
Seattle, WA 98119
(206) 298-0123

TODD ENGLISH
Olives
10 City Square
Charleston, MA 02129
(617) 242-1999

DEAN FEARING
The Mansion on Turtle
Creek
2821 Turtle Creek Boulevard
Dallas, TX 75219
(214) 559-2100

SUSAN FENIGER
Border Grill
1445 4th Street
Santa Monica, CA 90401
(310) 451-1655

MICHAEL FOLEY
Printer's Row
550 S. Dearborn Street
Chicago, IL 60605
(312) 461-0780

TED FONDULAS
Hemingway's
Route 4
Killington, VT 05751
(802) 422-3886

GALE GAND
Brasserie T
305 South Happ Road
Northfield, IL 60093
(847) 446-0444

CHRISTOPHER GARGONE
Remi Restaurant
145 West 53rd Street
New York, NY 10019
(212) 581-4242

VICTOR GIELISSE
Gielisse's CFI
(Culinary Fast Track)
6642 Garlinghouse Lane
Dallas, TX 75252
(214) 964-7757

ELKA GILMORE
Kokachin
21 East 52nd Street
New York, NY 10022
(212) 355-9300

KEVIN GRAHAM
Graham's
20 Magazine Street
New Orleans, LA 70130
(504) 524-9678

CHRISTOPHER GROSS
Christopher's
Biltmore Financial Center
2398 East Camelback Road
Phoenix, AZ 85016
(602) 957-3214

VINCENT GUERITHAULT
Vincent Guerithault on
Camelback
3930 East Camelback Road
Phoenix, AZ 85018
(602) 224-0225

GORDON HAMERSLEY
Hamersley's Bistro
553 Tremont Street
Boston, MA 02116
(617) 423-2700

TODD HUMPHRIES
Campton Place
Kempinski Hotel
340 Stockton Street
San Francisco, CA 94108
(415) 781-5555

JOHANNE KILLEEN
Al Forno
577 South Main Street
Providence, RI 02903
(401) 273-9767

BOB KINKEAD
Kinkead's
2000 Pennsylvania Avenue
Washington, DC 20006
(202) 296-7700

MARTIN KOUPRIE
Jump Cafe
2706-33 Wood Street
Toronto, Ontario M4Y 2P8
(416) 591-9221

GRAY KUNZ
Lespinasse
2 East 55th Street
New York, NY 10022
(212) 339-6719

RICK LAAKKONEN
The River Cafe
1 Water Street (East River)
Brooklyn, NY 11201
(718) 522-5200

EMERIL LAGASSE
Emeril's
800 Tchoupitoulas Street
New Orleans, LA 70130
(504) 528-9393

SUSAN MCCREIGHT
LINDEBERG
Morrison-Clark Inn
1015 L. Street, N.W.
Washington, DC 20001
(202) 898-1200

EMILY LUCHETTI
Chairwoman
International Association of
Women Chefs and
Restaurateurs
1010 Sutter Street
San Francisco, CA 94104
(415) 362-7336

WALDY MALOUF
The Rainbow Room
GE Building
30 Rockefellar Plaza
New York, NY 10112
(212) 632-5700

JACK MCDAVID
Jack's Firehouse
2130 Fairmount Avenue
Philadelphia, PA 19130
(215) 232-9000

ANDREW MCLAUGHLIN
Charlie Trotters
816 West Armitage Avenue
Chicago, IL 60614
(312) 248-6228

MARK MILETELLO
Mark's Place
2286 N.E. 123rd Street
North Miami, FL 33181
(305) 893-6888

MARK MILLER
Coyote Cafe
132 W. Water Street
Santa Fe, NM 87501
(505) 983-1615

MARK MILLER
Red Sage
605 14th Street, N.W.
Washington, DC 20005
(202) 638-4444

MARY SUE MILLIKEN
Border Grill
1445 4th Street
Santa Monica, CA 90401
(310) 451-1655

EMILY MOORE
Sweet Lips
8980 University Center Lane
San Diego, CA 92122
(619) 587-4600

WAYNE NISH
March
405 East 58th Street
New York, NY 10022
(212) 838-9393

PATRICK O'CONNELL
The Inn at Little Washington
Middle and Main Street
P.O. Box 300
Washington, VA 22747
(703) 675-3800

NANCY OAKES
Boulevard
1 Mission at Stewart
San Francisco, CA 94105
(415) 535-6084

BRADLEY OGDEN
Lark Creek Inn
234 Magnolia Avenue
Larkspur, CA 94939
(415) 924-7766

CHARLES PALMER
Aureole
34 East 61st Street
New York, NY 10021
(212) 319-1660

MARK PEEL
Campanile
624 S. La Brea Avenue
Los Angeles, CA 90036
(213) 938-1447

BRIAN POLCYN
Acadia
3880 Lapeer Road
Auburn Hills, MI 48326
(810) 373-7330

WOLFGANG PUCK
Chinois on Main
2709 Main Street
Santa Monica, CA 90405
(310) 392-9025

WOLFGANG PUCK
Postrio
Prescott Hotel
545 Post Street
San Francisco, CA 94102
(415) 776-7825

WOLFGANG PUCK
Spago
1114 Horn Avenue
West Hollywood, CA 90069
(310) 652-4025

STEPHAN PYLES
Star Canyon
3102 Oak Lawn Avenue
Dallas TX 75219
(214) 520-7827

MICHEL RICHARD
Citrus
6703 Melrose Avenue
Los Angeles, CA 90038
(213) 857-0034

DOUGLAS RODRIGUEZ
Patria
250 Park Avenue South
New York, NY 10003
(212) 777-6211

ANNE ROSENZWEIG
Arcadia
21 E. 62nd Street
New York, NY 10021
(212)223-2900

ANNE ROSENZWEIG
The Lobster Club
24 East 80th Street
New York, NY 10021
(212) 249-6500

CHRISTOPHER
SCHLESINGER
East Coast Grill
1271 Cambridge Street
Cambridge, MA 02138
(617) 491-6568

CHRISTOPHER
SCHLESINGER
The Blue Room
1 Hampshire Street
Cambridge, MA 02138
(617) 494-9034

JIMMY SCHMIDT
The Rattlesnake Club
300 River Place
Detroit, MI 48201
(313) 567-4843

ROXSAND SCOCOS
RoxSand
Biltmore Fashion Park
2594 East Camelback Road
Phoenix, AZ 85016
(602) 381-0444

JAMIE SHANNON
Commanders Palace
1403 Washington Avenue
New Orleans, LA 70130
(504) 899-8221

LINDSEY SHERE
Chez Panisse
517 Shattuck Avenue
Berkeley, CA 94701
(510) 548-5525

MICHAEL SMITH
The American Restaurant
2405 Grand Avenue
Kansas City, MO 64108
(816) 426-1133

SUSAN SPICER
Bayona
430 Dauphine Street
New Orleans, LA 70112
(504) 525-4455

BRAD STEELMAN
The Water Club
500 East 30th Street
New York, NY 10016
(212) 683-3333

ALESSANDRO STRATTA
Mary Elaine's
The Phoenician Resort
6000 East Camelback Road
Scottsdale, AZ 85251
(602) 941-8200

ALLEN SUSSER
Chef Allen's
19088 N.E. 29th Avenue
Aventura, FL 33180
(305) 935-2900

ELIZABETH TERRY
Elizabeth on 37th
105 E. 37th Street
Savannah, GA 31401
(912) 236-5547

JEREMIAH TOWER
Stars
150 Redwood Alley
San Francisco, CA 94102
(415) 861-7827

RICK TRAMONTO
Brasserie T
305 South Happ Road
Northfield, IL 60093
(847) 446-0444

CHARLIE TROTTER
Charlie Trotter's
816 West Armitage Avenue
Chicago, IL 60614
(312) 248-6228

JEAN-GEORGES
VONGERICHTEN
Vong
200 East 54th Street
New York, NY 10022
(212) 486-9592

ALAN WONG
Alan Wong's
1857 South King Street
Honolulu, HI 96826
(808) 949-2526

CHAPTER 1

Appetizers

"The discovery of a new dish
does more for human happiness
than the discovery of a star."

BRILLAT-SAVARIN
Physiologie du Goût

Asparagus Frittata Terrine

*G*reat for a rustic brunch, this terrine combines elements of European cuisine to celebrate the bounty of California asparagus. When asparagus spears are out of season, master chef Michel Richard recommends the use of leeks or sliced broccoli stalks to create this easy-to-make yet artistically impressive starter.

1   tablespoon olive oil

1   medium onion, peeled and finely diced

1/2   teaspoon sugar

3   large garlic cloves, peeled and minced

1   tablespoon champagne vinegar or white wine vinegar

    salt and freshly ground black pepper

11/2   pounds medium or thick asparagus spears, tough white end removed and peeled half way up the remaining stem

6   large eggs, room temperature

1   tablespoon fresh minced tarragon, dill, or mint

1. Make the onion mixture: Warm a small, heavy, nonstick skillet over low to medium heat and add the olive oil and onion. Cover the pan and sweat the onions about 10 minutes until translucent, stirring occasionally. Then add the sugar and stir at a medium-high heat until lightly browned, making sure the onions remain flattened. Add the garlic and vinegar and boil until the vinegar has evaporated. Season with salt and pepper to taste and stir occasionally. Cool.

2. Bring a large pot of water to boil. Add the thicker asparagus spears first, and then the thinner ones, and cook until tender when pierced with a knife. This could take about 3 to 4 minutes for the larger spears. Drain and shock in a water and ice bath. Dry by placing on a rack lined with paper towels. Season to taste with salt and pepper.

3. Preheat the oven to 325°F.

4. Make the terrine: Grease a loaf pan 8-inches-by-4-inches-by-21/2-inches and line with buttered parchment or waxed paper. Place the loaf pan in a larger baking pan sitting in water three-quarters of the way up the sides.

5. Trim the asparagus to fit the loaf pan; reserve the trimmings. Place a single layer of asparagus spears on the bottom of the loaf pan, alternating tips and ends. Fill in any spaces with the trimmings. Cover with one-third of the onions. Continue to make layers until the remaining asparagus and onion mixture are finished.

6. In a small bowl, whisk the eggs and then add the tarragon, salt and pepper to taste. Pour the egg mixture over the asparagus and move a knife between the asparagus spears, making sure the egg is evenly distributed. Lightly tap the loaf pan on the work surface, place it in the water bath, and cover with aluminum foil. Bake 50 minutes to 1 hour until the eggs are set and a knife inserted into the center comes out clean. Remove from the water bath. Let the terrine set for 15 minutes and then run a knife around the rim to unmold.

7. To serve, slice the terrine into 1/2-inch-thick pieces. Place several slices on each plate.

SERVES: 6

Beggar's Purses with Lobster and Black Truffles

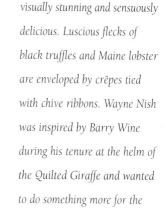

2 cups all-purpose flour
  kosher salt
3 cups milk, room temperature
8 extra-large eggs, plus 1 egg yolk
1/2 cup clarified butter, warm
1 heaping tablespoon finely chopped chives

FILLING:
7 ounces black truffles
3/4 pound cooked lobster meat, chopped

1/2 cup mayonnaise
1 1/2 tablespoons white vermouth
1 1/2 teaspoons fresh lemon juice
1/2 teaspoon rice vinegar
  salt and freshly ground black pepper

GARNISH:
24 chive spears

This ambitious starter is visually stunning and sensuously delicious. Luscious flecks of black truffles and Maine lobster are enveloped by crêpes tied with chive ribbons. Wayne Nish was inspired by Barry Wine during his tenure at the helm of the Quilted Giraffe and wanted to do something more for the filling than just opening a tin of caviar. He presents these majestic purses for special occasions.

1. Make the crêpes: In a stainless-steel bowl, combine the flour and a pinch of salt with 1 cup of milk. Whisk until a paste forms and all lumps are removed. Whisk in the remaining milk, eggs, and egg yolk until smooth. Let the batter rest under plastic wrap for 1 hour.

2. Stir the batter, then strain it through a fine sieve into a bowl sitting in a bath of warm water—a *bain-marie*. Stir the batter until it is warm to the touch. Whisk in 1/4 cup of the clarified butter and the chopped chives.

3. Dip a paper towel into the remaining clarified butter and wipe the inside of a 5-inch-wide nonstick crêpe pan. Fill a 2-ounce ladle and pour the batter into the crêpe pan and quickly move around to coat the bottom of the pan; return any excess batter to the bowl in the *bain-marie*. Cook the crêpes until the edges start to release from the pan. Use the top of a paring knife and your fingers to loosen the crêpe. Turn the pan at an angle and quickly remove the crêpe from the pan to a flat surface. Repeat the process until the batter is used up. Stack the crêpes one on top of the other, cooked-side down. Immediately wrap them tightly in plastic wrap and refrigerate until ready to use.

4. Blanch the chives in a pot of boiling salted water over high heat by stirring them quickly until submerged, approximately 10 seconds. Shock the chives in very cold tap water to stop the cooking process. Dry on a towel.

5. Chop the truffles into small chunks in a food processor. Place the lobster meat and truffles in the bowl and combine with the mayonnaise, vermouth, lemon juice, and rice vinegar. Season with salt and freshly ground pepper and refrigerate, covering with plastic wrap, until ready to use.

6. Bring the crêpes to room temperature and place them on top of each other on a piece of parchment or wax paper. Cut them with the top of a 500-gram caviar tin or 4 3/4-inch round cutter and use a knife to trim the edges.

7. Place 2 teaspoons of the truffle-lobster filling in the center of each crêpe. Carefully holding the edge of the crêpe farthest away from you between your forefinger and thumb, use your free hand to make small, even pleats in the edge of the crêpe, catching each pleat between your forefinger and thumb. Pleat the last section and tie the crêpe closed with a single chive in a double knot. Trim all but 1/2 inch from the chive ends.

8. Refrigerate the crêpe purses until ready to serve. Allow 3 crêpes per person.

SERVES: 8

Blini with Salmon and Horseradish Crème Fraîche

This star of American cuisine, David Burke, uses corn from America's heartland as the signature ingredient in these magical blini. The blini batter without the corn kernels makes equally good pancakes. Spiked with fresh grated horseradish and its oils, the blini glisten with Northwest salmon, which not only heightens the visual effect of the dish, but also adds a fragrant and distinctive texture to captivate the senses.

HORSERADISH OIL:

1/2 horseradish root, peeled and sliced into strips

1 cup soybean oil

BLINI: (Yield 12 three-inch blinis)

4 3/4 cups all-purpose flour

7 tablespoons granulated sugar

1 tablespoon salt

1 quart milk, tepid

1 1/2 ounces powdered yeast

5 eggs, separated

7 ounces salad oil

1/4 cup fresh corn niblets, blanched

1 tablespoon unsalted butter

HORSERADISH CRÈME FRAÎCHE:

1 cup crème fraîche

1 tablespoon grated horseradish

3/4 pound smoked salmon (30 slices)

1 bunch chives (1/2 bunch very finely diced, 1/2 bunch cut into 2-inch sticks)

8 radishes, (4 very thinly sliced, 4 finely julienned)

coarse salt and freshly ground black pepper

1. Make the horseradish oil: Place in the top of a double boiler the horseradish and soybean oil and bring water to high heat. Remove from heat and let steep overnight to infuse. Strain out the horseradish strips.

2. Make the blini: Sift together the all-purpose flour, the sugar, and the salt.

3. Warm the milk slightly and dissolve the yeast in it.

4. In a bowl, whisk the egg yolks and oil for several minutes, creating a mayonnaise. Add the milk and the sifted ingredients and let rise in a warm spot for 45 minutes.

5. Whip egg whites to soft peaks and fold into the mixture. Stir in the corn niblets.

6. Heat several 3-inch blini pans, melt the butter in them, pour 1/4 inch of batter in each, and cook for 2 minutes on both sides. Turn the blini with a small paring knife. (There will be extra blini. If preparing in advance, warm the blini in a toaster when ready to serve.)

7. Make the horseradish crème fraîche: Whip the crème fraîche to stiff peaks and then mix to incorporate the horseradish.

8. In a bowl, mix the salmon, 1/2 cup horseradish oil, chive sticks, thinly sliced radishes, and season with salt and freshly ground pepper to taste.

9. To serve, place one blini on each plate. Pipe with a pastry bag 3 mounds of horseradish crème fraîche 1 1/2 inch vertically in the center of the blini, top with 6 slices of salmon and then garnish with the radish julienne and diced chives.

SERVES: 5

Charlotte of Wild Mushrooms

CUSTARD:

1 tablespoon unsalted butter

1/2 medium onion, peeled and chopped

2 large eggs

1 3/4 cups heavy cream

1/8 teaspoon nutmeg

salt and freshly ground white pepper

MOLDS:

15 slices good quality white bread, crustless

1/2 cup (1 stick) unsalted butter, softened

2 tablespoons finely chopped parsley

nonstick spray

BRAISED WILD MUSHROOMS:

1/2 cup plus 2 tablespoons unsalted butter

2 medium shallots, peeled and finely chopped

2 large garlic cloves, peeled and minced

1 teaspoon fresh thyme leaves, finely chopped

1 pound assorted wild mushrooms, cleaned and sliced

1 cup dry white wine

1 cup chicken stock (see page 190)

salt and freshly ground black pepper

GARNISH:

6 fresh thyme sprigs

Charlottes, or rich, creamy fruitcake confections, reached their peak in popularity on American menus from 1830 to 1880. Waldy Malouf reinvents the charlotte in a savory version, with Hudson Valley mushrooms in a soft onion custard encased in a golden crust. Local mushroom foragers scurry year round for cèpe, shiitake, oyster, and pleurote mushrooms, and harvest chanterelles and morels in the spring. In this dish, the thyme-scented assorted wild mushrooms, braised in red wine and chicken stock, provide a hearty embellishment for toasty crowns of onion custard.

1. Make the custard mixture: In a sauté pan, melt the butter and, without browning, sauté the onion for 4 to 5 minutes until it is thoroughly cooked and translucent. In a bowl, combine the eggs, cream, nutmeg, salt, and pepper. Purée the onion in a food processor and stir it into the custard mixture.

2. Preheat the oven to 375°F.

3. Prepare the molds: Cut each bread slice horizontally into 4 strips. Spray each mold well with nonstick spray. Using a pastry brush, generously butter the bottom and sides of six 8-ounce ramekins (3 inches high and 3 1/2 inches in diameter), and sprinkle each with chopped parsley shaking out any excess. Line the sides of each mold with 4 or more bread strips, tightly fitted together so that the custard mixture does not run, by pressing the strips onto the butter. The ends of the bread pieces may extend about an inch above the tops of the ramekins.

4. Ladle the custard mixture into the ramekins, filling each one about half-full. Place the ramekins in a small roasting pan one-half filled with water and bring the water to a boil on top of the stove. Then place the pan on the bottom shelf of the oven and bake until golden brown and the custard is set for 20 to 30 minutes.

5. Make the mushrooms: In a large sauté pan, heat 1/2 cup of the butter until it is very hot. Quickly sauté the shallots and garlic and then sprinkle in the thyme. Add the mushrooms and cook 4 or 5 minutes until lightly browned, taking care not to burn the butter. Add the wine and boil until almost evaporated. Add the stock, stir well, and simmer the mushrooms until the liquid is reduced by two-thirds and thickens slightly. Season the mushrooms with salt and pepper to taste and finish with the remaining butter.

6. To serve, with a small paring knife gently remove each charlotte from the ramekin into your hand and place on a warm plate. Spoon equal amounts of the mushroom mixture into each charlotte and drizzle any extra around the charlottes. Garnish with fresh thyme sprigs. Serve immediately.

SERVES: 6

CHEF'S HINT: If preparing in advance, cover the charlottes with foil and reheat them for 10 to 15 minutes at 300°F.

Chipotle Shrimp with Corn Cakes

These shrimp scented with chipotle, or dried smoked chilies, provide a distinctively hot and smokey flavor which is mellowed on a bed of corn cakes flecked with crunchy corn kernels. The refreshing addition of salsa spiked with dark Mexican beer reflects the trend today towards spicier food in the true American Southwestern spirit.

CORN CAKES: (Yield: 20 cakes)

- $3/4$ cup all-purpose flour
- $1/2$ cup coarse cornmeal (polenta)
- $1/2$ teaspoon baking powder
- $1/2$ teaspoon baking soda
- 1 teaspoon kosher salt
- 1 teaspoon sugar
- $1 1/4$ cups buttermilk
- 2 tablespoons melted sweet butter
- 1 egg, lightly beaten
- 1 cup fresh corn kernels (3 ears of corn)
- 2 scallions, green and white parts, finely chopped

CHIPOTLE SHRIMP:

- $4 1/2$ tablespoons canned chipotle chilies, puréed
- $3/4$ pound jumbo shrimp (8–12 shrimp) peeled and deveined
- 1 cup softened unsalted butter
- 3 tablespoons unsalted butter

GARNISH:

- 2 scallions, peeled and chopped
- 1 cup salsa fresca (see page 201)
- $1/2$ ear of corn, blanched, optional

1. In a stainless-steel bowl, place the dry ingredients and mix together to incorporate. In a separate bowl, whisk the buttermilk and butter together. Add the egg and whisk to blend. Gradually add the dry ingredients to the buttermilk mixture and whisk until thoroughly incorporated.

2. Purée $1/2$ cup of the corn until it reaches a consistency of cooked oatmeal, and fold it into the batter with the whole kernels and scallions. Thin the mixture with extra buttermilk as needed. Let the batter rest for $1/2$ hour, until it has a pancake-like consistency.

3. In a stainless-steel bowl, toss shrimp with 3 tablespoons of chipotle purée to coat. Marinate, covered with plastic wrap in the refrigerator for $1/2$ hour.

4. Make the chipotle butter: Roughly purée the softened butter and $1 1/2$ tablespoons chipotle purée and set aside.

5. Ladle the corn cake batter into a heated 12-inch nonstick pan and form 3-inch cakes. Cook over medium heat until golden brown, about $1 1/2$ minutes on each side. (There will be extra batter remaining.)

6. On a griddle or in a frying pan, cook the shrimp in 3 tablespoons of melted butter over low heat for about 5 minutes, turning them once.

7. To serve, place 1 corn cake on each plate, top with 2 shrimps interlocked, and generously spread the chipotle butter over the shrimp. Garnish the shrimp with the chopped scallions. Serve with salsa fresca in 3 small mounds around the corn cake.

OPTIONAL: Cut the blanched ear of corn into quarters and arrange decoratively over the shrimp.

SERVES: 4

CHEF'S HINT: If using batter on the second day, add a little extra all-purpose flour and baking powder as a thickener. To make fresh chipotle chile purée, arrange 15 chipotle chilies on a sheet pan and roast at 200°F 3 to 4 minutes to bring out the oils. Place in a pot, cover with water, bring to a boil, and simmer for 20 minutes. Drain off the water. Add 3 tablespoons of fresh water and purée in a blender to a paste-like consistency. Strain.

Citrus-Crusted Shrimp with Ginger and Bourbon

MARINADE:

- 1 medium jalapeño pepper, seeded and chopped
- 3 tablespoons dried candied orange zest (see page 192)
- 3 tablespoons dried candied lemon zest (see page 192)
- 1 teaspoon lemon juice
- 1 teaspoon achiote powder
- 1 teaspoon cumin
- 1 teaspoon oregano
- 1 tablespoon fresh basil, stemmed and chopped
- 1 tablespoon coarse salt
- 1/4 cup bourbon

SHRIMPS AND SAUCE:

- 12 large shrimp, peeled, deveined, and diced
- 2 tablespoons olive oil
- 1 tablespoon minced ginger root
- 1 tablespoon minced garlic

- 2 star fruits, sliced

Allen Susser laces much of his Southern Florida cuisine with bourbon, a traditional flavoring for pecan pie and bread puddings. In these citrus-encrusted Gold Coast shrimp, the bourbon provides a well-balanced counterpoint to the pumpkin-colored achiote powder. Like others of his Floridian culinary peers, Susser has been a forerunner in introducing local American products, such as Florida citrus and local star fruit, to our pantries.

1. Make the marinade: Combine the jalapeño, orange and lemon zest, lemon juice, achiote, cumin, oregano, basil, coarse salt, and 1 tablespoon of the bourbon, and let stand for 1 hour.

2. Dip the shrimp in the marinade to form a citrus crust and marinate for 1/2 hour.

3. Heat the olive oil in a sauté pan, and sauté the shrimp. After 1 minute, add the ginger and garlic and cook another 1/2 minute. Add the star fruit and deglaze with the remaining bourbon.

4. To serve, divide the shrimp among 4 plates and pour the sauce over it. Artfully decorate the plate with the star fruit in the sauce.

SERVES: 4

AUTHOR'S NOTE: Achiote powder is made from the ancho chili, a dried red poblano pepper.

Corn Flan with Smoked Salmon and Chives

This fanciful corn custard encased in a delicate eggshell reflects the playfulness and gastronomic surprises of David Burke's cuisine. At the Park Avenue Cafe, attractive porcelain eggshell holders depicting Humpty Dumpty add to the charm of this dish. Its inspiration can be traced to Lyons, France, where culinary legend Paul Bocuse popularized scrambled eggs and caviar served in eggshells.

12 jumbo eggs with egg carton

FLAVORED CUSTARD:
1 cup fresh corn kernels (3 ears of corn)
1 pint heavy cream
4 large eggs
1 tablespoon salt
   freshly ground white pepper

FILLING:
2 tablespoon unsalted butter
1/2 cup fresh corn kernels, blanched (1 1/2 ears of corn)
1/4 pound smoked salmon, julienned or diced
1/2 cup chives, chopped
   salt and freshly ground white pepper

OPTIONAL GARNISH:
   carrot top greens

1. Preheat the oven to 325°F.

2. If fresh corn is available, husk the corn and grill the corn cobs until a light brownish color is reached. Remove corn from the cob.

3. Make the flavored custard: Cook the corn and cream over medium heat in a large stainless-steel pan until the mixture boils. Simmer for 6 to 8 minutes over low heat, stirring occasionally so that the corn infuses into the cream. Purée in a food processor or hand mixer and strain. Cool the mixture either in a water bath or in the refrigerator.

4. Whisk the 4 eggs and slowly incorporate the cream mixture. Season with salt and freshly ground white pepper to taste. Strain through a chinois or strainer if desired. Cover with plastic wrap until ready to use.

5. Cut the tops of the 12 raw eggs with egg scissors or use a tip from a pastry bag to remove the tops, emptying the egg. Remove ragged edges with your fingers and rinse the shells carefully by lightly pouring small amounts of water into the egg shell. Put the shell back into the egg carton, and place the carton in a small roasting pan. Fill each egg shell three-quarters of the way with the custard mixture. Pour boiling water halfway up the roasting pan, and cover the egg shells with aluminum foil. Cook in the oven for 45 to 55 minutes, or until the custard is just set.

6. Make the filling: In a small sauté pan, melt the butter, add the corn, season with salt and pepper, and heat thoroughly. Remove from the heat, add the salmon and all but 2 tablespoons of the chives, and toss over a low heat until warm.

7. Using a teaspoon, place a heaping spoon of filling on top of the custard. The filling should flow over the brim, creating height. Garnish with the remaining chives.

8. To serve, place the optional carrot top greens in an attractive porcelain egg holder or cut out one holder from the original carton. Place one egg in it and serve with a small teaspoon.

SERVES: 12

Duck Prosciutto with Melon Chutney and Foie Gras

A variation of the classic melon and prosciutto, this thinly sliced and cured duck with a melon vinegar chutney offers a sophisticated balance of flavors complimenting a lusty foie gras. Foie gras, the coveted fattened liver which reigns supreme in Gascony, is alluring and available in New York State's Hudson Valley and Northern California's Sonoma Valley. According to the Roman poet Horace, "The liver is the seat of the passions, particularly love and anger." Later the historian Suetonius concluded, "It is the center of the intelligence and the mind."

DUCK PROSCIUTTO:

1 (8-ounce) magret duck breast
1 1/2 tablespoons kosher salt
1/2 tablespoon granulated sugar
1/2 teaspoon paprika

MELON CHUTNEY:

1 large ripe cantaloupe
1/4 teaspoon chopped fresh ginger
1 1/2 tablespoons brown sugar
2 whole cloves
4 tablespoons white wine vinegar
4 tablespoons chopped white onion
1/8 teaspoon ground cinnamon

1 cilantro sprig
1/8 teaspoon cardamon
1/4 teaspoon cumin seed
1/4 teaspoon coriander seed
1/4 cup melon scrap (see step 2 below)

1 cup port wine
4 pieces (2 ounces each) of duck foie gras (1/2-inch thick)
coarse salt and freshly ground black pepper

GARNISH:

4 cilantro sprigs or 1/4 pound mache or baby field greens

1. Make the prosciutto: Trim the skin from the duck breast, leaving a thin, 1/8-inch layer of fat. Sprinkle the breast with the combined seasonings, completely coating the entire breast. Marinate overnight uncovered on a plate. The next day, wrap in cheesecloth and tie with twine, maintaining the natural shape of the breast. Hang in a dry area of the refrigerator for at least 10 days and up to 3 weeks. (It will become dryer and firmer when left to hang longer.)

2. Prepare melon garnish: Trim rind ends off the melon and peel sides, following the contour of the melon. Cut the melon lengthwise into four equal wedges and remove seeds. Using a 3-inch metal cookie cutter, cut a disc from the center of melon wedge (as large in diameter as possible). Punch out a smaller 1-inch hole from the center using a knife or disc (yielding four doughnut-shaped melon rings). Remove a thin slice of each side of the disc so the melon ring will sit flat. Reserve for final assembly. From the outer and inner trim of the doughnut, cut a medium dice. Reserve all remaining scrap (approximately 5 ounces) for the chutney base.

3. Make the chutney: Place all the chutney ingredients in a small saucepan. Cook the melon scrap approximately 3 minutes until tender. Purée in a blender for 1 minute until smooth.

4. Make the port wine syrup: In a small saucepan, slowly reduce the port wine to a syrup consistency for approximately 8 minutes. The port syrup should coat the back of a spoon.

5. Remove the duck from the cheesecloth and twine. In a hot skillet over low flame, place the duck fat-side down, allowing the skin to crisp for approximately 5 minutes. Do not allow the meat to continue cooking. Remove from the pan and rest at room temperature. Discard the excess fat from the pan.

6. Season the foie gras with salt and black pepper. Sear in the same pan on a high flame for 1 minute on each side. Remove and hold with the duck. Discard excess fat from pan.

7. Again in the same pan, sear the melon rings over a high flame for 30 seconds per side. Remove from the pan and reserve with the duck and foie gras.

8. Toss the diced melon in the same pan over medium heat. Add the chutney base and heat. Check the seasoning and keep warm.

9. To serve, place each melon ring on a plate and generously fill the center with the chutney. Slice the duck on a bias as thin as possible. Drape 3 slices, slightly overlapping each other, from each melon ring. Place the foie gras on top of the chutney, then drizzle the plate with the port wine syrup. Garnish with a fresh cilantro sprig or a bunch of mache.

SERVES: 4

11

Dungeness Crab Sushi with Sesame Dressing

DRESSING:

- 3 tablespoons sesame seeds (half black, half white)
- 1 teaspoon Asian sesame oil
- 1 cup mayonnaise
- 2 tablespoons lemon juice
- 1 teaspoon Asian oyster sauce
- 1 teaspoon soy sauce
- 1/4 teaspoon chopped garlic
- 1/4 teaspoon grated peeled fresh ginger root, or to taste
- 1/3 cup chicken stock (see page 190)

- 1/2 cup finely diced red bell pepper
- 1/2 cup finely diced green bell pepper
- 1/2 cup finely diced zucchini
- 1/2 cup finely diced carrots
- 3 ounces enoki-daki or oyster button mushrooms, trimmed and finely chopped
- 2 teaspoons sugar
- 2 teaspoons rice vinegar
- 1/4 teaspoon salt
- 1 pound fresh Dungeness (or lump) crab, picked over, 1/2 pound broken up into small pieces, the rest reserved for garnish
- 3 sheets, 8 by 7 1/2 inches, of toasted nori (seaweed), halved lengthwise
- 18 young lettuce leaves, a combination such as Belgian endive leaves, radicchio, and small spinach leaves

Dungeness crabs inhabit the Pacific coastline and impart a delicious flavor to Japan's most coveted dish—sushi. Kaspar Donier's rhapsodic version is presented with an aesthetic flair, embellished with graceful lettuce greens and a confetti of diced peppers, zucchini, and carrot.

1. Make the dressing: In a small skillet, toast the sesame seeds in the oil over moderate heat until golden brown. Cool. In a small bowl, stir the mayonnaise, lemon juice, oyster sauce, soy sauce, garlic, ginger root, stock, and sesame seeds. Cover and chill the mixture (may be made 2 days in advance).

2. In a small bowl, combine the bell peppers, zucchini, carrot, mushrooms, sugar, vinegar, and salt, and let stand for 15 minutes. Divide the mixture between 2 bowls. Chill and add the crab pieces to one of the bowls.

3. Place a nori sheet horizontally, with the long edge toward you. Bunch a few lettuce leaves together at the upper left corner, with the tops extending about 1 inch past the far edge of the nori. Spread the crab mixture across the long edge of the nori closest to you, up to about 1 1/2 inches from the far edge. Beginning at the left (the lettuce end), roll the nori tightly, jelly-roll fashion. Seal the seam with some water and cut each roll into 3 pieces with a sharp knife.

4. Spoon about 1/4 cup of the dressing in the center of each of 6 chilled plates and arrange the reserved vegetables around the edges. Arrange the 3 nori roll slices in the center of each plate and garnish with the reserved crab.

SERVES: 6

Ecuadorian Shrimp Ceviche

The national dish of Ecuador and Peru is ceviche. In this interpretation, the lightly blanched shrimp are "cooked" by the acidity of the lime, orange, and tomato juices. Roasting the sweet tomato and peppers heightens the flavor. Cornnuts and popcorn, traditional Ecuadorian accompaniments, adorn the ceviche and are a novel addition for American culinary enthusiasts.

SHRIMP CEVICHE:

- 1 pound shrimp, peeled and cleaned
- 1 large tomato, roasted, peeled and seeded
- 2 jalapeño peppers, roasted, peeled and seeded
- 2 red bell peppers, roasted, peeled and seeded
- 1/2 medium onion, roasted and peeled
- 3/4 cup fresh lime juice
- 1/2 cup fresh orange juice
- 1/4 cup fresh tomato juice

VEGETABLE GARNISH:

- 1 small whole red onion, peeled, halved, sliced into long strips
- 2 tablespoons chopped chives
- 2 tablespoons chopped scallions
- 4 cilantro sprigs, stemmed, coarsely chopped
- 1 large tomato, cored and diced

GARNISH:

- 1 avocado, peeled, pitted, sliced on the bias
- 1/2 cup cornnuts
- 1/2 cup popped popcorn

1. Make the ceviche: Place the cleaned shrimp into a pot of boiling salted water for approximately 2 minutes (no longer), then remove to an ice bath. Place all other shrimp ceviche ingredients in the blender and liquify. Pour over the shrimp and cover with plastic wrap. Chill for up to 1 1/2 hours.

2. Make the garnish: In a large bowl, toss all the vegetable garnish ingredients.

3. To serve, place the shrimp in a soup bowl, top with the ceviche liquid and vegetable garnish. Around the shrimp, place several slices of avocado. Place the bowl on a plate and randomly sprinkle the cornnuts and popcorn.

SERVES: 4

Grilled Calamari with Anchovies, Capers, Olives, Garlic, and Lemon in Brown Butter

16 calamari, with heads

1/3 pound unsalted butter

3 tablespoons olive oil

14 garlic cloves, peeled (12 whole and 2 finely chopped)

1/2 cup water or chicken stock (see page 190)

1 jalapeño pepper, finely chopped

    ground nutmeg to taste

    vegetable oil for the grill

3 anchovy filets, minced

1 heaping teaspoon capers

12 Gaeta olives (Greek black olives), pitted and quartered lengthwise

    juice of 2 lemons and finely chopped zest

2 scallions, peeled and sliced paper-thin on bias

The anchovies, capers, Gaeta olives, and garlic in this dish showcase squid at its best. Of the one hundred worldwide varieties of calamari or squid, one can differentiate between them by noting the country nearest the waters from where they are harvested. Thailand produces some of the best calamari. A highly nutritious food, calamari contains 18 percent protein.

The acidic lemon and nutty brown butter with roasted garlic in this grilled calamari lift the flavors to a harmonious height. The savory sauce can accompany many fish dishes.

1. Clean the calamari: Pull the skin off the body and remove the mantle. Rinse with water. Cut the head off just below the eyes and discard the eyes. Save the tentacles. By pressing between two fingers, separate the round sac containing the beak from the tentacles and discard. Remove the clear pen-like rudimentary shell from inside the body. Starting at one end with a small, sharp knife, cut "piano key" rings a quarter inch apart.

2. Make the brown butter: Place the butter in a small saucepan over high heat until the butter separates. Skim off any solids that form on the surface. When the butter turns a light, nutty brown, remove it from the heat and cool slightly. Using a ladle, remove the clarified nut butter into a clean saucepan, being careful not to disturb the sediments that have settled towards the bottom. (Make sure that all your equipment is thoroughly dry. The butter will splatter if it comes in contact with moisture.)

3. In a small pan, heat 2 tablespoons of the olive oil and sauté the whole garlic cloves until they are golden. Add the water or chicken stock and simmer until the garlic is tender. (Add more water as necessary to avoid scorching, allowing the water to cook away each time before adding more.) When the garlic is tender and sweet, spread it out on a tray and cool.

4. Toss the calamari in a bowl with the raw chopped garlic, jalapeño pepper, nutmeg, and olive oil. Wipe the grill with a rag soaked in vegetable oil and set the grill on high. Grill the calamari on each side for two minutes or until slightly charred.

5. Meanwhile, in a saucepan, add the anchovies, capers, olives, roasted garlic cloves, lemon juice, and zest to the brown butter and heat thoroughly.

6. To serve, divide the calamari slices and tentacles among four heated plates; spoon even amounts of the brown butter, including the braised garlic cloves, around and over the calamari and garnish with scallions.

SERVES: 4 (4 pieces each for an appetizer)

AUTHOR'S NOTE: Calamari is naturally tender but can become tough when overcooked. A grill or frying pan set to a high temperature and a short cooking time are the keys to your success. Oiling the grill surface immediately prior to cooking reduces the chances that the calamari will stick to it. If you are using a frying pan, be sure to preheat the pan.

When purchasing calamari, select the thick U-10 size (less than 10 pieces per pound) for best results.

Lip Chips with Chive Ginger Aioli

Root vegetable chips have given potato chips a healthy competition. The tang of the ginger juice and savory ginger potato purée add a piquancy of unrivaled dimension. Lip chips are a good-humored, lighthearted approach to appetizers inspired by the palate of Dada artist Man Ray, whose highly regarded picture depicts amorous lips floating over the Paris Observatory.

CHIVE GINGER AIOLI:

- 3 ounces potato garlic purée:
    - 1 Idaho potato
    - 1 garlic clove, peeled and minced
- 2 tablespoons ginger juice (1-inch piece ginger root), alternatively 1/2 teaspoon Dijon mustard
- 1/2 cup chive purée:
    - 1 ounce chives
    - 3 tablespoons water
- 2 egg yolks
- 3/4 cup olive oil
    - kosher salt
    - lime juice

VEGETABLES:

- 1 zucchini, cut on the bias
- 1 beet
- 1 yam
- 1 lotus root
- 1 russet potato
- 1 yucca
- 1 purple potato
- 1/2 cup potato starch
- 1 1/2 quarts canola or neutral oil

GARNISH:

- 2 Italian parsley sprigs, stemmed, finely chopped

1. Make the potato garlic purée: Preheat the oven to 375°F. Roast the potato for 45 minutes. Cool, remove skin, and mash it with garlic.

2. Make the ginger juice: With a small grater, rub the side of the ginger to remove the skin. Then grate into a bowl. Pass the pulp with the juice through a strainer or cheesecloth.

3. Make the chive purée: In a blender, process the chives with the water until well blended. Reserve.

4. Make the chive ginger aioli: In a food processor, combine the yolks and potato purée approximately 1 1/2 minutes until very fluffy. Slowly add the olive oil. Pour into a large stainless-steel bowl; fold in ginger juice and chive purée. Season to taste with salt and lime juice.

5. Heat the canola oil in a wok for about 20 minutes.

6. Using a mandoline, slice each vegetable very thinly and keep the slices separate. Slice the potatoes last, since they discolor quickly. Place the potato starch in a medium stainless-steel bowl, and dredge the zucchini, beet, and yam in starch, shaking off the excess.

7. Starting with the zucchini, deep-fry all the vegetables in small batches until a golden color appears. (While cooking these items, flip them over for even cooking.) Remove and drain on paper towels. Sprinkle with a teaspoon of salt. (These may be kept warm up to 45 minutes at 325°F.)

8. To serve, sprinkle an additional teaspoon of salt on the chips and gently toss by hand. Place the chips in a basket lined with a napkin. Sprinkle with parsley. Place sauce in a separate small bowl.

SERVES: 6

AUTHOR'S NOTE: Potato starch, lotus root, and purple potatoes are available at Asian markets.

CHEF'S HINTS: Chive purée can add flavor and color to many other dishes, including asparagus soup, sauces, and salad vinaigrette.

To test whether the oil is hot enough (after heating approximately 20 minutes), use a wok and heat the oil until a cube of bread browns in 20 to 40 seconds. If the oil is smoking and too hot, turn the heat down.

May River Oysters in a Cornmeal Crust

CRUST:

3/4 cup unbleached flour

1 1/2 teaspoons cornmeal

3 tablespoons (1 1/2 ounces) unsalted butter, chilled and cubed

2 2/3 tablespoons ice-cold water

FILLING:

2 tablespoons unsalted butter

1/4 cup country ham or prosciutto, minced

2 tablespoons good drinking bourbon

2 tablespoons all-purpose flour

1 cup heavy cream

1 tablespoon thyme, stem discarded, minced (parsley may be substituted)

2 cups leeks, scrubbed well, quartered and sliced (approximately 3 leeks)

2 pints small oysters, drained well
kosher salt and freshly ground white pepper

GARNISH:

1 tablespoon fresh tarragon, minced

General William Sherman was so mesmerized by the beauty of Old Savannah that it was spared on his 1864 march to the sea. Besides dusty-green moss, romantic gazebos, and a historic seaport, Savannah boasts the choicest briny sweet May River oysters. When draped in leeks and smoky minced country ham, these oysters are a fragrant hallmark of the new food of the Old South.

1. Make the crust: In a food processor, combine the flour, cornmeal, and the cubed butter. Process until the mixture resembles coarse meal. With the motor running, slowly pour in the water and process until the dough forms one mass. Remove dough and form a disc. Wrap in plastic wrap and refrigerate for 1/2 hour.

2. Preheat the oven to 400°F.

3. Roll the dough on a floured board until very thin. Cut out 6 discs 1 inch wider than the size of the opening of a coffee cup. Prick the crusts, place metal rings slightly larger than your coffee-cup opening on a buttered baking sheet, and lay the dough inside the rings so that it comes up the sides. Bake for about 7 minutes until golden and crisp. Set aside.

4. In a large skillet over high heat, melt 1 tablespoon of butter. Add the country ham and sauté until brown. Pour in the bourbon and stir. Add the flour and mix for 1 minute. Then whisk in the heavy cream and thyme and simmer while whisking until thick. (The sauce may be made ahead to this point; set aside to cool before refrigerating.)

5. In a large skillet over high heat, melt the remaining butter and sauté the leeks and oysters until the leeks turn bright green after approximately 1 minute. Rewarm the sauce in a small sauté pan. Add the leeks and oysters to warm sauce. Season with salt and white pepper to taste.

6. To serve, place a pastry cup on each plate and spoon the mixture among 6 plates. Top each oyster with minced tarragon.

SERVES: 6

CHEF'S NOTE: If oysters are unavailable, substitute chicken. Grill 3 skinless boned chicken breasts and then dice them.

Parfait of Salmon & Tuna Tartar, Caviar and Crème Fraîche

This buttery-textured parfait of tuna and salmon makes a refreshing starter for any special meal. The savory pearls of caviar topped with a sliver of crème fraîche combine elegantly with the piquant-flavored fish. In a towering presentation that echoes the best of Philip Johnson's skyscrapers, the taste rating of this edible architecture is awesome.

2 shallots, peeled and minced

3 tablespoons plus, extra virgin olive oil

10 ounces yellowfin tuna, cut into small dice

3 teaspoons mustard-flavored oil

2 teaspoons lemon zest

4 teaspoons soy sauce

2 tablespoons chopped coriander (cilantro), leaves only

1 teaspoon coarse salt

2 pinches freshly ground white pepper

10 ounces salmon filet, skinned and ground

2 teaspoons peeled, grated horseradish root

2 tablespoons chopped capers

2 tablespoons finely chopped chives
     salt and freshly ground black pepper

2 1/2 tablespoons osetra or other black-grained caviar

2 1/2 tablespoons salmon roe caviar

1 cup crème fraîche (see page 191)

GARNISH:

10 chive spears

1. Combine the shallots and 1 tablespoon of olive oil in a small saucepan, and sauté until the shallots are translucent.

2. In a medium bowl sitting on a bed of ice, combine half of the sweated shallots, all the tuna, half of the mustard oil, half of the lemon zest, all the soy sauce, 1 tablespoon of the olive oil, and all the coriander. Lightly season with coarse salt, season generously with the white pepper, and mix well with a large spoon.

3. In another medium bowl sitting on a bed of ice, combine the remaining shallots, mustard oil, lemon zest, and salmon. Mix with the remaining olive oil, horseradish, capers, chives, and salt and pepper to taste, and mix until all the ingredients are combined.

4. Line a sheet pan with waxed or parchment paper and lightly oil with fingers the inside of ten 2-inch-high-by-2-inch-diameter metal rings or molds, placing the molds on the sheet.

5. Place 1 1/2 tablespoons of the tuna mixture in each of the ten molds, making sure to smooth the mixture with the back of a spoon. If available, press down with the bottom of a Worcestershire or tabasco bottle. Then place 1 1/2 tablespoons of the salmon mixture on top, pressing down and smoothing the salmon mixture with the back of the spoon. Spoon approximately 1/2 teaspoon of osetra caviar on one half of the top of the salmon and approximately 1/2 teaspoon of salmon roe caviar on the other half, smoothing with the back of the spoon.

6. Whip the crème fraîche until thick, stiff peaks are formed. Add 2 tablespoons of the crème fraîche, smoothing with the blade of a flat knife or small metal spatula, making sure that the crème fraîche is level with the top of the mold. Chill the molds in the refrigerator for at least 20 minutes but preferably for 2 to 3 hours.

7. To serve, place each ring or mold on a dinner plate, and gently remove the mold by pulling ring upward, leaving the parfait intact. Garnish each parfait with one long chive spear placed at an angle over the parfait.

AUTHOR'S NOTE: Optional: Artfully add 3 dots of olive oil on top of the crème fraîche. Serve with slices of toasted French bread.

SERVES: 10

Squab, Black Trumpet, and Asparagus Terrine

Particularly adept at constructing terrines, Charlie Trotter shines as one of the star chefs of the Midwest. This delicate combination of squab, black trumpets, and asparagus presents a stunning mosaic of flavors and textures, illustrative of Trotter's global approach to gastronomy and a cornerstone of his meticulous cooking. The anise-like flavor of the pitch-black, trumpet-shaped mushrooms and the smoky quality of the squab present a harmonious composition.

6 whole deboned squabs or 12 breasts, remove tenderloins, reserving bones for squab glacé

SQUAB STOCK:

1/2 cup white wine

1 tablespoon olive oil

1/2 carrot, peeled and finely diced

3 celery stalks, finely diced

1 large white onion, peeled and finely diced

1 garlic clove, peeled and finely diced

3 black peppercorns

3 thyme sprigs

1/2 bay leaf

4 gelatin leaves

2 pounds black trumpet mushrooms (or portobellos), finely chopped

2 tablespoons olive oil

2 tablespoons shallots, peeled and finely minced

2 pounds thin asparagus, bottoms removed, peeled halfway

3 bunches spinach, stemmed and carefully washed

kosher salt and freshly ground white pepper

SHERRY VINAIGRETTE:

1/8 cup sherry vinegar

1/4 cup olive oil

1/4 cup canola, grapeseed, or neutral oil

SALAD:

1 head frisée, trimmed

1 bunch watercress, stemmed

1. Preheat the oven to 350°F.

2. Make the squab stock: Roast the squab bones in a roasting pan in the oven until evenly browned, approximately 25 minutes. Remove the squab bones and excess fat, and deglaze on top of the stove with 1/2 cup of wine by removing the squab bits on the bottom of the pan with a spoon. On top of the stove, heat a tablespoon of olive oil in a large soup pot and add the mirepoix of carrot, celery, onion, garlic, peppercorns, thyme sprigs, and bay leaf. Cook until caramelized. Add the squab liquid from the roasting pan, squab bones, and add water to cover the bones. Bring to a boil and then simmer over medium heat for approximately 2 hours, skimming the scum off the surface from time to time. Strain and then reduce to about 1 cup of glacé, for approximately 1 hour.

3. Soak the gelatin sheets in one cup of water for about 5 minutes to soften. Drain the sheets and add to the glacé.

4. Make the squab breasts: Generously season the squab breasts with salt and pepper and then grill them, remove their skins, and slice in half horizontally. Reserve. (If a grill is unavailable, place 1 tablespoon of olive oil in a saucepan and, when the oil smoking, sear the breasts.)

5. Season the mushrooms with salt and pepper. In a saucepan, heat the olive oil and sauté the mushrooms with the shallots for approximately 4 to 5 minutes, until the shallots are caramelized. Carefully purée in a food processor for a few seconds by pulsing slowly so that the consistency is not too fine but has some texture, like a duxelles.

6. Blanch the asparagus in salted boiling water for 4 minutes until tender. Shock in ice water, pat dry on a flat surface, and cover with paper towels.

7. Coat a 20-inch-long-by-2$\frac{1}{2}$-inch-high-by-2$\frac{1}{2}$-inch-wide terrine mold with olive oil and line with plastic wrap extending over the sides. Keep the terrine mold on a bed of ice while composing the terrine. Line the bottom of the mold with a thin layer of mushrooms, smoothing with the back of a tablespoon or spatula. Lightly brush the glacé over the mushrooms and each succeeding layer. Add a layer of asparagus tips placed inward toward each other overlapping a little. Then add one more layer of mushrooms, then squab breasts overlapping each other, then a very thin layer of mushrooms, the asparagus again, and then the mushrooms—each time adding a very thin layer, flattened with a spoon. Continue until reaching the rim of the terrine. Lightly brush the top of the terrine with the glacé. Fold over the plastic wrap tightly and press down with a weight for at least 2 hours or (preferably) overnight in the refrigerator.

8. Blanch the spinach in salted boiling water for 15 seconds. Shock the leaves in ice water. Set aside to wrap the terrine. Pat dry and lay on a flat surface, stem side up, facing you. Cover with a clean cloth.

9. Make the vinaigrette: In a medium stainless-steel bowl, whisk the sherry vinegar and oils. Season with salt and pepper.

10. On a flat surface, lay down a piece of plastic wrap a little larger than the terrine mold. Lay out spinach leaves vertically overlapping; on both sides, a little larger than the terrine, with the thicker part of the stem facing out. Season with kosher salt and freshly ground white pepper.

11. Unwrap the terrine, placing terrine on the bottom end of the spinach wrap. Turn each end onto the spinach wrap until the entire terrine is completely wrapped. Fasten the plastic wrap until ready to serve. Refrigerate for 1 hour. With a very sharp knife, slice the terrine into $\frac{1}{2}$-inch pieces.

12. To serve, toss the greens in a very small amount of vinaigrette. Place a mound of greens a little off-center and arrange two overlapping slices of the terrine, touching the greens. Drizzle the vinaigrette around the terrine slices.

SERVES: 20 (2 slices each)

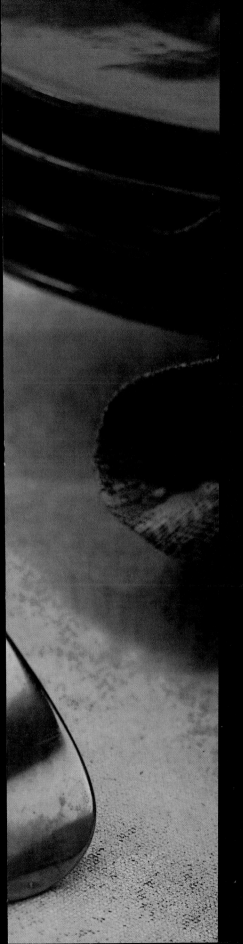

Soups

"Only the pure of heart can make a good soup."

LUDWIG VAN BEETHOVEN

"Of soup and love, the first is best."

SPANISH PROVERB

Baby Clams in Light Broth with Sake

If neither New England nor Manhattan clam chowder is your cup of tea, try this lighter temptation: a silky broth shimmering with diminutive New Zealand littleneck clams or "cockles." The hint of sake and bok choy suggests a beguiling taste of the Far East.

2¹/2 pounds New Zealand littleneck clams (72–80)

2 cups chicken or fish stock (see page 190, 194)

¹/2 cup sake

8 red cherry tomatoes, quartered

1 cup packed baby bok choy, snow pea shoots, or other tender young greens, coarsely chopped

¹/4 cup extra virgin olive oil

GARNISH:

4 tablespoons mixed herb sprigs: chives, chervil, tarragon, parsley, basil

1. Place the clams, stock, sake, cherry tomatoes, bok choy, and oil in a large skillet and bring to a boil. Cook over medium heat covered for approximately 2 minutes until the clams open.

2. Pour the clams and broth into 4 heated soup plates. Garnish each with a tablespoon of herb sprigs.

SERVES: 4

AUTHOR'S NOTE: If New Zealand clams are unavailable, any small baby clam such as Manilas, East Coast littlenecks, or Italian vongole can be used.

Cannellini Bean and Swiss Chard Soup

1¹/₄ cups dried cannellini beans

1 teaspoon white vinegar

3 tablespoons olive oil

³/₄ cup finely diced onion

¹/₂ cup finely diced carrot

¹/₂ cup finely diced shiitake mushrooms

10 cups chicken stock (see page 190)

1 herb sachet (1 bay leaf, 1 thyme sprig, 6 black peppercorns, and 8 parsley stems, wrapped in cheesecloth and tied with a string)

8 roasted garlic cloves

³/₄ pound fresh Swiss chard, stemmed ribs removed, diced into 1-inch squares

8 fresh basil leaves, fine chiffonade (strips)

coarse salt

freshly ground pepper

¹/₄ cup freshly grated Pecorino-Romano cheese

A taste of Italy accents this hearty soup, filled with nutritious cannellini beans and Swiss chard. Swiss chard, a beet variety, has an appealing tartness which added to the cannellini beans makes a satisfying main-course lunch or a light supper dish.

1. In a soup pot, place the beans in cold water to cover. Add the vinegar and soak for at least 6 hours. Drain well and set aside.

2. In a medium stockpot, heat the olive oil over medium-low heat. Add the onions, carrots, and mushrooms and sweat their moisture for about 5 minutes or until just softened. Add the beans and stir to coat. Stir in the stock and herb sachet. Raise the heat and bring to a boil. Lower the heat and allow to barely simmer for about 35 minutes or until the beans are tender but still hold their shape. (Do not overcook.)

3. Remove the garlic from the skin. Add to the beans with the Swiss chard and basil. Discard the herb sachet. Season to taste with salt and pepper. Remove from the heat.

4. To serve, ladle equal portions into each of 6 warm, flat soup bowls. Sprinkle tops with cheese and serve immediately.

SERVES: 6

CHEF'S NOTE: If you want to prepare this soup a day or two before serving, do not add the vegetables. Cook the beans until just tender. Refrigerate until ready to serve. Prepare the garlic, chard, and basil, and add just before serving so that they retain their individual flavors.

Chilled Tomatillo Soup with Goat Cheese Tamales

The predatory coyote, with a mating call as powerful as a herd of Texas Longhorns, is the namesake of Mark Miller's Southwestern showcase, Coyote Cafe. The tart, citrusy, lime-colored tomatillos are the canvas for the bold flavors of the chilies and herbs, balanced and enhanced by the goat cheese tamales in their rustic corn-husk wraps.

TAMALES:

- 4 dried corn husks
- 1 tablespoon baking powder
- 1 teaspoon salt
- 1 cup corn masa (stone-ground cornmeal flour)
- 1/2 cup lukewarm water
- 1 tablespoon unsalted butter, melted
- 4 tablespoons goat cheese, rolled into a log

TOMATILLO SOUP:

- 25–30 tomatillos (green tomatoes)
- 1 red onion, medium, peeled
- 2 garlic cloves, peeled
- 2 poblano chilies, roasted, peeled and seeded
- 20 cilantro sprigs, leaves only
- 1 English cucumber, chopped (or 2 regular cucumbers, peeled and seeded)
- 3–4 serrano chilies
- 1 tablespoon sugar
- kosher salt
- 1/2 cup crème fraîche (see page 191)

GARNISH:

- 8 lime wedges

1. Make the tamales: Soak the corn husks in a deep container covered with hot water and cover for 1 hour. In a separate bowl, place the baking powder, salt, and corn masa, and whisk in the lukewarm water. Then add the melted butter to achieve a dough consistency. (If it crumbles, add water. If too moist, add a little flour. If you can make a thumbprint on the mass, it is ready.) Wrap in plastic and refrigerate for 10 to 15 minutes. Remove from the wrap and divide the dough into 4 pieces, flattening each piece to 1/2-inch thickness. Divide the goat cheese into 4 pieces and place one in the middle of each piece of dough and then place that in the middle of a corn husk. Roll the corn husks around the tamales and tie with a string. Refrigerate until ready to serve.

2. In a pot of boiling water with a steamer, steam for 1 hour. Remove from the pot and untie the string; cut off one end of the husk and peel back.

3. Peel the tomatillos and wash them under hot water. (Alternatively, soak in a bowl of cold water for an hour and then remove skins.) Coarsely chop the tomatillos, saving 4 unblemished ones for the garnish, and process in a blender until smooth.

4. Add three-fourths of the onion, garlic, poblanos, and cilantro, and process approximately 5 minutes until the consistency is smooth.

5. Add three-fourths of the chopped cucumbers to the tomatillos mixture and purée. Season with salt. Pour in a bowl, cover with plastic wrap, and chill thoroughly.

6. Make the salsa garnish: Mince very finely the remaining tomatillos, onion, cucumber, and serranos. In a bowl, combine with sugar and salt to taste. Chill covered with plastic wrap.

7. To serve, divide the tomatillo soup in chilled bowls. Place in each a tamale with a dollop of crème fraîche or Mexican crema in a zig zag decoration and a tablespoon or more of the salsa. Garnish with lime wedges.

SERVES: 4

AUTHOR'S NOTE: An artistic way of presenting the cream is to pour it into a plastic paint or squeeze bottle and make a zigzag over the green tomatillo soup. If poblano chilies are unavailable for the chilled tomatillo soup, anaheim chilies can be substituted.

Chicken and Coconut Soup

This Thai-inspired classic galangal-flavored soup is reconstituted with chicken breast chunks, shiitake instead of straw mushrooms, and an explosive spice-infused broth. The sweet-sour balance typical in Thai food is provided by the sweet coconut and sour-tinged lime juice. A yin yang combination of hot, cold, and crunchy, bursting with aromatic flavors, brings Thai food to elevated heights.

3 cups chicken stock:
   bones of 3 chickens
1 bunch scallions, ends trimmed
4 cups water

1 tablespoon unflavored oil
1 large white onion, peeled and medium dice
$^1/_4$ pound galangal (similar to ginger), peeled and cut into 1-inch x $^1/_8$-inch batons
1 teaspoon red curry paste

BOUQUET GARNI TIED WITH STRING:
2 lemongrass stalks, smashed
3 cilantro sprigs, stemmed
6 lime leaves, optional

1 bird chili, stemmed
3 cups coconut milk
14 ounces chicken breasts, skinned, cut into $^1/_2$-inch cubes
$^3/_4$ pound shiitake mushrooms, stemmed, sliced $^1/_4$-inch thick
2 tablespoons nam pla (fish sauce)
$^1/_4$ cup freshly squeezed lime juice

GARNISH:
4 scallions, sliced at exaggerated diagonal
1 bird chili, stemmed and finely chopped (serrano or jalepeño can be substituted)
8 cilantro sprigs
4 lime leaves (optional)

1. Make the chicken stock: In a medium soup pot, place the bones of 3 chickens with the bunch of scallions and just barely cover with the water. Bring to a boil, skimming off the scum from time to time for about 2 hours. Strain into a bowl.

2. Make the broth base: In a soup pot, heat 1 tablespoon of unflavored oil and sweat the onions, galangal, and red curry paste. Add the chicken stock and the bouquet and bird chili, bring to a boil, and then slowly simmer for 30 minutes. Remove the bouquet garni and strain.

3. In a soup pot, add the broth base, coconut milk, chicken cubes, and mushrooms. Cover and bring to a boil. Simmer for 5 minutes. Remove from the heat and stir in nam pla and lime juice.

4. To serve, use a slotted spoon to divide the chicken and mushroom among 4 large soup plates. Then divide the soup and garnish equally with scallions, chili, and cilantro sprigs, and decorate each bowl with a lime leaf.

SERVES: 4

AUTHOR'S HINTS: Smashing the lemongrass with the side of a large knife releases its essential oils for a more fragrant bouquet. Lime and lemon leaves can be purchased at most Asian grocers.

Galangal, which looks like ginger, has a pine flavor and is used in Thai and Indonesian cooking as a flavoring for soups and sauces.

On a heat scale of 1 to 10, bird chili is about 7, whereas habañero or Scotch bonnet is rated 10. These are red or green chilies with a short thin stem. For less heat, remove the seeds.

Cream of Potato Soup with Avocado, Chicken, and Corn

4   tablespoons unsalted butter

2   cups white onions, peeled and chopped

2   tablespoons ground cumin

5   cups (approximately 4 large) russet or Idaho potatoes, peeled and diced

6   cups plus chicken stock (see page 190) and up to 2 cups more

1–1$^{1}/_{2}$ cups heavy cream

1$^{1}/_{2}$ pounds whole, boneless, skinless chicken breasts, cut into bite-size pieces

   salt and freshly ground white pepper

GARNISH:

3   avocados, seeded, peeled, and cut into $^{1}/_{2}$-inch cubes

3   tablespoons minced fresh chives

2   cups corn kernels (6 ears, husked and blanched)

In this robust soup, the all-American standard russet or Idaho potato gets dressed for dinner with a California favorite, the avocado. This tropical, pear-shaped fruit provides a smooth texture and well-balanced counterpart to the full-textured potato soup.

1. Melt the butter in a large saucepan. Add the onions and cook until translucent, 10 to 15 minutes. Stir in the cumin and cook for 1 to 2 minutes. Add the diced potatoes and 4 cups of the chicken stock and bring to a boil. Reduce the heat and simmer for about 20 minutes, until the potatoes are very tender. Purée in a blender.

2. Return the soup to the saucepan and simmer. Whisk in the cream to taste. If too thick, add up to 2 additional cups of chicken stock to taste.

3. In a separate saucepan, simmer the remaining 2 cups of chicken stock. Add the chicken pieces and poach until just cooked through.

4. To serve, divide the soup among 6 soup bowls. Season with salt and pepper to taste. Pour the chicken pieces and liquid in the bowls. Garnish with the avocado, chives, and corn.

SERVES: 6

Mushroom Tawny Port Soup

2 quarts chicken stock (see page 190)

1/8 cup peanut oil

1/2 pound domestic mushrooms, cleaned and stemmed, finely sliced

1/2 pound crimini mushrooms, cleaned and stemmed, finely sliced

1/2 pound shiitake mushrooms, cleaned and stemmed, finely sliced

1 teaspoon kosher salt

1/2 teaspoon white pepper

1/2 cup tawny port

GARNISH:

1/2 bunch scallions, green part only, thinly sliced on bias

Start your meal with the traditional Southern welcome of a tawny soup brimming with woodsy mushrooms. This Colonial soup features port, following a tradition appropriated by Southern cooks from the British during the American Revolution, modernized with an addition of exotic mushrooms and scallion bits.

1. In a large saucepan, heat the chicken stock.

2. Heat a medium saucepan, add peanut oil, and, when hot, sear the mushrooms in batches in order not to crowd them and cook for 5 minutes until lightly browned. Season with salt and pepper.

3. Remove the mushrooms to the pan with the chicken stock, add the tawny port and simmer for 40 minutes. Season with salt and white pepper.

4. Serve soup piping hot and garnish each soup bowl with scallion greens.

SERVES: 6

Painted Soup

RED SOUP:

1 tablespoon virgin olive or corn oil

1 white onion, peeled and sliced

2 garlic cloves, peeled and minced

1 teaspoon black peppercorns

1 tablespoon coriander seeds

1 bay leaf

1 chili arbol or cayenne chili, stemmed and seeded

2 gajillo or New Mexican red chili

2¹/4 pounds large red tomatoes, cored and halved

2¹/4 pounds Roma plum tomatoes

1 cup water

¹/2 bunch cilantro, stemmed

kosher salt and freshly ground black pepper

juice of 1 lemon

1 teaspoon red habañero (bottled salsa), optional

YELLOW SOUP:

1 tablespoon olive or corn oil

1 large white onion, peeled and sliced

2 garlic cloves, peeled and minced

1 teaspoon coriander

1 teaspoon fennel seeds

1 cup water

3 pounds yellow tomatoes, cored and halved

zest from ¹/2 lemon, finely chopped

juice from 1 lemon

salt

¹/2 teaspoon tomato red Coyote Cocina Howlin' Hot Sauce (optional)

GARNISH:

8 green chilies or parsley sprigs

¹/4 cup crème fraîche or Mexican crema (see page 191)

¹/4 cup salsa fresca (see page 201)

Piquant green chilies balance well and paint a colorful canvas with this fruity yellow and red tomato soup heightened with the pungency of coriander. Mark Miller is particularly interested in the psychological reaction to food and the body's responses to temperature, texture, and taste. Inspired by Arizona's painted desert and its colored bands of sunset, this painted soup bursts with refreshing flavors.

1. Make the red soup: In large saucepan, add the oil and heat. Add the onions and cook until well caramelized. Add garlic, black peppercorns, coriander seeds, bay leaf, and chilies (mince them up into smaller pieces). Once a full aroma is created, add gajillo.

2. To the pan, add the tomatoes, a cup of water, cilantro, salt and freshly ground black pepper to taste, and juice of 1 lemon. Cover and simmer over low heat for 20 to 30 minutes until the tomatoes soften. (Pierce the tomato with a fork until there is no resistance.) Cool in an ice bath. Remove the bay leaf.

3. Purée in a blender for one minute and then push through a sieve into a bowl. Chill the soup and check seasoning before serving. Add red habañero if desired.

4. Make the yellow soup: In a large saucepan, heat the oil and sweat the onion over medium heat until translucent. Add the garlic, coriander, and fennel seeds. Deglaze with a cup of water. Add the yellow tomatoes, reduce the heat, and cover. Cook for 25 to 30 minutes until the tomatoes are soft. Strain out the seeds and stems and blend long enough to break down the tomatoes. Cool and season with lemon zest, lemon juice, salt, and optional Coyote Cocina Howlin' Hot Sauce.

5. To serve, pour a large ladle of each soup preparation simultaneously into opposite sides of a large soup plate. Place crème fraîche in a plastic squeeze bottle and make a design in a zigzag pattern. In the center, garnish with a green chili or parsley sprig and salsa fresca.

SERVES: 8

AUTHOR'S NOTE: Gajillo is a dried chili, similar in heat to the New Mexican chili. It is characteristically more fruity.

Porcini Broth with Soft Polenta, Taleggio Cheese, and a Poached Egg

PORCINI BROTH:

4 ounces dried porcini mushrooms

3^{1}/$_{2}$ cups chicken stock (see page 190)

^{1}/$_{2}$ cup Marsala wine

   kosher salt and freshly ground pepper

POLENTA:

3 cups water

^{1}/$_{2}$ cup coarsely ground cornmeal

2 tablespoons grated Parmesan cheese

2 tablespoons white vinegar

6 extra-large eggs

^{3}/$_{4}$ cup Taleggio or other semisoft cheese (e.g., Fontina), coarsely sliced

3 teaspoons truffle (optional) or extra virgin olive oil

GARNISH:

6 herb sprigs such as dill, parsley, rosemary, carrot-green tops

Jody Adams approaches food from an anthropological point of view so that each element and texture melds well together. The Taleggio cheese provides a nutty flavor and the porcini broth a wonderfully scented aroma to this delicately constructed temptation.

1. Make the porcini broth: Soak the dried porcini in a bowl of warm water just to cover. When soft, trim the stems and chop the mushrooms coarsely. Rinse thoroughly. To remove the dirt, strain the porcini juices through a fine mesh strainer into a medium saucepan. Add the mushrooms, chicken stock, and Marsala, and simmer for 45 minutes. Season with salt and pepper to taste and strain the broth through a fine strainer or, if desired, a coffee filter. Keep warm.

2. Make the polenta: Bring the water to a boil in a medium saucepan. Add the cornmeal in a steady stream and whisk constantly to prevent lumps for about 20 minutes. Stir with a long wooden spoon until the polenta is thick and shiny and comes easily away from the sides of the pot. Add the cheese, season with salt and pepper to taste, cover, and keep warm in a water bath.

3. Fill a shallow 8-inch sauté pan with water. Bring to a boil and simmer. Add the vinegar and a pinch of salt. Crack each egg, one at a time, into individual teacups and then tip into the simmering water. Using the cup, fold the whites over the yolk to form a compact shape. Poach for 4 minutes. Set on a cloth tea towel until ready to serve.

4. To serve, heat 6 large soup bowls. Divide the hot polenta among the bowls, making a mound by taking 2 large spoons and rounding into shapes. Press a piece of cheese into each mound of polenta. Heat the eggs in the porcini broth and, using a slotted spoon, scoop them out of the broth and place on top of the cheese. Pour hot broth into each bowl around the polenta mound. Drizzle with truffle or extra virgin olive oil. Top with an herb sprig.

SERVES: 6

AUTHOR'S NOTE: Vinegar helps eggs to coagulate.

Roasted Onion Soup with Roasted Garlic and Ham Hock Croutons

Bradley Ogden has great respect for the onion, a cultivated root vegetable with a several thousand year history of its own in promoting good health. As to the infusion of garlic, Alexander Dumas opined while walking the streets of Marseilles, "The air of Provence is impregnated with a scent of garlic which makes it very healthy to breathe." This richly colored broth, scented with roasted onions and garlic, provides an explosive flavor and is food for thought for any culinary enthusiast.

3 medium white onions, peeled

3 tablespoons plus 1 teaspoon olive oil kosher salt and freshly cracked black pepper

1 tablespoon unsalted butter

7 large garlic cloves, unpeeled

1 small carrot, peeled and sliced

1/2 celery stalk, sliced

3 thyme sprigs (or 1/4 teaspoon dried)

1/2 bay leaf

3 cups chicken stock (see page 190)

2 cups water

2 tablespoons malt vinegar

1/2 pound ham hock

12 slices baguette, 3/4-inch-thick rounds

1. Preheat the oven to 350°F.

2. Rub the onions with 1 tablespoon of the olive oil and season with 1/2 teaspoon each kosher salt and black pepper and place in a small roasting pan. Roast in the oven for 1 1/2 hours. Cool.

3. Make the roasted garlic: In a small roasting pan, over low heat, melt the butter and add the remaining 2 tablespoons of olive oil. Add the garlic cloves, season with salt and pepper, and cover the pan with foil. Roast in the oven for 30 minutes, until the garlic is very tender. Cool the garlic, squeeze it from the husks, and mash with a fork to form a paste. Reserve the garlic oil remaining in the roasting pan. Keep the oven on.

4. Meanwhile, heat a heavy-bottomed medium saucepan over moderate heat. Add 1 teaspoon olive oil, carrots, and celery, and sauté for 3 to 4 minutes. Add the herbs, chicken stock, water, vinegar, and ham hock. Bring to a boil, reduce heat, and simmer for 1 1/2 hours. Remove ham hock and cool. Strain the broth. Remove meat from the bones and trim off all fat. Shred.

5. Combine the ham-hock shreds with the garlic paste.

6. Deglaze the onion pan with one cup of the ham-hock broth and return it to the stock. Remove outer layers of the onions and chop coarsely. Simmer the onions in the reserved broth for an additional 30 minutes. Purée the onions and broth in a blender and season with kosher salt to taste.

7. Brush the sliced baguettes with the reserved garlic oil and place on a sheet pan. Bake in the oven until lightly browned around the edges.

8. To serve, reheat the soup to a simmer. Spread garlic and ham paste on the bread slices. Ladle the soup into 6 warm bowls and place 2 ham croutons on each serving.

SERVES: 6

Roast Yellow Pepper Soup with Basil

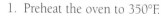

1   tablespoon virgin olive oil
6   yellow bell peppers
1   red bell pepper
4   large shallots
1   quart vegetable or chicken stock
    (see page 190)

¹/₂ cup lowfat plain yogurt
     sea salt and freshly ground white pepper

GARNISH:

4   teaspoons lowfat plain yogurt
¹/₄ cup basil, chiffonade (cut into fine strips)

This fragrant soup, subtly complemented with roasted yellow peppers and shallots, is a seductive introduction to any meal. Yellow and red bell peppers are most frequently available in summer and fall. The roasted shallots add a rich explosion of flavor.

1. Preheat the oven to 350°F.

2. In a shallow pan, lightly drizzle oil over the peppers and shallots. Roast in the oven for 40 minutes. Remove the charred skin and the seeds from the peppers and peel the roasted shallots. Finely chop the yellow peppers and shallots.

3. Purée the red pepper in the food processor.

4. In a saucepan, bring the vegetable stock to a boil. Season well with salt and freshly ground white pepper. Simmer to obtain a stronger flavor. Increase the heat to medium, add the shallots and yellow peppers, and cook until hot. (Do not allow to boil again.)

5. Place the mixture in a blender for a few seconds. Add the yogurt and blend to incorporate. Adjust the seasoning.

6. To serve, ladle soup into warm bowls, decoratively drizzle with a tablespoon of red pepper purée, and place a teaspoon of yogurt in the center of the soup. Sprinkle the basil chiffonade on top of the soup.

SERVES: 4

Tropical Gazpacho

In Latin America and Southeast Asia, fruits are frequently utilized in savory dishes. Such equatorial favorites as papaya and mango are mixed with diced bell peppers to create bold, innovative combinations. The sweetness of the mangoes and pineapple and the sharpness of the limes and Tabasco inflame this refreshing gazpacho with a burst of flavor.

6 cups tomato juice

1 cup papaya juice

2 medium mangoes or papayas, peeled and small dice

1/2 medium pineapple, peeled, cored and small dice

1/2 red bell pepper, seeded and small dice

1/2 green bell pepper, seeded and small dice

juice of 4 limes

4 dashes Tabasco sauce

1/2 cup chopped cilantro

salt and freshly cracked black pepper

GARNISH:

juice of 1 lime

6 cilantro sprigs

1 lime, cut into thin wedges

1. In a large bowl, combine the tomato and papaya juice. Add the remaining ingredients, season with salt and pepper to taste, stir, and cover with plastic wrap. Refrigerate from 4 to 6 hours.

2. To serve, divide among 6 bowls, add juice of lime, garnish with cilantro sprig and lime wedges.

SERVES: 6

Turnip Cream Soup with a Swirl of Apple Purée

4 tablespoons unsalted butter	9 cups water
2 large Spanish onions, peeled and thinly sliced	2 teaspoons kosher salt
1 large Westport turnip, peeled and diced	6–8 Empire apples
	2 cups heavy cream

1. In a stockpot, melt the butter and add the onion slices. Cook, covered, over low heat approximately 15 to 20 minutes until the onions are very soft.

2. Add the diced turnip, 7½ cups of water, and the salt. Raise the heat, bring to a boil, and reduce the heat to a simmer. Cook covered for about 1 hour until the turnips are very soft and break up easily when pressed with the back of a spoon.

3. While the turnips are cooking, quarter and core the apples, leaving the skins on. Cut each quarter in half horizontally. Combine the apples and the remaining water in a small saucepan. Bring to a boil and cook, uncovered, until the apples disintegrate, stirring constantly. Raise the heat and cook until the water has evaporated. Purée the apples in a blender, remove any excess skin, and reserve.

4. Purée the turnips with their liquid in a blender and return the purée to a clean pot. Over low heat, add the cream. Bring to a boil, stirring constantly. Ladle the soup into heated bowls. Place the apple purée in a squeeze bottle and swirl in the center.

SERVES: 8

New England produces the smooth-skinned Westport turnip, a variation of the root vegetable rutabaga, and the Empire apple, a mildly sweet, medium-size, cherry-red fruit. The apple purée is delicately swirled throughout the white turnip soup to create a fragrant, rosy-hued comfort dish.

CHAPTER 3

Salads

"To make a good salad is to be a brilliant diplomat—
the problem is entirely the same in both cases.
To know how much oil one must mix with one's vinegar."

OSCAR WILDE

"Lettuce is like conversation; it must be fresh and crisp,
and so sparkling that you scarcely notice the bitter in it."

CHARLES DUDLEY WARNER

Bulgarian Salad of Roasted Peppers, Onions, and Walnuts

A tower of roasted red peppers, red onions, and California walnuts, buttressed by verdant arugula greens, is flanked with crumbly feta cheese. This colorful salad illustrates some of the international influences on California cuisine, one of our most distinguished culinary meccas. Joyce Goldstein was a pioneer of the popular California trend of using home-grown, seasonal vegetables accompanying a diet lower in fat.

2   medium unpeeled red onions
     olive oil for rubbing
2   large red bell peppers
1   cup walnuts, shelled

GARLIC VINAIGRETTE:
1/3   cup virgin olive oil
1/3   cup olive oil
2   tablespoons red wine vinegar
1/2   teaspoon finely chopped garlic
1   teaspoon salt
1/2   teaspoon freshly ground pepper

4   small handfuls arugula, well cleaned

1   cup feta cheese, crumbled

1. Preheat the oven to 400°F.

2. Rub the onions with olive oil and roast in a baking dish until tender, 45 minutes to 1 hour. Cool, then peel and cut into 1/2-inch strips.

3. Char the peppers in a broiler or over a direct flame, turning often with tongs until blackened on all sides. Transfer to a plastic container with a lid or a paper or plastic bag. Cover the container or close the bag for about 15 minutes. Remove the skins with your fingers or with a knife blade. Cut the peppers in half, remove the stems, seeds, and ribs, and slice the peppers into 1/2-inch-wide strips.

4. Place the walnuts on a baking sheet and toast in the oven 7 to 10 minutes. Remove and coarsely chop.

5. Make the garlic vinaigrette: Whisk all the vinaigrette ingredients in a bowl.

6. To serve, toss the arugula with about one-third of the vinaigrette and place it on a platter or on individual serving plates. Toss the roasted peppers and onions with some of the remaining vinaigrette and place on top of the arugula. Top with toasted walnuts and crumbled feta cheese. Drizzle with the rest of the vinaigrette to taste.

SERVES: 4

Charred Lamb Salad with Cucumber and Mint

LAMB JUS:

- 1 tablespoon olive oil
- 1/4 teaspoon red curry paste
- 1 quart lamb stock (see page 197)

CHILI VINAIGRETTE:

- 1 cup white vinegar
- 2 teaspoons sugar
- 1 garlic clove, peeled and finely minced
- 1 bird chili pepper, stemmed (serrano or jalapeño are good alternatives)
- 1 teaspoon kosher salt

SALAD:

- 3/4 pound jicama, peeled and cut into 1/2-inch dice
- 2 carrots, peeled, julienned
- 1 English (seedless) cucumber, washed, skin on, very thinly sliced
- 1/4 cup fresh bean sprouts
- 2 lemongrass stalks, smashed, finely minced
- 1 bunch mint, stemmed and chiffonade (cut in thin strips)
- 2 teaspoons nam pla (fish sauce)
- 1 tablespoon unflavored oil
  One 3/4-pound boneless lamb loin
  kosher salt

GARNISH:

- 8 cilantro sprigs

Here the personalized cuisine of Jean-Georges Vongerichten is redirected so that the essential taste of the charred lamb provides a pure flavor to the dish. The vinaigrette harmonizes well with the richness of the lamb in this twist on the classic Thai beef salad with lemongrass. As in most Thai food, the seasoning is in the liquid. The fish sauce heightened by ginger, lemon grass, and mint simultaneously provides a fiery hotness and refreshing coolness.

1. Make the lamb jus: In a hot deep skillet over medium heat, heat the olive oil and the red curry paste, mashing it for a few minutes. Add the lamb stock and reduce to 1 cup for approximately 40 minutes to 1 hour.

2. Make the chili vinaigrette: In a bowl, combine the vinegar, sugar, garlic clove, bird chili, and salt to taste, and infuse for 1 hour.

3. Make the salad: In a stainless-steel bowl, combine the jicama, carrots, cucumber, bean sprouts, minced lemongrass, and mint.

4. In a very hot iron skillet, add the unflavored oil and sear the lamb on both sides for 3 minutes each. Remove with tongs and rest for 5 minutes. Thinly slice the lamb across the grain. Season with kosher salt.

5. To serve, dress the salad with the vinaigrette and nam pla and place a pile in the center of each dinner plate. Pile and cascade 6 lamb slices over each salad. Garnish the plates with 2 cilantro sprigs and drizzle lamb jus over the top of the lamb.

SERVES: 4

Charred Venison Salad with Wild Mushrooms and Fresh Herbs

Wayne Nish is a master at fusing East and West, producing dishes exalting the world's finest ingredients. The salt and acid content of the soy sauce and lime juice marinade provide the cure for the venison, creating an exhilarating complement to an earthy herb and mushroom salad. The availability of high-quality, tender venison has spurred increased demand for this robust, lean, and low-cholesterol game. New Zealand's best venison is cervena, from deer allowed to roam free.

One 2-pound venison leg (separate muscles)

WET CURE:

2 1/2 cups Japanese soy sauce

3/4 cup rice vinegar

6 tablespoons lime juice (approximately 8 limes)

3 tablespoons Ryori (cooking) sake or dry sake for drinking

3 tablespoons shin mirin (sweet cooking rice wine)

2 teaspoons harissa or Vietnamese chili sauce

8 garlic cloves, peeled and very thinly sliced

1/2 teaspoon freshly ground black pepper

BEET AND TOMATO CONDIMENT:

3 medium beets, halved, stemmed

1/2 cup extra virgin olive oil

kosher salt and freshly ground black pepper

1 tablespoon water

1 cup roast tomato purée (see page 200)

1/4 cup prepared horseradish in vinegar

WILD MUSHROOMS:

3/4 pound portobello mushrooms, carefully wiped cleaned, stems removed and split lengthwise, ends trimmed and reserved

1 cup first-press extra virgin olive oil

2 ounces fresh herbs, parsley, thyme, rosemary, sage, singly or in combination

clarified butter for basting

GARNISH:

24 chives

1/2 chervil bunch

1/2 parsley bunch

1. Pat the venison dry. Cut each venison muscle into long, narrow pieces not more than 2 inches wide by 3 inches long. Combine all of the ingredients in the wet cure and mix well. Add the meat and refrigerate tightly covered with plastic wrap for 24 hours or up to 5 days.

2. Preheat the oven to 275°F.

3. Make the beet and tomato condiment: Place the beets in a small roasting pan, coat lightly with extra virgin olive oil, and season with salt and pepper. Add 1 tablespoon of water and roast the beets covered with aluminum foil in the oven for 1 hour or until soft. Cool, peel, and chop coarsely. Place the beets, tomato purée, and horseradish in a blender and process until smooth. Adjust seasonings and set aside.

4. Turn the oven down to 250°F.

5. Make the mushrooms: Arrange the caps, gill-side up, and the stems in a shallow medium roasting pan. Season liberally with kosher salt and black pepper, then pour over the extra vir-gin olive oil to a level of 2¼ inches from the bottom of the pan. Bruise 1 or 2 hand-fuls of fresh herbs, including parsley, thyme, rosemary, and sage, singly or in combination. (Bruising releases the oils from the herbs.) Sprinkle the herbs over the mushrooms. Cover the pan with aluminum foil and cook in the oven for 45 minutes until the mushrooms are soft to the touch. Drain the mushrooms with a sieve and strain out the fragrant oil. Reserve for remaining use in sauces or salad dressings or a dressing for grilled meats. Slice the mushrooms into thin strips and serve at room temperature.

6. Make the venison: Remove venison from the wet cure and blot dry with paper tow-els. Baste generously with clarified butter and season generously with salt. Char the meat on the hottest part of a grill. When brown, turn and char the other side for sev-eral minutes. Alternatively, in a smoking, heavy-bottomed pan, sauté on both sides. Thinly slice the meat across the grain.

7. Lump 3 chives together on a slice of venison and roll. Press the seam to seal, moistening with water, as needed. Repeat the process.

8. To serve, place one roll vertically on each dinner plate. Fan out several mushroom slices around the meat and intersperse with herb sprigs. Spoon out the beet and tomato condiment adjacent to the venison roll.

SERVES: 8

AUTHOR'S NOTES: If harissa or Vietnamese chili sauce is unavailable, other hot sauces will substitute well.

Grilled Scallop Salad with Frizzled Tortillas

Two 6-inch blue corn tortillas
(see page 195, use blue cornmeal
instead of all-purpose flour)

Two 6-inch yellow corn tortillas
(see page 195, use yellow cornmeal)

1/2 cup olive oil

1 tablespoon each—red, green, and yellow
bell peppers, cored, seeded, and diced

1 tablespoon fresh ginger, peeled and
julienned

2 tablespoons chopped basil, stemmed

2 tablespoons sherry wine vinegar
kosher salt and freshly ground pepper

1 tablespoon diced tomato, peeled and
seeded

1 pound assorted greens (mache, red oak
leaf, arugula, watercress)

1 pound fresh scallops, tendons removed

Frizzled blue and yellow corn tortilla strips provide a crunchy contrast to the tender, fleshy, moist scallops. Tortillas, standard fare in a southwestern pantry, are increasingly available nationwide and are giving potato chips healthy competition. Deftly dotted with fresh peppers, this exhilarating salad bursts with a confetti of color.

1. Heat the olive oil until it reaches 350°F. To frizzle tortillas, run the blue and yellow corn tortillas through a pasta machine to make thin julienne strips. Sauté the strips in the olive oil until crisp. Drain thoroughly and reserve warm olive oil for the dressing.

2. In a large salad bowl, combine the bell peppers, ginger, basil, sherry wine vinegar, and warm olive oil, reserving 2 tablespoons of the olive oil for the scallops. Toss and season with salt and pepper to taste. Add tortilla strips, diced tomato, and assorted greens. Gently toss and divide into 4 equal servings.

3. Brush the scallops lightly with olive oil and grill over a very hot fire for approximately 1 minute.

4. Place each heap of greens on the plates and surround artfully with the scallops.

SERVES: 4

Red Jalapeño Caesar Salad with Shrimp Diablo Tamale

These warm diablo shrimp, spiced as "hot as the devil," gracefully pose with their tails in the air, with corn husks encasing a sweet corn filling. The pomegranate garnish adds a tart burst of flavor to this cool, crisp jalapeño pepper Caesar salad. The balance of the cool salad with the hot shrimp provides a perfect harmony in the Texan plains.

DIABLO SAUCE:

- 1 tablespoon vegetable oil
- 3 shallots, peeled and chopped
- 3 garlic cloves, peeled and chopped
- 3 habañero or Scotch bonnet chilies, stemmed, seeded, and chopped
- 1 teaspoon cumin seed
- 1 tablespoon finely grated fresh ginger root
- 2 red bell peppers, seeded, ribs removed, and chopped
- 1/2 mango, peeled, pitted, and diced
- 1 cup chicken stock (see page 190)
  salt and lime juice

CORN PUREE:

- 4 ears fresh yellow corn, shucked and cleaned
- 1 teaspoon maple syrup (optional)
  salt and lime juice

- 4 dried corn husks

RED JALAPEÑO CAESAR DRESSING:
(Yield: 1 1/2 cups)

- 2 large egg yolks
- 4 garlic cloves, peeled and minced (if possible, smoke over hickory chips on a grill)
- 2 shallots, peeled and minced

- 4 boneless anchovy filets, roughly chopped
- 2 tablespoons Dijon mustard
- 1 tablespoon Worcestershire sauce
- 2 teaspoons Tabasco sauce
- 2 teaspoons balsamic vinegar
- 1/4 cup canola oil
- 1/2 cup extra virgin olive oil
  salt and freshly ground black pepper
- 1 roasted red jalapeño pepper, stemmed, seeded, and finely chopped
- 2 tablespoons finely chopped cilantro, stemmed

- 3 tablespoons vegetable oil
- 1 tablespoon salt
- 12 large shrimp, peeled and deveined
- 2 heads of romaine lettuce, trimmed and cut into 1-inch pieces
- 1/4 cup Mexican Cotija cheese, crumbled (if unavailable, use a good-quality Romano, Parmesan, or dried feta cheese)
- 1/4 cup pueblo dried corn
- 1/4 cup pomegranate seeds
- 1/4 cup pumpkin seed powder
- 4 tablespoons pico de gallo (spicy red salsa) (see page 199)
  Two 8-inch flour tortillas, cut in half and rolled into a cone (see page 195)

1. Make the diablo sauce: In a heavy-bottomed skillet, heat the oil until it is lightly smoking. Sauté the shallots and garlic until light brown. Add the chilies, cumin, ginger, and red peppers, stirring for a few seconds. Add the mango and stir for a few seconds. Add the chicken stock, bring to a boil, reduce the heat, and simmer for 20 to 30 minutes. Purée in a blender until the mixture is free of chunks, and put the sauce through a fine sieve. Season with salt and lime juice.

2. Make the corn purée: Using a large hole grater, grate the corn on the cob until all the pulp is extracted. Break up the kernels and place in a heavy-bottomed cast-iron skillet. Over low heat, stir approximately 10 minutes until the corn is thick and cooked through, turning from a mildly yellow to deeper yellow color. If the corn is not sweet, add the maple syrup. Otherwise, season to taste with salt and lime juice.

3. Cover the corn husks in plastic wrap and soak in warm water at room temperature for 30 minutes. Remove from the water and pat dry. Peel off 2 narrow strips of each husk horizontally to make ties. Fill each tamale with the corn purée and tie both ends to create a boat.

4. Make the red jalapeño Caesar dressing: In a blender on low speed, whisk the egg yolks, garlic, shallots, anchovies, Dijon mustard, Worcestershire, Tabasco, and balsamic vinegar, and purée until smooth, slowly drizzling in the oils. Season to taste with salt and fold in roasted red jalapeño and cilantro.

5. Heat the vegetable oil in a sauté pan. Season the shrimp with salt and when the pan is hot sear until the shrimp are three-quarters cooked. Add ³/₄ cup diablo sauce or enough to coat the shrimp, and continue cooking another 2 minutes until the shrimp are done to create a final glazing.

6. In a bowl, toss the romaine lettuce with about 1 cup of the Caesar dressing. Reserve any remaining for another use.

7. To serve, place the corn husks in the middle of a dinner-size plate. Stand the shrimp tails up in the husk. Place the Caesar salad on the plate next to the stuffed tamale. Sprinkle the salad with cheese, dried corn, and pomegranate seeds. Dust the outer rim of the plate with pumpkin seed powder. Stand the tortilla cone vertically between the corn husk and the salad, and spoon the *pico de gallo* around the base of the tortilla.

SERVES: 4

CHEF'S HINTS: The golden-orange Mexican habañero chilies, also known as King of the Yucatan, are the hottest chili peppers in the world. Jamaican or Caribbean Scotch bonnet, a little less spicy, are a good substitute.

Seared Duck Salad
with Tart Port and Caper Sauce

Wisconsin is the industry leader in bratwurst, beer, and duck cultivation. The savory taste of duck, the earthy salad, and the flavorful sauce enlivened with balsamic vinegar, port, and capers, fashions a lusty treasure. Sanford D'Amato's philosophical approach to cooking recommends acid such as balsamic vinegar to heighten flavor and balance the sweetness of the port.

Six 5-ounce Peking duck breasts, boneless and skinless
kosher salt and freshly ground black pepper
2 tablespoons olive oil

PORT AND CAPER SAUCE:

4 tablespoons finely chopped shallots
2 tablespoons chopped garlic
1/4 cup balsamic vinegar
3/4 cup port wine
1 cup duck stock (see game stock, page 196)
2 1/2 tablespoons capers

BALSAMIC VINAIGRETTE DRESSING:

3/4 cup extra virgin olive oil
1/2 cup balsamic vinegar
kosher salt and freshly ground black pepper

SALAD:

6 portobello mushrooms, grilled, brushed with 2 tablespoons of olive oil and sliced 1/4-inch thick
6 plum tomatoes, blanched, skinned, seeded, cut julienne style
1 head frisée, cleaned and separated into leaves
1 head red oak leaf lettuce, cleaned and separated into leaves
12 radishes, blanched and quartered
30 pieces fiddlehead ferns, blanched and trimmed
12 large spears asparagus, blanched and peeled, cut into quarters, cut on the bias

1. Season the duck breasts with salt and pepper. In a hot smoking saucepan, add 2 tablespoons of olive oil and sear the duck breasts until medium-done. Reserve in warm spot.

2. Make the sauce: In the same pan, discard the excess oil, cook over medium heat, add 2 tablespoons of the shallots, and sauté for 1 minute. Add 1 tablespoon of garlic and sauté an additional minute. Deglaze with balsamic vinegar by scraping the bits and reduce by one-half for approximately 2 to 3 minutes. Add the port and duck stock and bring to a boil. Cook for approximately 5 minutes until the sauce has the consistency of just clinging to the spoon. Add the capers during the last 2 minutes of the reduction. Season to taste with salt and pepper, keeping in mind that the capers have a salt content. (Add a few drops of balsamic vinegar if your taste buds require more acidity.)

3. Make the vinaigrette: In a medium stainless-steel bowl, whisk the olive oil and balsamic vinegar and season with salt and pepper to taste.

4. In a small stainless-steel bowl, marinate the portobellos in one half of the balsamic dressing. In a large stainless-steel bowl, marinate the tomatoes in the remaining balsamic dressing.

5. In a saucepan, heat 2 tablespoons of the olive oil and add the remaining shallots, garlic, salt, and pepper, and sauté for an additional minute until the garlic and shallots are translucent.

6. In the bowl with the tomatoes, place the frisée, oak leaf, radishes, fiddlehead ferns, and asparagus. Toss the ingredients from the pan in step 5 and season with salt and pepper.

7. To serve, divide the salad among 6 warm plates, arranging it with some height. Slice the duck breast at an angle and fan out around the salad in the center of the plate. Place the portobello mushrooms in a pile near the salad and drizzle the port caper sauce around the plate.

SERVES: 6

AUTHOR'S NOTE: Blanch the radishes, fiddlehead ferns, asparagus, and tomatoes separately in boiling salted water. Shock in ice water to stop the cooking process.

Shrimp and Bean Sprout Salad

This warm shrimp and cold bean sprout salad, with a fragrant citrus yogurt, provides a subtle balance of Oriental influences and domestic flavors. It typifies the lighter cuisine of renowned chef Jean-Georges Vongerichten who, although French-trained, absorbed the flavors from his sojourn in Bangkok, and also helped popularize lighter oils and vinaigrettes in the United States.

MUSHROOM SALAD:

1/4 pound domestic mushrooms, stemmed, skin peeled, and quartered

1/4 cup plain lowfat yogurt

1 1/2 tablespoons heavy cream

1/2 teaspoon lemon juice

coarse salt

SHRIMP SALAD:

24 jumbo shrimp (approximately 1 pound), peeled, deveined, rinsed

coarse salt and freshly ground black pepper

2 tablespoons unsalted butter

2 shallots, peeled and finely chopped

1 small garlic clove, peeled and minced

4 teaspoons chopped chives

4 tablespoons soy sauce

1/2 pound bean sprouts

2 tablespoons hazelnut oil

1 red bird chili (or 1/2 jalapeño), seeded and chopped

1/8 cup chopped unsalted peanuts

GARNISH:

1/4 bunch mint, stemmed and chopped

1/4 bunch coriander, stemmed and chopped

1. Make the mushroom salad: Season the mushrooms with salt. Whisk the yogurt and cream in a stainless-steel bowl to blend well with lemon juice. Toss the mushrooms with 4 tablespoons of the yogurt and cream mixture. (Use the rest if you prefer more.)

2. Make the shrimp salad: Season both sides of the shrimp with salt and pepper. In a sauté pan, melt 1 tablespoon of butter and sauté the shrimps over medium heat for 2 minutes. Stir in the shallots and garlic. Turn the shrimps over and cook an additional 2 minutes. Toss in the chives to coat with the warm oil. Deglaze with soy sauce and quickly remove the contents from the pan to a bowl.

3. In a stainless-steel bowl, place the shrimp mixture and cooling liquid with bean sprouts, hazelnut oil, chilies, and peanuts. Season with salt and pepper and toss.

4. To serve, on each of 4 dinner-size plates, place the mushroom salad in 3 lines at the 2 o'clock, 6 o'clock, and 10 o'clock positions. Place 2 shrimps in each of the spaces. Arrange a heap of bean sprouts over each pair of shrimp, and spoon the juice from the shrimp mixture over the bean sprouts. Garnish the shrimp with chopped mint and coriander.

SERVES: 4

Southern Fried Chicken Salad with Mustard Vinaigrette

This tasty salad of greens and succulent chicken pieces coated with buttermilk and bread crumbs reflects Bradley Ogden's commitment to comfort food. The strong taste of the Dijon mustard enlivened with thin crispy crumbles of pancetta truly satisfies the soul.

SEASONING SALT:

- 8 garlic cloves, peeled and crushed with a knife
- 1 cup kosher salt
- 2 teaspoons freshly cracked black pepper
- 1 tablespoon minced fresh thyme
- 2 tablespoons finely chopped fresh sage
- 1 teaspoon ground nutmeg

MARINADE:

- 1/4 cup Dijon mustard
- 1/2 teaspoon freshly ground black pepper
- 2 pinches cayenne pepper

MUSTARD VINAIGRETTE:

- 1 teaspoon Dijon mustard
- 1/2 teaspoon seasoning salt
- 1/4 teaspoon freshly cracked black pepper pinch cayenne pepper
- 1 tablespoon red wine vinegar
- 3/4 cup extra virgin olive oil

- 2 boneless chicken breasts, sliced into 4 bias-cut pieces
- 2 boneless chicken thighs trimmed, sliced into 4 bias-cut pieces
- 1/2 cup buttermilk
- 2 cups breadcrumbs
- 6 thin slices pancetta or bacon
- 1 pinch cayenne
- 1/2 cup peanut oil

- 2 quarts salad greens (such as spinach, curly endive, baby lettuces, radicchio), cut into bite-size pieces

1. Make the seasoning salt: Place garlic cloves, kosher salt, black pepper, thyme, sage, and nutmeg in a food processor and blend until medium coarseness. Reserve in a sealed glass jar and refrigerate until ready to use.

2. Make the marinade: In a stainless-steel bowl, whisk together the Dijon mustard, 1/2 teaspoon seasoning salt, black pepper, and a pinch of cayenne.

3. Flatten the chicken pieces with a pounder and coat with the marinade. Cover and refrigerate until ready to cook.

4. Make the mustard vinaigrette: Whisk together the Dijon mustard, seasoning salt, fresh cracked black pepper, cayenne, red wine vinegar, and extra virgin olive oil.

5. Remove chicken pieces from the marinade and coat first with the buttermilk, next with the breadcrumbs seasoned with salt and pepper, pressing the crumbs firmly into the chicken.

6. In a skillet, lightly brown the pancetta. Drain and crumble. Immediately mix together with the remaining breadcrumbs 1 teaspoon of seasoning salt and a pinch of cayenne.

7. In a medium skillet, heat the peanut oil until it is almost smoking. Fry the chicken in 2 batches until golden brown on both sides. This will take approximately 20 minutes altogether. Drain the chicken on paper towels and place on a warm plate.

8. Toss the salad greens with the mustard vinaigrette.

9. To serve, arrange the salad greens on a dinner plate. Position the fried chicken pieces on top of the greens. Sprinkle with crumbled pancetta.

SERVES: 6

AUTHOR'S NOTE: Although you can buy seasoning salt, it is always best to make it fresh. It can be kept for up to 2 weeks, refrigerated in an airtight jar. Bradley Ogden suggests this preferred (though more lengthy) method to using a food processor: Place the garlic and salt in a small bowl and rub the mixture with a mortar or fingertips until the salt is moist. Discard the remaining garlic pieces and add the pepper, thyme, sage, and nutmeg. Thoroughly blend the ingredients.

Thai-Inspired Shrimp Salad with Spicy Peanut Vinaigrette

One of the hallmarks of a great California meal is the plentitude of regional, organic greens and vegetables. This refreshing mélange of shrimp, spinach, carrots, cucumbers, and red cabbage is enlivened by a spicy peanut vinaigrette of Thai inspiration.

SPICY PEANUT VINAIGRETTE:

5 tablespoons rice wine vinegar

3 tablespoons sugar

2–3 jalapeño peppers, finely minced, or 1 teaspoon cayenne pepper

3 tablespoons soy sauce

1/2 cup peanut or mild olive oil

salt

1/2 cup dry roasted unsalted peanuts, coarsely chopped

30 medium-to-large shrimp, shelled and deveined

white wine or water for poaching

6 cups small spinach leaves, well washed and dried

1 1/2 cups peeled and julienned carrots (2 inches long by 1/4-inch wide)

2 cups peeled and diced cucumbers (1/2 inch)

1 1/2 cups thinly sliced red cabbage

1. Make the spicy peanut vinaigrette: In a small bowl, whisk together the vinegar, sugar, cayenne or jalapeño peppers, soy sauce, and oil. Season to taste with salt. Stir in the peanuts.

2. In a large saucepan, poach the shrimp over low heat in white wine or water to cover for about 5 minutes, until just cooked through. Remove from the poaching liquid and cool. Cut the shrimp in half lengthwise.

3. To serve, toss the spinach and lightly coat with vinaigrette. Divide among 6 salad plates, creating some height. Then toss the carrots, cucumbers, red cabbage, and shrimp with the remaining vinaigrette as needed and arrange on top of the spinach.

SERVES: 6

AUTHOR'S NOTE: The spicy peanut vinaigrette also makes a good sauce for stir-fry shrimp.

Tournedos Rossini Salad

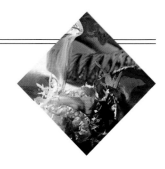

SAUCE:

- ³/₄ cup balsamic vinegar
- ¹/₂ cup cassis (currant liqueur)
- 1 cup game or veal stock (see page 196)

- 1 head radicchio, cleaned
- 1¹/₂ ounces baby mesclun greens
- ¹/₄ cup mustard greens
- ¹/₄ pound shiitake mushrooms
- ¹/₄ cup extra virgin olive oil
- 4 teaspoons clarified butter
- 1 pound beef fillet, cut into 16 medallions

GARNISH:

- 1 carrot, peeled and julienned
- ¹/₂ endive head, julienned
- 8 chive sticks, sliced vertically
- 5 tablespoons mousse of foie gras (optional)

These petite tournedos of beef, duck foie gras, and an elegant arrangement of baby greens make an inspiring special lunch. The namesake of tournedos Rossini is the composer Gioacchino Rossini, highly acclaimed for his last opera's overture, William Tell. This American twist on the classic Rossini salad could improve the vocal chords of any soprano.

1. Make the sauce: In a medium saucepan, add the balsamic vinegar and reduce by half. Then add the cassis and reduce until syrupy (to approximately ¹/₄ cup). Add the veal stock and reduce to ¹/₂ cup. (The consistency should be able to coat the back of a spoon.)

2. Preheat the oven to 350°F.

3. On each large plate, take 2 leaves of radicchio and place together to form 1 large cup. Fill with baby greens.

4. On a sheet pan, roast the shiitake mushrooms coated with extra virgin olive oil for approximately 20 minutes until tender. When cooled to room temperature, slice the mushrooms. Add about 1 tablespoon of mushrooms to each salad.

5. In a preheated pan, heat the clarified butter over high heat, and sear each fillet medallion on both sides, approximately 2 minutes all together.

6. Reheat the sauce slightly in the top of a double boiler. Be careful not to burn the sauce.

7. Spike each salad with approximately 5 pieces each of julienned carrots and endives. Top each one with 1 tablespoon extra virgin olive oil and place 2 chive sticks in each vertically.

8. To serve, on each plate place 4 medallions topped with a teaspoon of mousse of foie gras and drizzle sauce over and around the meat.

SERVES: 4

Walnut Bread Salad

This crusty peasant loaf, boldly woven into a panzanella, or Italian bread salad, is fragrantly tossed with oils and juicy plum tomatoes, and flecked with mint and parsley. Since California is the source of 99 percent of our country's walnut supply, walnut breads and salads sprinkled with walnuts are favored here.

VINAIGRETTE:

1^1/$_2$ tablespoons walnut oil

2^1/$_2$ tablespoons extra virgin olive oil

4 garlic cloves, peeled and minced

1 tablespoon lemon juice

1 tablespoon white wine or sherry vinegar

^{1}/$_4$ teaspoon coarse salt

^{1}/$_2$ teaspoon coarsely ground black pepper

1^1/$_2$ tablespoons extra virgin olive oil

1^1/$_2$ tablespoons walnut oil

1 garlic clove, peeled and minced

4 cups 1-inch walnut bread cubes with crusts (alternatively wheat bread)

6 tablespoons chopped flat-leaf parsley

1 tablespoon chopped mint

2 cups seeded and diced plum tomatoes

^{1}/$_2$ cup toasted walnut halves

2–3 cups (loosely packed) arugula leaves

1. In a small bowl, whisk together the vinaigrette ingredients. Let infuse for 1 hour.

2. Preheat the oven to 300°F.

3. In a large skillet, heat the olive and walnut oils, and add the garlic. Toss in the bread cubes and stir until the bread is lightly browned. Transfer to a baking sheet and place in the oven for 20 minutes to crisp. Remove and let cool to room temperature.

4. In a large bowl, combine 4 tablespoons of the parsley with the mint, tomatoes, walnuts, and arugula. Add the bread cubes and spoon on half of the vinaigrette. Toss well and add the remaining vinaigrette as needed. Sprinkle with the remaining parsley.

SERVES: 5

AUTHOR'S NOTE: To toast walnuts, preheat the oven to 350°F. Line a baking sheet with foil. Spread the nuts on the sheet and roast for 10 to 15 minutes.

Warm Salad of Lobster and Avocado

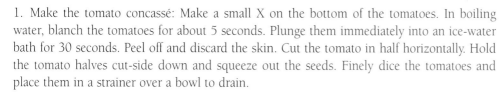

1/2 cup tomato concassé (2 1/2 ripe tomatoes, cored)

Two 1-pound lobsters

2 ripe avocados, halved and pitted

1/2 cup lobster essence (see shellfish essence page 202)

1/4 pound unsalted butter

2 tablespoons chopped shallots

1/2 cup fish stock (see page 194)

12 tarragon leaves thinly sliced

salt and freshly ground white pepper

1. Make the tomato concassé: Make a small X on the bottom of the tomatoes. In boiling water, blanch the tomatoes for about 5 seconds. Plunge them immediately into an ice-water bath for 30 seconds. Peel off and discard the skin. Cut the tomato in half horizontally. Hold the tomato halves cut-side down and squeeze out the seeds. Finely dice the tomatoes and place them in a strainer over a bowl to drain.

2. Prepare the lobster: Place the lobsters in a pot and cover with cold water by 6 inches. Cook over high heat until just before the water boils. Turn off the heat and let sit 7 minutes for a 1-pound lobster and 12 minutes for a 2-pound lobster. Remove the lobsters and cover with ice to stop cooking.

3. Cut each avocado half crosswise into 1/8-inch slices. Press gently down on and across each avocado half to make a fan. Lift the avocado fans onto 4 warm plates.

4. Heat the lobster essence in a saucepan and whisk in 4 tablespoons of butter. Keep warm.

5. Heat 1 tablespoon of butter in a sauté pan. Add the shallots and 2 tablespoons of the fish stock. Cover and sweat the shallots over very low heat for 10 minutes. Remove the cover, add the rest of the stock, tarragon, and tomato concasse, and cook for 2 minutes over high heat. Add the remaining butter and cook an additional minute. Add the lobster and cook another minute only. Season to taste with salt and pepper.

6. To serve, place the lobster slices in the center of each plate with the tomato and juice mixture, arrange the avocado fans on both sides of the lobster, and spoon the lobster essence around the avocados.

SERVES: 4

Harvard-trained architect and a prince of California cuisine, Jeremiah Tower artfully constructs a well-balanced warm lobster salad heightened with the intensity of avocado and a refreshing tomato concassé. This tender mound showcases the natural affinity between lobster and avocado, a vegetable plentiful in Southern California, America's avocado capital.

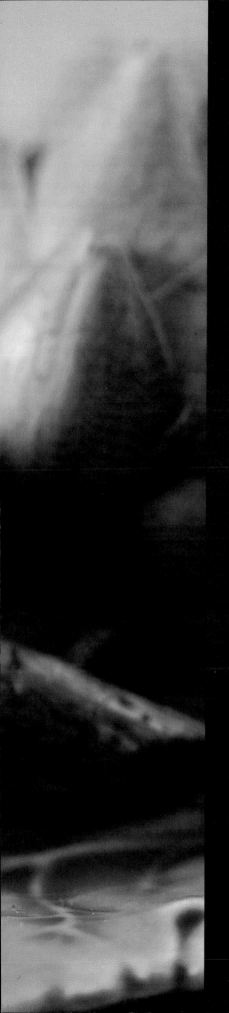

CHAPTER 4

Vegetables

*"Then a sentimental passion of a vegetable fashion
must excite your languid spleen."*

PATIENCE BY GILBERT AND SULLIVAN

*"Eating an artichoke is like
getting to know someone really well."*

WILLI HASTINGS

Artichoke Bottoms Stuffed with Fava Bean Purée

*F*ava beans, otherwise known as broad beans or horse beans, have become increasingly popular in today's lowfat, high-fiber health orientation. The beans produce a satisfying, meat-like stuffing for the delicately petaled artichoke globes abundant in California. Located on the San Francisco coast, Castroville, the artichoke capital of the world, produces 75 percent of the U.S. crop. Look into the heart of arti-chokes and you will find these green globes enchanting.

6   large yellow bell peppers
6   large red bell peppers
1/3 cup olive oil
4   pounds fresh fava (broad bean) pods
2   sprigs fresh savory or thyme

2   cup chicken stock (see page 190)
4   large artichokes
1   lemon, halved
1/2 pound unsalted butter
    salt and freshly ground pepper

1. Make the pepper purées: Preheat the oven to 350°F. Rub the red and yellow peppers with the oil and place them on a baking pan. Cover with aluminum foil and cook for about 45 minutes until soft. Remove from the oven and let stand covered until cool. Remove the skin from the peppers and discard the stems and seeds. Purée the yellow and red peppers separately in a food processor and pass separately through a fine sieve or food mill. Season to taste with salt and pepper. Reserve separately.

2. Make the bean purée: Remove the outer pale green skins from the fava beans. In a soup pot, place all but 1/2 pound of the beans and the savory, and cover with the chicken stock. Bring to a boil over high heat, then simmer for 8 minutes. Drain, reserving the cooking liquid and beans separately. Purée the beans either with the medium blade of a food mill or in a food processor, using up to half the cooking liquid. Press the purée through a fine sieve. Cover and set aside.

3. Cut off half the top of each artichoke with a stainless-steel paring knife, rotating each artichoke in your hand as you cut about 1 inch from the top, until the bases of the leaves remain on the bottom of each artichoke. Remove the chokes or center fibers with the knife. Trim the stems to 1/8 inch. Squeeze the juice from the lemon halves into a pot of salted water and add their rinds. Bring to a boil, add the artichoke bottoms, and simmer for 10 minutes. Remove artichokes and plunge into ice water for 5 minutes. Drain well and set aside.

4. In a sauté pan just large enough to hold the artichokes, add the remaining bean liquid, 1 tablespoon of the butter, and artichoke bottoms. Cover and simmer over low heat for 10 minutes. While cooking, heat the bean purée in a double boiler. When hot, add 1/2 cup of the butter and stir to incorporate. Season, remove from the heat, and keep warm.

5. In separate sauce pans, place the pepper purées, bring to a boil, cover, and turn off the heat. Divide the remaining butter in half and whisk one-half into each purée.

6. To serve, spoon some of the yellow pepper purée onto the center of each warm plate. Spread the red pepper purée around the edges. Fill the artichoke bottoms with the bean purée and place 1 in the center of each plate. Heat the remaining 1/2 pound of the fava beans for 1 minute over boiling water and spoon them around the artichokes.

SERVES: 4

AUTHOR'S NOTE: The yield on the yellow and red pepper purées is 11/2 cups, while only 1/2 cup of each purée is needed for this dish.

Baby Artichokes Stuffed with Quinoa and Nuts

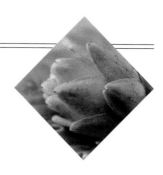

QUINOA AND NUT STUFFING:

1¹/2 cups cooked quinoa

2 tablespoons walnuts or pecans, finely chopped

2 tablespoon hazelnuts, finely chopped

2 tablespoons pistachio nuts, finely chopped

2 tablespoons minced fresh mint leaves

¹/3 cup extra virgin olive oil

3 tablespoons fresh lemon juice

1 teaspoon freshly ground black pepper

¹/4 cup finely diced tomato

1 tablespoon finely diced black olives

ARTICHOKES:

24 baby artichokes, washed and bottom stems trimmed

¹/2 cup virgin olive oil

¹/2 peeled and finely diced yellow onion

1 garlic clove, peeled

1 teaspoon red pepper flakes

1 bay leaf

1¹/2 cups white wine

2¹/2 cups chicken stock (see page 190)

¹/2 cup fresh lemon juice

    salt and freshly ground black pepper

¹/2 cup freshly grated Parmesan cheese

Skilled at cooking with grains in a flavorful way, Kevin Graham presents a savory tender baby artichoke with a quinoa and nut stuffing. Quinoa, an ancient grain with religious importance to the Incas, is replete with iron and protein.

1. Make the quinoa and nut stuffing: In a medium bowl, combine all the stuffing ingredients. Leave at room temperature.

2. Make the artichokes: With sharp scissors, remove the spiked tips and outer leaves. In a heavy pot, heat ¹/4 cup of the olive oil over medium heat. Add the onion, garlic, red pepper flakes, and bay leaf, sauté about 3 minutes until the onion is translucent. Add the artichokes to the pot and sauté for 1 minute, stirring constantly. Add the white wine, chicken stock, lemon juice, salt and pepper to taste, to the pot. Lower the heat, cover, and simmer for about 10 minutes, until the artichokes are tender. Remove the pot from the heat, uncover, and cool for 15 minutes.

3. Drain the artichokes. Gently open the center of each artichoke and fill with quinoa and nut stuffing. Sprinkle with Parmesan cheese and remaining olive oil.

SERVES: 6

Caramelized Vidalia Onions

4 jumbo Vidalia onions, whole

FILLING:

8 tablespoons unsalted butter, softened

1/4 cup light brown sugar

1 tablespoon chopped garlic

2 tablespoons chopped shallots

1/4 cup sherry vinegar

1/4 cup balsamic vinegar

1/4 cup beef or chicken stock (see page 190)

4 teaspoons fresh rosemary, stemmed and chopped

4 teaspoons fresh thyme, stemmed and chopped

2 tablespoons olive oil

4 shiitake mushrooms, stemmed and diced finely

1/2 cup cooked country ham, finely diced

1 ripe tomato, blanched, cored, seeded, and finely diced

salt and freshly ground white pepper

GARNISH:

2 tablespoons chopped chives

Vidalias are like champagne. They are so precious and special that an entire region is named after them, a name that can only be legally used for the product made in that region. The onions in Vidalia, a city and county in Georgia, are particularly sweet and plentiful. Dotted with brown sugar and glazed with an herbaceous vinegar coating, these baked onions make a sumptuous repast.

1. Preheat the oven to 350°F.

2. Prepare the onions: Keeping the outer layers on the onions, remove the stem and using a paring knife, make 6 vertical cuts around the onion, 2 layers deep, and pull down the 6 sections forming a crown on top.

3. In a bowl, mix the filling ingredients except for the mushrooms. Divide the filling ingredients in the center of four 12-inch-by-12-inch pieces of aluminum foil.

4. Hold the crown of each onion and place on top of the filling ingredients. Draw the squares of aluminum foil from 4 corners to the top center like a pyramid with the crown sticking out. Seal well by pressing in the foil.

5. Place the onions on a sheet pan and bake in the oven for about 1 hour and 10 minutes, or until soft.

6. Make the sauce: In a small, hot skillet, heat the olive oil and sauté the mushrooms until soft. Add the cooking juices from the onions in the aluminum foil and the contents of the onion pouch (but not the onions themselves) and gently heat with the ham and tomato. Season to taste with salt and pepper.

7. To serve, spoon the sauce up to the rim of a dinner plate. Place the onion in the center, and garnish with fresh chopped chives.

SERVES: 4

AUTHOR'S NOTE: If Vidalia onions are unavailable, Maui onions grown in volcanic soil in Maui, Hawaii, and Walla Wallas from Washington State are similarly sweet and juicy. If using onion bulbs with long green stems, serve the two crisscrossed on the plate.

Eggplant Caviar and Tapenade

This aromatic eggplant caviar flecked with basil and parsley has the New Orleans' French Quarter in arms. The olives, capers, and anchovies are characteristic flavors of Provence, and the ancient name for caper *tapena* is the namesake of the tapenade, heightened in flavor by the tingle of Dijon mustard.

EGGPLANT CAVIAR

1 large eggplant

1/4–1/2 small red onion, peeled and finely chopped

1/2 teaspoon garlic, peeled and minced

1/2 tomato, peeled, seeded and diced

2 tablespoons olive oil

1/2 lemon, juiced

2 tablespoons chopped parsley
kosher salt and freshly ground black pepper

1 tablespoon fresh basil, stemmed and chopped

TAPENADE:

1 1/2 pounds black olives, pitted

1/4 cup capers

1/4 cup anchovies

2 tablespoons Dijon mustard

4 tablespoons extra virgin olive oil

GARNISH:

1/2 cup feta cheese cubes

1. Prick the eggplant several times with a fork. Then, using an oven preheated to 400°F (cook at least an hour), a flattop, or a grill, roast the eggplant until the skin begins to blacken, the juices turn syrupy, and the pulp becomes completely soft. When the eggplant is cool enough to handle, peel off the skin and dice the pulp.

2. In a bowl, add the eggplant and the rest of the eggplant caviar ingredients. Stir until smooth. (Add more olive oil or lemon juice to taste as needed.)

3. Make the tapenade: Rinse the black olives, capers, and anchovies. Place in food processor and purée into a paste for 3 to 4 minutes. While the machine is still on, add the mustard and slowly adjust with water if the consistency is too thick, then add the oil. Season with salt and pepper to taste.

4. To serve, spoon the eggplant caviar on each plate. Dot the tapenade on the plate. Sprinkle with feta cheese cubes.

SERVES: 4

Fava and Chanterelle Ragout

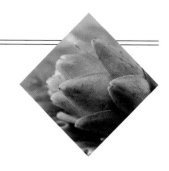

1/2 pound haricots verts, picked and cut into 1-inch lengths

1/2 cup fava beans (shelled but not peeled)

8 tablespoons unsalted butter

4 large shallots, peeled and finely diced

4 small garlic cloves, peeled and minced

1/2 pound chanterelles, cleaned and sliced lengthwise

1/2 cup water

2 tablespoons summer savory (picked from stems), bottom veins removed, finely chopped

kosher salt and freshly ground black pepper

GARNISH:

1/2 bunch fresh parsley, stemmed and chopped

1. Bring 2 small pots of salted water to a boil. In one pot, blanch the haricots verts until *al dente*; in the other blanch the favas for a few minutes. When both are tender, strain and soak immediately in an ice water bath. Strain again.

2. Peel the outer skin of the favas and reserve the fava beans.

3. In a sauté pan, melt 2 tablespoons of the butter and heat until foaming. Add the shallots and cook until transparent. Add the garlic and the chanterelles and cook 3 minutes or until the chanterelles are lightly browned. Add the fava beans and haricots verts and cook on low heat for 2 minutes until heated through.

4. In a small sauce pan, bring 1/2 cup of water to a boil. Add the savory and whisk in the remaining butter. When smooth, add to the fava mixture and season with salt and pepper. Garnish with chopped parsley and serve immediately.

SERVES: 6

The fava bean, found in the Swiss Lake Dwelling archeological sites, is one of the earliest cultivated vegetables. The combination of this earthy bean with haricots verts and woodsy mushrooms in Robert Kinkead's ragout keeps cosmopolitan Washingtonians fueled from meeting to meeting. The scent of summer savory, reminiscent of thyme, adds fragrance and pungency to this satisfying vegetarian delight.

Grilled Morels with Garlic, Chives, and Balsamic Vinegar

This beguiling mushroom dish is favored in spring, when woody, conical morels are plentiful in the Northern Midwest. Michigan's agricultural bounty provides the fundamental richness to this dish. Morels are compatible with a wide range of herbs, as demonstrated here with parsley and chives.

1¹/2 pounds morel mushrooms, stems removed
   2 tablespoons extra virgin olive oil
   2 garlic cloves, peeled and finely minced
      salt and freshly ground black pepper
¹/4 cup flat parsley leaves, stemmed and minced
¹/4 cup snipped fresh chives
¹/4 cup balsamic vinegar

GARNISH:

   4 chives or parsley sprigs

1. Preheat the grill or broiler.

2. In a medium bowl combine the morels, olive oil, and garlic. Season with salt and a generous dose of black pepper, mixing well to combine.

3. Spread the morels evenly on an oiled grill to ensure consistent cooking. Grill for about 3 minutes until well seared. Turn the mushrooms over with a metal spatula or tongs, cooking another 3 minutes until tender. With a spatula, transfer the mushrooms back to the bowl.

4. Add the parsley, chives, and vinegar to the mushrooms and toss to combine. Adjust the seasoning as necessary.

5. Divide the morels among 4 plates. Garnish with a chives spear or parsley sprig.

SERVES: 4

Portobello Mushroom Pizzaiola

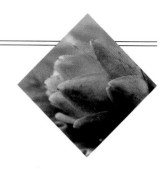

2 red bell peppers

2 green bell peppers

4 tablespoons olive oil

$1/4$ teaspoon chopped garlic

$1/2$ teaspoon kosher salt

4 portobello mushrooms (about 5 inches in diameter), stemmed

4 tablespoons chopped red onions

1 tablespoon capers

8 kalamata olives, pitted and halved

8 Roma tomatoes, blanched, skinned and seeded, cut into $1/2$-inch cubes

2 fresh artichoke bottoms, quartered or 4 hearts, quartered, cut into small wedges

8 basil leaves

pinch chili flakes

8 thin slices mozzarella cheese

8 anchovy filets, optional

A savory pizzaiola topping of onions, capers, olives, tomatoes, and artichoke bottoms coats the highly prized, cultivated portobello mushroom. The spicy tomato sauce makes an equally gracious complement to a tender steak.

1. Preheat the oven to 500°F.

2. Roast the red and green peppers in a roasting pan for about 7 minutes, or until skin is slightly burned. Cool in plastic bag and then remove skins. Halve the peppers and remove the seeds.

3. In a small bowl, combine 2 tablespoons of the olive oil with garlic and salt, and sprinkle on the underside (gill) of the mushrooms.

4. In a nonstick pan, sauté the mushrooms, first on the gill for 2 minutes. Turn and cook an additional 2 minutes. Transfer the mushrooms onto a cookie sheet.

5. Make the sauce: In the same saucepan, heat the remaining 2 tablespoons of olive oil. Sauté the onions, capers, and olives for several minutes until the onions are transluscent. Add the blanched tomatoes, artichoke bottoms, basil leaves, and chili flakes, and cool for several minutes.

6. Lower the oven to 375°F.

7. Lay half of the red pepper and half of the green pepper on each mushroom cap. Spoon $1/4$ of the sauce over each mushroom cap. Top each with 2 slices of mozzarella and 2 anchovy filets, crisscrossing each other.

8. Bake in the oven for approximately 12 to 15 minutes, until heated through, and the cheese is slightly browned.

SERVES: 4

CHEF'S HINT: Saffron angel hair pasta pairs well with this portobello mushroom pizzaiola.

Potato Bhujia with Mint and Cilantro Chutney

In India, potato bhujias are addictive afternoon snacks for children. This flavorful, highly seasoned version can be regarded as an appetizer for cocktail parties or a satisfying main dish for the vegetarian. The chickpea batter adds a complex flavor, and the chutney with cilantro, mint, ginger, garlic, and chilies creates a refreshingly spicy topping.

POTATO BHUJIA: *(Yield: 30 –35 rounds)*

- 2 pounds Idaho potatoes, peeled (approximately 4 potatoes)
- 2 tablespoons black mustard seeds
- 3 tablespoons whole cumin seeds
- 3 tablespoons clarified butter
- 3 tablespoons crushed curry neem leaves (alternatively, chopped cilantro)
- 2 large Spanish onions, peeled and finely diced
- 2 tablespoons minced garlic (approximately 9 cloves)
- 2 teaspoons turmeric
- 1/4 cup chopped cilantro leaves (packed)
- 2 serrano chilies, diced with seeds
- 1 teaspoon salt
- 2 teaspoons ground black pepper

MINT AND CILANTRO CHUTNEY:

- 3 bunches cilantro, stems trimmed and finely chopped
- 1 small bunch fresh mint, leaves only, finely chopped
- 2 garlic cloves, peeled and minced
- 1 1/2 tablespoons freshly grated ginger
- 1–2 serrano chilies, finely chopped, with seeds
- 1/2 teaspoon kosher salt
  juice of 1 small lemon
- 1/2 tablespoon peanut oil

- 1 quart vegetable oil

CHICKPEA BATTER:

- 1 1/2 cups chickpea flour
- 1/3–1/2 cup water
- 3/4 teaspoon ground cumin
- 1/2 teaspoon cayenne
- 3/4 teaspoon turmeric
  salt and freshly ground black pepper
- 1/4 cup plain yogurt

1. Make the potato bhujia: Grate the potatoes on the large side of a grater. In a saucepan, cook the potatoes in 1 quart of salted water until soft. Drain and cool. Pop mustard seeds and roast cumin seeds in a preheated dry pan. Stir in the clarified butter and crushed neem leaves. Add the onions and cook until browned. Add the garlic and turmeric and cook for a few minutes to incorporate. Off the heat, add the cilantro, serranos, salt, and black pepper. Gently mix the potatoes with the onions and spices. Press tightly with your hands into half-dollar discs (1 1/2-inches wide by 1/2-inch thick). Use a falafel-forming tool if available. Place on a sheet pan lined with parchment paper, cover, and chill at least 2 hours or overnight.

2. Make the mint and cilantro chutney: Mix the chutney ingredients in a bowl. Turn out onto a wooden board and chop until a paste is formed.

3. Heat 1 quart of vegetable oil in a large pot for 20 minutes.

4. Make the chickpea batter: In a bowl, moisten the chickpea flour with 1/3 to 1/2 cup water.

Mix until smooth. Add the cumin, cayenne, turmeric, salt and pepper to taste. Dip the potato fritters in the batter and fry them in the vegetable oil approximately 10 minutes until golden crispy. Drain on paper towels.

5. To serve, divide the potato fritters among the plates and serve with mint and cilantro chutney. Add a dollop of yogurt.

SERVES: 5 (25 fritters)

CHEF'S HINTS: To form the potato mixture into mounds, it is easiest to press into a falafel-maker, available at Armenian stores. The oil must be hot enough so that the fritters float on top of it; otherwise, the oil will seep inside the fritters and they will be too greasy.

AUTHOR'S NOTE: Chickpea flour is flour made out of chickpeas. In Indian shops and in specialty shops, it is known as grain flour, besan, or *farine de pois chiches*.

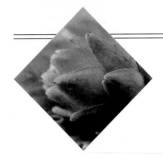

Potato Napoleon with Assorted Seasonal Vegetables

The potato, once a humble root vegetable, is treated here with great reverence. This low fat delicacy contains a splash of garlic mashed potatoes sandwiched between crispy galettes accented with baby vegetables. It would have made Emperor Napoleon Bonaparte proud to be this dish's eponym.

POTATO GALETTES:

5 medium size Russet potatoes, peeled

3 tablespoons olive oil

   salt and freshly ground white pepper

VEGETABLES:

1/2 pound baby beets

1/2 pound baby squash

1/2 pound string beans, stemmed

1/2 pound assorted wild mushrooms, stemmed and sliced

1/2 cup olive oil

2 tablespoons chopped thyme

2 tablespoons chopped parsley

MASHED POTATOES:

5 cups chicken stock (see page 190) or water

10 medium size Russet potatoes, peeled and quartered

6 garlic cloves, peeled

1/4 cup salt

3/4 cup lowfat milk

3 tablespoons unsalted butter

   salt

1. Preheat the oven to 350°F.

2. Make the galettes: Using a mandoline or vegetable slicer, slice the potatoes about 1/16-inch thick. (Do not rinse.) Toss with the olive oil, and season with salt and pepper. Lightly brush 2 baking pans or cookie sheets, 10 by 15 inches, with 1 tablespoon olive oil, and line with parchment paper. Divide potatoes among the baking sheets. Lay slices evenly in pans to cover bottoms, overlapping slices about 1/4 inch. Continue laying rows of potato slices, overlapping the row above about 1/4 inch, until both sheets are filled.

3. Bake in the oven approximately 20 to 35 minutes, until potatoes are crisp and golden. If the potatoes brown unevenly, cover the dark parts lightly with foil. Cool galettes slightly, then loosen with a spatula and break each sheet into 12 random shapes of approximately equal size. Alternatively, cut with scissors into triangles or squares about 4 inches per side. (If making in advance, cool in pans and cover airtight for up to 4 hours. To reheat, uncover and return to 350°F for about 5 minutes until crisp and hot to the touch. Keep the oven on.)

4. In separate medium pots of boiling, salted water, blanch the baby beets, baby squash, and string beans until cooked *al dente*. Cool in a bowl of ice water. Toss with 1/4 cup olive oil, 1 tablespoon thyme, and 1 tablespoon of chopped parsley. Season with salt and pepper.

5. In a bowl, toss the mushrooms in remaining olive oil, chopped thyme and parsley, and season with salt and pepper. Roast in the 350°F oven for 20 minutes.

6. Make the mashed potatoes: In a 5- to 6-quart pan, combine the stock, potatoes, and garlic. Add salt and bring to a boil over high heat, cover and simmer until potatoes and garlic are very tender when pierced, approximately 20 to 30 minutes. About 5 minutes before the potatoes are tender, combine milk and butter in a 1- to 1¹/₂-quart pan. Warm over medium heat until the butter melts. Keep warm.

7. Drain the potatoes, reserving the broth. In a pan, mash the potatoes with a masher or a mixer, adding warm milk and butter and ¹/₄ cup of the reserved broth. (For creamier potatoes, add more broth in small quantities until potatoes are desired consistency.) Season with salt and pepper to taste.

8. To serve, in the center of 8 dinner plates, layer equal amounts of mashed potatoes and place on top of warm galette pieces, extending dramatically beyond the mashed potatoes. Place a galette piece standing upright (reserve your smallest galettes to use on top). Serve at once because galettes soften quickly. Surround the napoleon with hot roasted vegetables.

SERVES: 8

Roasted Beet Terrine with Smoked Salmon and Horseradish Sauce

This ruby root terrine is artfully surrounded with napa cabbage leaves and topped with slivers of salmon and crème fraîche. Beets are a particularly nutritious source of quick energy, containing multiple vitamins and minerals, and the horseradish adds a fibrous exhilaration.

5 cups roasted beets, sliced into rounds (approximately 5 large beets)

2 cups of lobster or chicken stock (see page 194 or 190)

1 cup red wine

1¼ cups balsamic vinegar

1½ tablespoons granulated unflavored gelatin

10 napa cabbage leaves, core removed

1 large leek, cleaned, tops of greens removed, root trimmed

3 tablespoons prepared drained white horseradish

2 cups crème fraîche (see page 191)

2 shallots, peeled and finely diced
juice of ¼ large lemon
coarse sea salt and freshly ground white pepper

GARNISH:

¼ pound smoked salmon, sliced thinly on the bias

3 tablespoons chopped Italian parsley

1 lemon, cut into 12 rounds or zest

1. Preheat the oven to 375°F.

2. Roast the beets in an ovenproof shallow pan. Sprinkle with salt and pepper and cook in the oven, covered until very tender, about 2½ hours. Cool and peel the beets and slice into ¼-inch-thick pieces.

3. In a medium saucepan, over medium-high heat, combine the stock, wine, and vinegar, and reduce until 1¾ cups remain, after approximately ½ hour. Season with salt and pepper and add gelatin slowly in a fine stream, constantly stirring with a whisk.

4. Blanch the cabbage in boiling salted water until just tender, approximately 3 to 4 minutes, and refresh in cold water. Pat dry with a clean towel and reserve.

5. Split the leek in half lengthwise, but keep the root attached, and soak in warm water for 10 minutes. Remove and boil the leek in a pot of salted boiling water approximately 8 to 10 minutes until tender. Drain and cool in cold water, and then slightly trim the root end (not so much that leek falls apart).

6. Lightly coat a 9-inch-by-4-inch loaf pan with olive oil or cover with plastic wrap, folding over the edges. Line the bottom and sides with overlapping cabbage leaves. Layer the beets next until the mold is half full; then place the leek down the center of the mold lengthwise so that the root of each leek half touches the other in the same direction as it originally did intact. Lightly season with salt and pepper. Pour half of the stock mixture into the mold on top of the beets. Then layer the remaining beets until the loaf pan is level-full. Lightly season with salt and pepper. Pour the remaining stock mixture over the top. Fold the leaves draping over the loaf pan towards the center so that they cover the top (set a spare leaf on top to fill if there is a gap). Place plastic wrap over the top and set the pan on a cookie sheet or plate larger than the loaf pan since some of the stock will seep out. Place a 1-pound weight (for example, a quart of milk) on top of the pan and refrigerate for 6 to 8 hours or overnight.

7. Make the horseradish sauce: In a stainless bowl, whisk the horseradish with the crème fraîche, shallots, lemon juice, sea salt, and white pepper, just to incorporate.

8. Slice the terrine into 1/2-inch to 3/4-inch pieces with a serrated or electric knife, and place the pieces in the center of each plate. Spoon the horseradish sauce at the base of the terrine. Make a rosette out of the salmon slices by rolling tightly from one end to the other and place one next to the pool of sauce. Sprinkle with parsley over and around the terrine and garnish with lemon slices.

SERVES: 5 (2 slices each)

AUTHOR'S NOTE: Kosher salt is smaller than coarse sea salt, but either one works fine here. Napa cabbage is America's most common Chinese cabbage with pale-green, elongated leaves that are wrapped around one another.

Sweet Corn Flan with Wild Mushroom Ragout

Patrick Clark proudly presents a new twist on a homey Southern favorite: corn flan. Corn has been an American staple for years, and the wild mushroom ragout artfully adorns this crunchy custard flan.

3 tablespoons unsalted butter

1/2 whole large white onion, peeled and chopped

2 corn ears, husked, peeled, and kernels removed and separated

1 1/2 cups heavy cream

1/4 teaspoon kosher salt

   pinch of cayenne pepper

1 whole egg

1 egg yolk

VEGETABLE GARNISH:

4 tablespoons unsalted butter

1 portobello mushroom, stemmed and cut into 1/2-inch pieces

4 button mushrooms, stemmed and cut into 1/2-inch pieces

1 ear corn, husked and roasted

2 tablespoons parsley, stemmed and chopped

MUSHROOM COULIS:

2 tablespoons olive oil

7 crimini mushrooms, quartered

3 thyme sprigs

1 shallot, peeled and chopped

6 tablespoons unsalted butter

1/2 cup chicken stock (see page 190)

   salt and freshly ground black pepper

GARNISH:

5 chervil or parsley sprigs

1. Preheat the oven to 350°F.

2. Make the corn flan: In a stainless-steel pan, place the butter and onions, and cook over medium heat for 1 to 2 minutes. Add all but 5 teaspoons of the corn, stirring occasionally with a metal spoon to absorb the butter. Pour in the cream and cook for 5 minutes. Place in a flat pan sitting in an ice bath. Add the salt and cayenne pepper and stir.

3. Add everything in a blender, including the eggs, and blend on a high speed for 2 minutes. Then add the corn kernels.

4. Place 5 six-ounce aluminum foil ramekins 2-inches-high-by-5-inches wide, well-sprayed with vegetable oil spray and then well-buttered, in a small roasting pan filled halfway with water. Fill with the custard mixture three-quarters of the way up and cover with well-buttered parchment paper. There will be some custard mixture remaining. Cook in the oven for about 20 to 30 minutes until lightly browned. Place the custards in a cool water bath for 5 minutes.

5. Make the vegetable garnish: In a sauté pan, melt 1 tablespoon of butter and sauté the mushrooms with salt and pepper until light brown. With a knife, gently remove the roasted

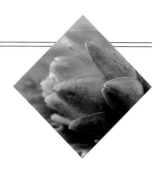

corn from the cob. In a separate pan, coat the corn with remaining 3 tablespoons of butter and season with salt and pepper. Add the chopped parsley and heat.

6. Make the mushroom coulis: In a hot sauté pan, heat the olive oil and sauté the mushrooms with the thyme sprigs until a little after the *al dente* stage, approximately 8 to 10 minutes. Finish by sweating the shallot over low heat. Remove the sprigs and place mixture in a blender with the butter and chicken stock. Season with salt and pepper to taste until the mixture reaches a loose consistency.

7. To serve, alternate the mushroom quarters and roasted corn around the inner rim of the plate. Unmold the flan by tapping the bottom of the ramekin on a hard surface; position in the center of a dinner plate and top with a chervil or parsley sprig. Spoon the mushroom coulis around the flan.

SERVES: 5

Strange Flavor Eggplant

Barbara Tropp has been at the forefront of the new California Chinese cuisine, as evidenced here in one of her spicy hallmark dishes. This aromatic eggplant caviar uses Western eggplant rather than the Chinese or Japanese variety because of its more assertive flavor.

1–1¹/₄ pounds large Western eggplant, leaves removed

AROMATICS:

  1 tablespoon finely minced garlic

  1 tablespoon finely minced fresh ginger

  ¹/₄ cup thinly sliced green and white scallions

¹/₄–¹/₂ teaspoon dried red chili flakes

SAUCE:

  3 tablespoons soy sauce

  3 tablespoons packed brown sugar

  1 teaspoon unseasoned Japanese rice vinegar

  2 tablespoons corn or peanut oil

  ¹/₂ teaspoon Japanese sesame oil

  6 pieces of garlic toast, optional

GARNISH:

  thinly sliced green and white scallions

1. Preheat the oven to 475°F. Place the rack in the middle position.

2. Using the tip of a sharp knife or a fork, prick the eggplant in several places. Place on a baking sheet and bake from 20 to 40 minutes until tender. (Test by piercing with a fork.) Turn once during the cooking process. Remove from oven.

3. Cut in half lengthwise, remove tough stem end, and peel, scraping off and retrieving any pulp. Cube the pulp and process it with its baking liquid until smooth.

4. In a small bowl, combine the aromatics.

5. In another bowl, combine the sauce ingredients, stirring to dissolve the sugar.

6. Over the high heat, heat a wok or large heavy skillet for at least 10 minutes so that a pearl of water will evaporate upon contact. Add the corn or peanut oil to cover the bottom of the pan. Add the aromatics and stir-fry about 15 seconds until fragrant. Add the sauce ingredients and stir. Bring to a simmer. Then add the eggplant, stir well to blend, and heat throughout. Remove from the heat, adjust seasoning with chili flakes, brown sugar, or vinegar, if needed. Stir in the sesame oil.

7. Cool, stirring occasionally. Refrigerate overnight, sealed airtight. Serve at room temperature with garlic toast (optional) and sprinkle with scallion rings.

SERVES: 6

Two Potato Terrine with Potato White Truffle Sauce

2¹/₂ cups large spinach leaves, stemmed

2 medium sweet potatoes, unpeeled

1 large russet potato, unpeeled, ¹/4-inch lengthwise slices

MOUSSELINE:

¹/₂ pound chicken breast, skinless

1 egg white

4 tablespoons cognac, reduced to 2 tablespoons by boiling

1 cup heavy cream
kosher salt and freshly ground white pepper

SAUCE:

1 large potato, peeled and diced

2 cups chicken stock (see page 190)

¹/₂ cup milk
salt and freshly ground white pepper

¹/4 cup fresh white truffle gratings or if unavailable, Westphalian smoked ham, finely diced

GARNISH:

2 tablespoons chopped chives

1 cup potato sticks

The farmlands of the Midwest abound with potatoes, an American staple that highlights a tradition with years of colorful history. The versatile potato plays perfect host to other flavors. It can be served soft, as in the sauce, heightened with the perfume of white truffles, firm, as in the mosaic of terrine layers topped with verdant spinach leaves; or crisp, in the garnish.

1. Preheat oven to 350°F.

2. Steam spinach leaves in boiling water. Drain and shock in ice water. Pat dry by laying side by side, stem side down, on an absorbent cloth and reserve.

3. Place the sweet potatoes with the skin on in a roasting pan in the oven and cook until tender. Cool, peel, slice into ¹/4-inch slices lengthwise, set aside.

4. In a saucepan, cover the russet potatoes with salted water, and boil until tender. Drain, cool, and set aside.

5. Make the mousseline: Clean the chicken breast of any fat or sinew and cut into small pieces. Place in a food processor with the egg white. Process until smooth. Add the reduced cognac. While processing, add the cream, and salt and pepper to taste.

6. Line a 2-quart terrine mold 3-inches-by-10-inches-by-2¹/₂-inches with plastic wrap. Lay the spinach leaves on the wrap. Place a small amount of mousseline on the bottom with the back of a large metal spoon, then alternately layer each potato with mousseline in between until the mold is full. Cover the top with spinach leaves. Cover with foil and bake in a water bath in the oven for 20 to 25 minutes, or until the internal temperature reaches 125°F. Cool slightly before unmolding. To unmold, turn the mold pan upside down onto a cutting board and slice with a sharp knife.

7. Make the sauce: Cover the potatoes with chicken stock and bring to a boil. Simmer until the potatoes are very tender. Place in blender and purée until smooth. Whisk in the milk to desired consistency. Season with salt and pepper to taste, and fold in truffle gratings. Keep warm.

8. To serve, sauce the plate, sprinkle with chopped chives, place a slice of warm terrine on top of the sauce, and garnish with crisp potato sticks for texture.

SERVES: 12

AUTHOR'S NOTE: Optional potato sticks: 1 small russet potato, peeled and cut into shoestring sticks. Rinse the potatoes in cold water and immediately pat dry. Fry in 2 cups of peanut oil at 350°F until crispy. Drain on paper towels.

Torte of Whipped Mascarpone and Porcini Essence

Bunker Hill inflamed the Revolutionary War, but the restaurant Olives situated at its base has ignited a culinary sensation. Inspired by a Venetian-Austrian technique of using crêpes instead of lasagna noodles to layer this earthy torte, this olivaceous specialty of mascarpone and grilled exotic mushrooms is surrounded by spinach mounds dotted with an optional black truffle oil.

MUSHROOM STOCK:

- 1/4 cup olive oil
- 1 medium Spanish onion, peeled and chopped
- 2 garlic cloves, peeled and finely chopped
- 2 celery stalks, chopped
- 1 small carrot, peeled and chopped
- 2 cups domestic mushrooms, with stems, chopped
- 1/2 cup roasted tomatoes
- 2 cups red wine
- 2 cups water
  salt and freshly ground black pepper

FILLING:

- 4 tablespoons olive oil
- 1 large Spanish onion, peeled and sliced
- 1 garlic clove, peeled and sliced
- 2 cups domestic mushrooms and stems
- 2 cups portobello mushrooms, stemmed
- 3 porcini mushrooms, stemmed
- 2 cups tomatoes, cored and roughly chopped
- 1 cup red wine
- 3 fresh rosemary sprigs, stemmed and roughly chopped
- 1/4 cup heavy cream
- 1 cup mascarpone cheese

- 1 cup fontina cheese, grated
  approximately 10 crêpes (see page 192)

BECHAMEL:

- 4 tablespoons unsalted butter
- 1/4 cup all-purpose flour
- 1 pint milk, warm
  salt and freshly ground black pepper
  pinch nutmeg

  four 8-ounce bags flat leaf spinach

- 2 tablespoons olive oil
- 2 garlic cloves, peeled and sliced vertically
- 2 cups wild mushrooms (shiitake, chanterelle, black trumpet), cleaned, stemmed, and chopped

GARNISH:

- 4 Italian parsley sprigs
  black truffle oil, optional

1. Make the mushroom stock: In a large heavy-bottomed pan, heat the olive oil and sauté the onion, garlic, celery, carrots, and mushrooms until the onions become translucent. Add the roasted tomatoes and red wine, and reduce the red wine by half. Season generously with salt and pepper, then add enough water to cover the ingredients. Reduce by half; this should take approximately 15 to 20 minutes. Strain out the solids and reserve the stock. (This should yield 2 cups.)

2. Preheat the oven to 375°F.

3. Make the filling: In a large heavy-bottomed skillet, heat the olive oil and sauté the onions, garlic, mushrooms, and stems until the onions become translucent. Add the tomatoes, red wine, and mushroom stock. Generously season with salt and pepper. Reduce by 3/4 until mixture thickens, and the sauce glazes the mushrooms, approximately 15 to 20 minutes. After 10

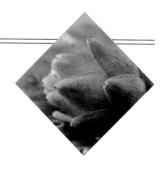

minutes, add the rosemary. When 5 minutes remain, add the heavy cream to thicken. Place in a food processor and pulse a few times to achieve a smooth consistency (a duxelles), but do not purée. Cool to room temperature.

4. Assemble in a loaf pan approximately 6-inches-by-4-inches-by-3-inches in size. Butter the pan and place a thin layer of mushroom filling to cover the surface. Add a layer of the crêpes (overlap them if need be), a layer of mushrooms about 1/4-inch thick, and a few dollops of mascarpone. This process should be repeated 3 to 4 times until you reach the rim of the pan. Sprinkle with the fontina cheese. Cover with plastic wrap or parchment paper and then aluminum foil.

5. Bake in the oven for 15 to 20 minutes, then raise the temperature to 425°F and bake another 5 to 7 minutes.

6. Make the spinach quenelles: Make a bechamel sauce by melting the butter in a small saucepan and then whisking in the flour (the roux) over low heat for 5 minutes, stirring constantly with a wooden spoon. Whisk in the warm milk, season with salt and pepper to taste, add a pinch of nutmeg, and cook gently over a low flame for 15 minutes, stirring constantly.

7. Meanwhile, blanch the spinach in boiling salted water for 3 or 4 minutes. Shock in cold water and pat dry. Place in the food processor. Pulse slowly and then gradually add the bechamel sauce. If the mixture is too tight, adjust with heavy cream.

8. With a 3-inch-high-by-2-inch-diameter metal ring, cut out 4 rounds of the torte and place in an iron pot. In a 375°F oven, heat for approximately 10 minutes until the tortes start to bubble. Remove and, with a paring knife, loosen from metal rings.

9. In a separate pan, heat 2 tablespoons of olive oil and sauté the garlic until golden. Add the wild mushrooms and cook until tender.

10. To serve, place the torte in the middle of a large plate with the spinach mixture, forming 3 quenelles or oval shapes that should be spread evenly around the plate. Intersperse with the warm mushrooms. Garnish each plate with a sprig of Italian parsley and the optional black truffle oil.

SERVES: 4

Wild Mushroom Enchiladas with Avocado-Tomatillo Salsa

Wild mushrooms distinguish this Southwestern staple. The mélange of spicy ancho chilies, tangy lime, cool-textured avocado, and feta cheese is the perfect foil for the avocados, tomatoes, and cilantro salsa. The maestro of the New Texas cuisine, Stephan Pyles, believes that "avocados, tomatoes, and cilantro have a natural affinity for each other." This spicy salsa is a counterpoint to the wild mushroom enchilada, but also comports well with tortilla chips and a pomegranate margarita.

AVOCADO-TOMATILLO SALSA:

- 2 large avocados, peeled, pitted, and diced
- 1 teaspoon diced red bell pepper
- 1 teaspoon diced green bell pepper
- 1 tablespoon diced scallions
- 4 tomatillos, husked, rinsed, and diced
- 1 garlic clove, peeled and minced
- 2 tablespoons cilantro leaves
- 2 serrano chilies, seeded and diced
- 2 teaspoons fresh lime juice
- 3 tablespoons olive oil
  salt

WILD MUSHROOM ENCHILADAS:

- 5 ancho chilies
- 1 cup heavy cream
- 2 garlic cloves, peeled and minced
- 2 teaspoons fresh lime juice
  coarse salt
- 1 tablespoon unsalted butter
- 1/2 white large onion, peeled and diced
- 3/4 cup wild mushrooms, preferably mixture of morels, shiitakes, oysters, and portobellos, sliced
- 1/2 avocado, peeled, pitted, and cut into 1/4 inch dice
- 6 tablespoons queso fresco or feta cheese, crumbled
- 1 tablespoon chopped cilantro
- 1 tomato, blanched, peeled, seeded, and diced
- 6 corn tortillas (see page 195 - flour tortillas and replace all-purpose flour with cornmeal)

1. Make the avocado-tomatillo salsa: In a large mixing bowl, combine the avocados, bell peppers, scallions, and half the tomatillos. Place the garlic, cilantro, serranos, lime juice, and remaining tomatillos in a blender, and purée until smooth. Slowly drizzle in the oil. Pour the purée into the mixing bowl, combine thoroughly and season with salt to taste. Let sit for 30 minutes.

2. Preheat the oven to 375°F.

3. Make the ancho chile purée: Roast the ancho chilies on an oiled baking sheet in the oven for 1 minute. Soak in a bowl of warm water for 30 minutes. Purée and add a little soaking liquid. Reserve.

4. Make the cream purée. In a skillet, bring the cream, ancho chile purée, and garlic to a boil and simmer for 2 minutes. Transfer to a blender and purée for 1 minute. Add the lime juice and season with salt. Strain the purée into a bowl and reserve.

5. In a large saucepan, heat the butter and sauté the onion and mushrooms for 2 minutes over medium heat, until the onion is translucent and the mushrooms are soft. Add the avocado, cheese, cilantro, and tomato, heating thoroughly. Add 2 tablespoons of reserved cream purée and stir gently. Add salt to taste and simmer for 3 minutes.

6. In a saucepan, warm each tortilla. In another saucepan, heat the remaining purée to a simmer. Place the tortillas one at a time into the cream purée for 15 seconds to soften, and place

adjacent to one another on a sheet pan. Return tortillas to the saucepan one by one, dividing the mixture among the tortillas, spreading evenly down the middle. Fold in 2 vertical sides and then roll with your hands. If not serving immediately, cover the tortillas on sheet pan with foil and reheat at 350°F for 10 minutes.

7. To serve, place the enchiladas on dinner plates seam-side down. Serve with the avocado-tomatillo salsa.

SERVES: 6

AUTHOR'S NOTE: Serrano chilies are available in most supermarkets.

CHAPTER 5

Pasta and Grains

"Everything you see I owe to spaghetti."

SOPHIA LOREN

"He who looks at magnitude is often mistaken.
A grain of pepper angers lasagna with its strength."

TACOPONE DA TODI

Angel Hair Pasta with Roast Tomato Broth and Jumbo Lump Crabmeat

Light air-spun threads of angel hair pasta are flecked with juicy morsels of lump crabmeat and basil leaves. The flavorful tomato broth made with roasted tomatoes produces a moist delicate sauce. This capellini of quiet distinction is a sensation all year round, although sun-ripened tomatoes are at their prime in summer.

TOMATO BROTH:

- 8 pounds (11 large) ripe red tomatoes, cored and halved
- 2 tablespoons plus 1/2 cup olive oil
- 1/2 tablespoon coarse salt
  freshly ground white pepper
- 1 small white onion, peeled and chopped
- 1/2 cup fresh basil leaves

SAUCE:

- 1/4 cup olive oil
- 1/4 cup (6 tablespoons) finely diced leeks
- 1 jalapeño pepper, cored and chopped
- 3/4 pound angel hair pasta (capellini)
- 4 teaspoons finely chopped chives
- 1 pound jumbo lump crabmeat (snow crab), shells removed

GARNISH:

- 1/2 bunch chives
- 1/2 bunch fresh basil leaves

1. Preheat the oven to 350°F.

2. Place the tomato halves on a baking pan and coat the tomatoes with 2 tablespoons of the oil. Season with 1/2 tablespoon coarse salt and freshly ground white pepper. Roast approximately 45 minutes until charred. Remove the skin from the tomatoes and chop all but 6 tomato halves. Reserve skins from the 6.

3. Make the tomato broth: In a medium saucepan, add 1/2 cup of the olive oil, and sweat the onions over low heat until translucent. Then, add the roasted chopped tomatoes and simmer for 2 minutes, pressing down on the tomatoes to extract the juice. Add a handful of basil leaves. Add the removed skin from the 6 reserved tomato halves, squeeze in their juice and seeds, and simmer covered for 15 minutes. Strain the sauce through a colander into a bowl, pressing down on the solids to extract the juice. (This should yield 4 cups of tomato broth.)

4. Make the sauce: In a large sauté pan, add 1/4 cup of olive oil, leeks, and jalapeño, and sweat the leeks until translucent.

5. In a pan of rapidly boiling salted water, add the pasta and cook for approximately 2 minutes. It should be barely tender yet firm to the bite. Drain the pasta.

6. Continue making the sauce by adding the tomato broth to the sauté pan of leeks and jalapeño along with the capellini and chives and season with salt and pepper to taste. Add the crabmeat and simmer for 30 seconds.

7. To serve, divide the pasta and crabmeat among large soup plates and serve immediately with a garnish of chives and fresh basil leaves.

SERVES: 3 as a main course, 6 as an appetizer

AUTHOR'S NOTE: Add the crabmeat right before serving so that it only heats a bit and does not cook.

ELKA GILMORE

Caviar Noodles

VINAIGRETTE:

1/2 cup canola oil

1 teaspoon grated ginger

1/4 cup rice wine vinegar

1 teaspoon finely chopped shallots

4 ounces osetra or other black caviar
(reserve 1 teaspoon for garnish)
salt and freshly ground pepper

NOODLES:

1/2 pound high-quality dry soba noodles

1/4 cup finely julienned carrots

1/4 cup finely julienned daikon radishes

4 scallions, finely shredded

Elka Gilmore's cuisine is distinguished by combining European techniques and Asian ingredients. The crunchy textured scallions, daikon, and ginger mixed with salted sturgeon eggs and soba noodles creates what has been called a "rich man, poor man's dish."

1. Make the caviar vinaigrette. In a medium bowl, combine all the caviar vinaigrette ingredients and whisk gently.

2. In a pot of boiling salted water, cook the soba noodles for 5 minutes. Drain, chill in a bowl, and cover with plastic wrap.

3. Combine noodles, carrots, radishes, and scallions, and toss with vinaigrette.

4. To serve, divide the caviar noodles among plates and garnish their center with the remaining caviar.

SERVES: 4

Fig and Taleggio Pizza with Sage and Honey

Figs, those sweet ambrosial fruits, showcase well with the nutty, full-flavored taleggio cheese and sage, another traditional Italian favorite. Throughout history, sage has been sought after, not only for its beguiling flavor but also because of its longevity and healing powers.

PIZZA DOUGH:

- 1 cup warm water
- 1 package yeast
- 1 tablespoon salt
- 1/4 cup extra virgin olive oil
- 3 cups all-purpose unbleached flour
  cornmeal, for dusting

TOPPING:

- extra virgin olive oil
- 9 ounces fresh ricotta cheese
  salt and freshly ground black pepper
- 9 ounces taleggio cheese, trimmed and cut into 1 1/2-inch cubes
- 6 large fresh or dried figs, quartered
- 24 medium sage leaves
- 3/4 cup freshly grated Parmesan cheese
  good quality honey to taste

1. Prepare the pizza dough: Place 1/4 cup warm water in a large bowl. Add the yeast and stir until dissolved, allowing the yeast to proof. Add the remaining water, salt, and olive oil, and mix well. Using a wooden spoon, add the flour, 1 cup at a time. When the dough is too stiff to stir, place on a clean board and knead about 7 minutes until smooth and elastic. (This dough should be a little sticky.)

2. Place the dough in an oiled bowl, cover with plastic wrap, and allow to rise in a warm area about 2 hours until it has doubled in bulk. Punch down and let rise again by the same method for 45 minutes. Cut the pizza dough into 3 equal pieces and roll into balls. Cover with plastic wrap and let it rest for 40 minutes.

3. Preheat an oven containing unglazed tiles or a pizza stone to 500°F.

4. Make the pizza: Roll each of the 3 pizza doughs into 8-inch circles 1/4-inch thick. On a lightly floured board hold the dough in your hands and turn, pulling lightly outward with your hand, making a 1/2-inch-high border with your thumb. Place on peel or plate sprinkled with cornmeal. Brush the dough with olive oil. Spread one-third of the ricotta on each of the doughs, leaving a 1/2-inch border, and season with salt and pepper. Distribute the taleggio, figs, and sage leaves evenly over the pizzas. Sprinkle with the Parmesan cheese.

5. Slip the pizzas from the wooden peels or plates to the tiles or stone (which makes for easier baking) and bake approximately 10 to 12 minutes or until crispy, bubbly, and brown. Remove the pizzas from the oven with the peel, transfer to a cutting board, and cut each pizza into 4 pieces. Move the pizzas to a plate and drizzle with honey.

SERVES: 6

CHEF'S HINTS: For a more flavorful dough, after the second rising refrigerate overnight. Bring to room temperature before using. If you don't have tiles or a stone and/or you want to cook all the pizzas at the same time, bake them on a cornmeal-sprinkled sheet pan.

Lobster Ravioli with Goat Cheese and Basil

RAVIOLI:

1½ pounds lemon-dill pasta dough
   (see page 197)

1 cup goat cheese

1 pound fresh cooked lobster meat
   cornmeal for dusting

SAUCE:

2 cups heavy cream
   red, green, and yellow bell pepper, seeded
   and diced (1 each)

4 whole tomatoes, peeled, seeded and diced

1 tablespoon fresh basil chopped
   kosher salt and freshly ground white
   pepper

Ravioli stuffed with spinach and cheese is a trademark of Italian gastronomy. This pasta dough is flavored with a magical combination of lemon and dill and then pocketed with goat cheese and lobster chunks. Lemon and dill partner well with the lobster, while the diced pepper and spicy basil make an unusually arresting sauce.

1. Prepare the ravioli: On a floured work surface, roll out the pasta dough to ⅛-inch thickness. Mark sheet in rounds with a 1-inch cutter about ⅛-inch apart, making about 50–60 rounds. Place 1 teaspoon of goat cheese and lobster meat on each round. Roll a second sheet of pasta dough as above and place over the first sheet, completely covering the rounds of cheese and lobster meat. Cut each ravioli with a 1½-inch cutter, pinch the edges securely, and place the ravioli on a sheet pan. Sprinkle lightly with cornmeal or flour to prevent sticking. Reserve, cover with plastic wrap, and refrigerate until ready to cook.

2. Make the sauce: In a bowl, mix the cream, bell peppers, tomatoes, and basil. Season to taste with salt and pepper. Place in a medium saucepan and heat until hot.

3. Meanwhile, drop the ravioli into a quart of boiling water for 7 to 9 minutes or until tender (*al dente*); drain.

4. Simmer the ravioli for 2 to 3 minutes in the sauce and serve immediately.

SERVES: 8

Lobster Taco with Yellow Tomato and Jicama Salad

Dean Fearing has popularized such local Texan bounty as jicama, spicy jalapeño Jack cheese, and serrano chilies. Jicama, a popular tuber indigenous to Mexico and Central America, adds a refreshing crunchy texture similar in taste to water chestnuts. Lobster morsels buttressed by a towering salad of jicama picqued with lime juice and yellow tomato salsa provide a counterpoint to the crispy-textured taco.

YELLOW TOMATO SALSA:

- 2 pints yellow cherry tomatoes or 1 pound yellow tomatoes, stemmed
- 1 large shallot, peeled and very finely minced
- 1 large garlic clove, peeled and very finely minced
- 2 tablespoons minced fresh cilantro
- 1 tablespoon champagne or white wine vinegar
- 2 serrano chilies, stemmed, seeded, and minced
- 2 teaspoons lime juice
  kosher salt
- 1 tablespoon maple syrup (optional)

  Four 1-pound Maine lobsters

JICAMA SALAD:

- 1/2 small jicama, peeled and finely julienned
- 1/2 small red bell pepper, seeded and finely julienned
- 1/2 small yellow bell pepper, seeded and finely julienned
- 1/2 small zucchini, skin only and finely julienned
- 1/2 small carrot, peeled and finely julienned
- 4 tablespoons cold-pressed peanut, olive, or canola oil
- 3 tablespoons lime juice
  cayenne pepper
  kosher salt
  Six 7-inch flour tortillas (see page 195)
- 3 tablespoons corn oil
- 1 cup cleaned, stemmed, and shredded spinach leaves, chiffonade
- 1 cup grated jalapeño Jack cheese

1. Make the tomato salsa: In a food processor, using the steel blade, process the tomatoes until chopped well. Add the shallot, garlic, cilantro, vinegar, chilies, lime juice, and salt, and then pulse once or twice. Adjust the seasoning and add maple syrup if the tomatoes are not sweet enough. Place in a bowl covered with plastic wrap and refrigerate from 2 to 8 hours.

2. Preheat the oven to 300°F.

3. Fill a large pot with lightly salted water and bring to a boil over high heat. Add the lobsters. Bring to a boil and cook for about 3 to 4 additional minutes. Drain and shock in cold water. Carefully remove the lobster meat and cut into chunks.

4. Make the jicama salad: Combine the jicama, peppers, zucchini, carrots, peanut oil, lime juice, and cayenne, and toss well. Add salt when ready to serve.

5. Mold the tortillas into cylindrical shapes and wrap tightly in foil (all together). Heat in the oven for about 15 minutes. Keep warm until ready to use.

6. In a medium sauté pan, heat the corn oil over medium heat and warm the lobster medallions until just heated through. Add the spinach, melt the jalapeño Jack cheese, and season with salt and pepper.

7. To serve, horizontally place a warm cylindrically shaped tortilla in the center of each dinner plate with the opening on top. Place the lobster mixture into the tortilla, folding one side over the other. Place the yellow tomato salsa around the tortilla plate and garnish with a small mound of jicama salad.

SERVES: 6

Red Pinto Bean and Bulgur Salad

1   quart chicken stock (see page 190)
½   pound red pinto beans
4   fresh thyme sprigs
4   tarragon leaves
½   pound bulgur wheat
3   ounces cherry juice
3   ounces freshly squeezed orange juice

GARNISH:
1   quart peanut oil
4   branches kale, ribs removed

1. In large saucepan, soak beans in 1 quart chicken stock and refrigerate overnight.

2. In the saucepan, simmer the beans with thyme sprigs and tarragon leaves approximately 1 hour until tender.

3. Make the bulgur: In a saucepan, bring 2 cups of water to a boil. Season with salt, pepper, add the bulgur, and stir. Cover and remove from the heat. Let sit for 15 minutes. (There should be almost no water left.)

4. In a bowl, combine the bean-bulgur mixture, add the cherry and orange juices, stir, and let sit for 15 minutes.

5. In very hot peanut oil (approximately 350°F), fry the kale for approximately 4 minutes. Remove and pat dry.

6. To serve, place a piece of kale in the center of each plate and mold the bean salad into 4 small ramekins, pressing in for a few minutes, and then turn upside down onto the kale.

SERVES: 4

Red beans and bulgur are the consummate high-energy food for any health-conscious eater. These fibrous grains sweetened with a dash of cherry and orange juice are scented with harmonizing savories.

Risotto with Saffron and Dried Cherries

Kevin Graham deftly presents this cross-cultural savory risotto speckled with saffron and dried cherries. He is known for adding fruit to grains, providing fragrance while maintaining firmness.

6–8 cups chicken stock (see page 190)

4 tablespoons extra virgin olive oil

pinch of saffron threads

1 large white onion, peeled and finely chopped

2 cups Arborio rice (Italian long-grain rice)

1 cup dry white wine

salt and freshly ground black pepper

1 cup dried cherries

1. In a large saucepan, add the chicken stock and heat to a simmer.

2. Meanwhile, in a large, heavy saucepan, heat the oil until hot. Add the saffron and stir for 1 minute. Add the onion and sauté about 2 minutes until translucent. Add the rice to the pan and cook, stirring constantly, until the grains are white in the center and clear towards the edges. Add the wine, reduce the heat to medium, and stir until the wine is absorbed. Then add 1 cup of the hot stock. Stir constantly until the stock is absorbed. Then add the stock in 1/2-cup portions until each 1/2 cup is absorbed. After a total cooking time of approximately 15 minutes, the rice will be slightly *al dente*. Remove the pan from the heat.

3. Season with salt and pepper to taste. Cover the pan and let the risotto rest for 2 minutes. Fold in the cherries.

4. To serve, spoon the risotto into bowls and serve immediately.

SERVES: 4

Roasted Quail and Wild Mushroom Risotto

1/4 cup olive oil

1/2 large white onion, peeled and small diced

2 garlic cloves, peeled and minced

2 cups Arborio rice

6 quails, boneless, halved

1 quart chicken stock (see page 190)

1/4 cup shallots, peeled and minced

3/4 pound wild mushrooms (crimini, shiitakes, portobellos), wiped, stemmed, and coarsely chopped

4 tablespoons unsalted butter

  kosher salt and freshly ground black pepper

2 branches thyme

1/2 cup chopped herbs, equal parts (tarragon, chives, parsley)

1 1/2 tablespoons olive oil

This roasted quail risotto flecked with savory wild mushrooms illustrates the culinary wizardry of one of America's Midwestern epicureans. The perfumed liquid released from the mushrooms tempered with a rich chicken stock combine to provide an arresting broth.

1. Make the risotto: In a wide, hot saucepan, heat 2 tablespoons of the olive oil and sauté the onions and garlic until caramelized. Add the Arborio rice. Stir in one direction only with a wooden spatula or spoon (otherwise you might break the grain and it will become gummy).

2. Add 1/4 cup of the chicken stock and continue to stir constantly until almost absorbed into the rice, making sure that the rice does not stick to the bottom of the pan. Add another 1/2 cup of chicken stock and follow the same procedure until 1/2 quart of the stock is absorbed into the rice.

3. In a sauté pan, heat the remaining olive oil, add the shallots and mushrooms, and sauté until they start to release the liquid. Add them to the risotto. Add the butter and stock if it is too dry. Season with salt and pepper.

4. Make the sauce: Heat the remaining 1/2 quart of stock and reduce by three-quarters for approximately 1/2 hour. Season to taste with salt and pepper and infuse with thyme branches for 45 seconds. Remove the thyme branches.

5. Preheat the oven to 350°F.

6. Rub the quail with olive oil and sprinkle with 1/2 of the herbs, salt, and pepper.

7. In a hot saucepan, heat 1 1/2 tablespoons of olive oil until hot and sear the quails on both sides for 2 minutes each. Then roast in the oven for 5 minutes.

8. Divide the risotto among 6 plates. Spoon the risotto in the center of the plates. Arrange the quail on top of the risotto. Spoon the sauce over the quail and sprinkle with the remaining herbs.

SERVES: 6

Spicy Chicken Pizza

pizza dough (see page 199)

MARINADE:

$3^1/2$ tablespoons lime juice

2 teaspoons chopped jalapeño pepper

   pinch of chopped cilantro

3 cups skinless chicken cubes

$^1/2$ cup plus 1 tablespoon olive oil

   salt

TOPPING:

3 cups grated mozzarella cheese

2 cups grated fontina cheese

1 pound (about 6) plum tomatoes, ends removed, thinly sliced

$^1/2$ cup cubed eggplant, sautéed or grilled

2–3 grilled onions, peeled and chopped, to yield $^1/2$ cup

$^1/2$ cup chopped chives

4 teaspoons grated Parmesan cheese

Impresario Wolfgang Puck is often noted for popularizing and raising the status of pizza in America. He uses a combination of mozzarella and fontina cheeses and a spicy chicken marinade enhanced by the chili and garlic-oiled crust.

1. Make the marinade: In a medium bowl, combine the lime juice, jalapeño pepper, and cilantro, by lightly whisking. Add cubed chicken and toss, using $^1/2$ cup of the olive oil. Season lightly with salt. Marinate for about 1 hour, refrigerated.

2. Remove the chicken and in a skillet large enough to hold the chicken in one layer, heat the remaining 1 tablespoon of oil. Sauté the chicken just to brown on all sides.

3. Preheat the oven to 525°F.

4. Prepare the pizza as directed on page 199, brushing lightly with 2 tablespoons of the chili and garlic oil or olive oil.

5. Place the topping in order by spreading the layers of: mozzarella, fontina, tomato, eggplant, onion, chopped chives, grated parmesan, and then the chicken.

6. Bake for 15 to 20 minutes, until nicely browned. Transfer to a firm surface and slice with a pizza cutter. Serve immediately.

SERVES: 6

Seared Sea Scallops with Black Squid Ink Pasta in a Mango Vanilla Bean Sauce

This riveting combination of sea scallops and fruit sauce could fix the crack in the Liberty Bell. Using fruit with fish was pioneered in southern France, but this pairing is served to increased demand in the United States. The mango-orange sauce is particularly refreshing in spring and summer, when mangos are juicy and sweet. It is the perfect complement to the squid ink pasta, flecked with crunchy scallions.

1 bunch scallions, green part only, finely julienned

16 large sea scallops, tendons removed
salt and freshly cracked black peppercorns

2 tablespoons olive oil

3 whole ripe mangos, peeled, pitted, and cut into 1/4-inch dice

2 cups freshly squeezed orange juice

2 vanilla beans

1 teaspoon chopped shallots
freshly ground white pepper

1 pound fresh black squid ink pasta

1 tablespoon unsalted butter

1 tablespoon chopped garlic

1. Soak the scallions in ice water for at least 7 minutes. Drain and pat dry with paper towels. Reserve.

2. Wash the scallops and pat dry in towel. Season with salt and freshly cracked black peppercorns.

3. In a medium, hot sauté pan, add the olive oil and, when the oil is almost smoking, sauté the scallops over medium heat for 4 to 5 minutes until both sizes are caramelized. Set aside.

4. In a saucepan, combine the mango cubes with orange juice, vanilla beans, and shallots. Cook approximately 5 minutes until the mangos are soft. Purée in a food processor until very smooth. Season with salt and white pepper to taste. Set aside.

5. In a quart of boiling salted water, cook the fresh pasta for 2 1/2 to 3 minutes. Drain.

6. In a saucepan, melt the butter and sweat the garlic until aromatic and translucent. Mix in pasta and season with salt and pepper. Heat until piping hot.

7. To serve, spoon a 3-ounce portion of sauce to cover up to the rim and evenly coat the dinner plates. Take a quarter of the pasta in the fork and twist it into a turban. Place the turban vertically in the center of the plate and arrange 4 scallops evenly around the pasta. Place a bunch of julienned scallions on top of the pasta turban.

SERVES: 4

Truffled Mushroom Risotto

MUSHROOMS:

1 tablespoon unsalted butter

1 tablespoon olive oil

2 cups assorted mushrooms, (shiitake, portobello, morel, chanterelle, oyster, black trumpet)

1 garlic clove, peeled and minced

2 tablespoons white wine

dash of fresh lemon juice

1 teaspoon finely chopped sage

1/2 teaspoon minced shallot

salt and freshly ground black pepper

RISOTTO:

2 tablespoons olive oil

3 tablespoons unsalted butter

1 cup diced Spanish onion

1 bay leaf

3 garlic cloves, peeled and minced

2 cups superfine Arborio rice or long grain rice

1 1/2 cups white wine

4 1/2 cups double strength chicken stock, heated (see page 190)

1 teaspoon balsamic vinegar

3/4 cup Parmigiano-Reggiano cheese, grated

1 teaspoon truffle oil

salt and freshly ground black pepper

A favorite dish among contemporary chefs, this wild mushroom risotto rises to the top of the culinary box office charts. The tangy lemon juice and acidic balsamic vinegar balance the creamy short-grained Arborio rice to create a bewitching risotto of earthy, wild mushrooms and grated Parmesan cheese.

1. Make the mushrooms: In a large saucepan, heat the butter and oil, add the mushrooms and cook until caramelized. Add the minced garlic and deglaze with white wine and lemon juice. Add the sage and shallot and season with salt and pepper.

2. Make the risotto: In a large, heavy saucepan, heat the olive oil and 2 tablespoons of the butter. Add the onion, bay leaf, and garlic, and cover tightly. Cook for about 3 minutes or until the onions are translucent. Add the rice, stirring constantly with a wooden spoon, for approximately 2 minutes. Add the white wine and wait for the first bubbles to appear. Add 1 cup of chicken stock and balsamic vinegar; cook, stirring constantly, until the vinegar is almost completely absorbed.

3. Add 1/2 cup stock at a time until all the stock has been added and the risotto is creamy but still slightly firm to the tooth (*al dente*).

4. Fold the mushrooms into the risotto. Gently stir in the remaining butter and 1/2 cup Parmigiano-Reggiano.

5. To serve, spoon the risotto into heated dishes, drizzle with truffle oil, and serve at once. Pass the remaining cheese separately.

SERVES: 3 as a main course, 5 as an appetizer

Tortelli of Butternut Squash with Sage-Brown Butter and Parmesan

This lighter American interpretation of an Italian classic substitutes finely grained orange-fleshed butternut squash for pumpkin because squash is more consistent and flavorful. The addition of crumbled amaretti cookies provides a subtle texture to an otherwise smooth filling.

BUTTERNUT SQUASH FILLING:

2 cups butternut squash, peeled and seeded (1 medium)

1/2 cup ground amaretti cookies
  pinch of nutmeg
  salt and freshly ground black pepper

1 pound egg pasta dough (see page 193)

1 egg, whisked

2 tablespoons unsalted butter

1 teaspoon fresh sage, stemmed and julienned

1 1/2 tablespoons freshly grated Parmesan cheese

GARNISH:

4 sage leaves

1. Make the butternut squash filling: Dice the squash into large chunks, cover with salted water, and boil approximately 10 to 15 minutes until tender. Strain well in a colander, then purée in a food processor. Add the ground cookies, nutmeg, salt and pepper to taste, pulsing slowly for 1 minute. Let cool uncovered in refrigerator until ready to use (at least 1/2 hour; if more than 1 hour, cover after cooled).

2. On a lightly floured, flat, hard surface, roll the pasta until the dough is very thin, or pass through a pasta machine until the dough is the desired thickness. (A pasta machine is preferable for this recipe). Lay 18-inch-long-by-7-inch-wide sheets of pasta and cut in half down the middle, then cut into 3 1/2-inch squares. Using a pastry brush, paint thin strips of egg around the outer edge to serve as a sealant.

3. Place a teaspoon of squash in the center of each square. Fold in half diagonally, corner to corner, forming a triangle.

4. Next fold the longest flat edge one-third of the way toward the top of the triangle, leaving the top third of the triangle (1/2 inch) exposed. Place thumbs on either side of the squash pocket and gently press to seal. Place in a container with a lot of flour to prevent sticking. Freeze until ready to use.

5. In a pot of salted boiling water, cook the tortelli for 1 minute or until they float. Remove with a slotted spoon to 4 soup plates, arranging 5 pastas per portion.

6. Make the sage-brown butter: In a medium sauté pan, melt the butter until it browns. Add 1 tablespoon of the pasta water to the pan along with the sage and cook approximately 3 minutes. Add the grated Parmesan cheese to the sauce.

7. To serve, pour the sage-brown butter over the tortelli and garnish with a sage leaf.

SERVES: 4

AUTHOR'S NOTE: 10 tortellis should be served for a main course and 5 for an appetizer.

Vegetable Couscous

*N*ew Orleans, the Crescent City, is in its glory with Susan Spicer, whose trademark vegetable cous cous is in constant demand from vegetarians to culinary enthusiasts alike. Couscous, or cracked wheat, conjures up visions of Arabian nights and treasures. It is a staple in such countries as Morocco, Tunisia, and Libya, and is made by moistening 100% durum wheat semolina flour with olive oil and water.

$^1/_2$ cup chickpeas

VEGETABLE STEW:

1   medium onion, peeled and chopped

1   small green bell pepper, seeded and diced

1   small red bell pepper, seeded and diced

2   tablespoons olive oil

2   medium tomatoes, peeled, seeded, and diced

$1^1/_2$ quarts flavored stock (see page 190) (save 1 cup for hot sauce, if desired) pinch saffron

1   cinnamon stick, tied with parsley and cilantro stems

1   medium carrot, peeled and diced

1   cup butternut or acorn squash, peeled, seeded, and diced

1   medium zucchini, diced

COUSCOUS:

$^1/_2$ pound ($^1/_2$ box) instant dry couscous kosher salt

2   tablespoons olive oil or butter (or a combination of the two)

2   tablespoons parsley, chopped (save stems for cinnamon-herb bundle)

2   tablespoons cilantro, chopped (save stems)

$^1/_2$ bunch scallions, thinly sliced

HOT SAUCE:

1   cup vegetable or chicken stock (see page 190)

1   teaspoon chili paste

$^1/_2$ teaspoon garlic, minced

1   teaspoon lemon juice

$^1/_2$ teaspoon cumin

1   tablespoon olive oil

$^1/_2$ bunch fresh parsley, stemmed and chopped

$^1/_4$ bunch cilantro, stemmed and chopped

1. Soak the chickpeas overnight in water to cover, and cook for 45 minutes. Drain and peel.

2. Make the vegetable stew: Sweat the onion and peppers in hot olive oil for 10 to 15 minutes. Add the diced tomato, stock, saffron, and cinnamon-herb bundle. Bring to a boil and then reduce to a simmer. Add all other vegetables in sequence of cooking time needed, and simmer for 20 to 30 minutes until the vegetables are tender.

3. Make the couscous: In a bowl, coat couscous with 1 tablespoon of olive oil either by hand or with a spoon. In a saucepan, mix the couscous with 1 cup of boiling water and season with salt. Stir, cover with plastic, and set aside 5 to 10 minutes. Uncover, break up any lumps, and stir in olive oil or butter, herbs and scallions. Season to taste with salt and pepper. Keep warm.

4. Make the hot sauce: Mix the stock, chili paste, garlic, lemon juice, cumin, and olive oil. Add parsley and cilantro.

5. To serve, place the couscous in the middle of the plate, top with the vegetables, and spoon the hot sauce on the side.

SERVES: 6

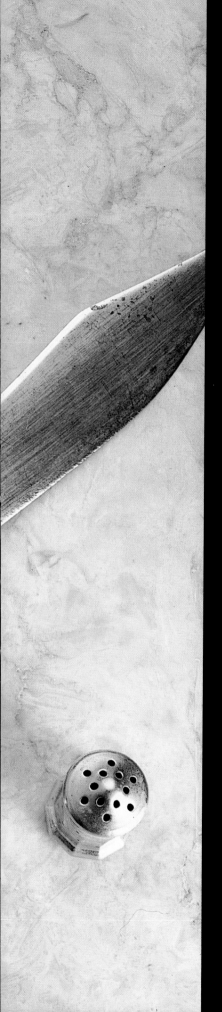

CHAPTER 6

Chicken and Meat

"Poultry is for the cook what canvas is for the painter."

BRILLAT-SAVARIN

Barbecued Kalbi Beef with Spicy Soba Noodles

Soba noodles are hospitable to a wide range of ethnic seasonings, including soy, molasses, and tahini. Flecked with verdant scallion bits, this visually arresting heap of spicy soba noodles makes an excellent vegetarian meal in itself, served with cucumber marinated in a cider vinegar preparation. The Kalbi beef preparation, Korean-style, is tenderized in honey, water, soy, and ginger. The moist rillettes of ribs are tender, and the marinade imparts a spicy underpinning.

1 1/2 pounds beef ribs (12 bones cross-cut beef flank and rib, sliced 1/2-inch thick)

KALBI MARINADE:

4 tablespoons fresh diced ginger

1 1/2 cups soy sauce

2 tablespoons chopped white onions

2 tablespoons toasted sesame seeds

1/2 cup water

1 1/4 pounds honey

1/4 tablespoon fresh chopped garlic

MARINATED CUCUMBERS:

1 European (seedless) cucumber, thinly sliced

1 garlic clove, peeled and minced

3 tablespoons minced ginger

3/4 cup sugar

3/4 cup cider vinegar

SPICY SOBA NOODLES:

1/3 cup soy sauce

1 tablespoon molasses

1/4 cup sesame oil

1/4 cup tahini (Middle Eastern sesame paste)

1/4 cup brown sugar

1/4 cup chili oil

3 tablespoons balsamic or red wine vinegar

1/2 bunch scallions, white and green parts, thinly sliced

salt

1/2 pound soba or Japanese buckwheat noodles

1. Make the Kalbi marinade: In a bowl, combine the marinade ingredients. Marinate the ribs at least 24 to 48 hours in the kalbi marinade.

2. Make the marinated cucumbers: Marinate the cucumber, garlic clove, ginger, and sugar for 1 hour. Then add cider vinegar; continue marinating for up to 3 hours.

3. Make the spicy soba sauce: Place the soy sauce in a pan over high heat and reduce by half. Turn the heat to low; stir in the molasses and warm briefly. Transfer to a mixing bowl. Add the sesame oil, tahini, brown sugar, chili oil, vinegar, and scallions, and whisk to combine. Season to taste with salt, if desired.

4. Bring a large pot of salted water to a rapid boil. Add the noodles. Return to a boil and cook, stirring occasionally until they just begin to soften after about 3 minutes. (Soba noodles can overcook very quickly, so stay nearby.)

5. Prepare a large bowl of iced water. Drain the noodles, plunge in iced water, and drain again. Place in a colander and rinse well under cold running water. Combine the noodles and the spicy soba sauce. Toss well and chill.

6. Place the ribs on a hot oiled grill until well barbecued or place in a preheated 375°F oven for 30 minutes.

7. To serve, heap spicy soba noodles on a plate and surround with beef ribs in a star design around the noodles. Garnish with marinated cucumbers.

SERVES: 4

Crispy Roast Chicken with Wild Mushroom Hash

Anne Rosenzweig was one of the first women stars on the contemporary American culinary scene. Her technique of pan searing to retain the chicken juices and roasting on high heat creates poultry to perfection. This very American mushroom hash complements a tender, juicy chicken that could easily become a daily indulgence.

Three 3¹/₂-pound chickens

MUSHROOM HASH:
- ¹/₂ pound bacon slab, minced
- 2 large onions, peeled and minced
- 1 pound assorted wild and/or domestic mushrooms, sliced
- 2 tablespoons fresh chopped thyme
- 3¹/₂ pounds baking potatoes, peeled and diced into ¹/₂-inch cubes
- 2¹/₂ cups chicken stock (see page 190)

- 1 cup heavy cream to taste (optional)
  salt and pepper
- ¹/₄ cup chopped parsley
- ¹/₄ cup chopped chives
- 2 tablespoons butter

- 1 pound spinach, stemmed and thoroughly washed
  salt

1. Remove wings and drumsticks. Using a boning knife, remove breast and thigh in one piece from each side of the chicken. Season with salt and pepper.

2. If using dried mushrooms, soak in enough water just to cover and add strained liquid when adding cream in step 6.

3. Preheat oven to 475°F.

4. Heat a large sauté pan over high heat and add a small amount of oil. Place the chicken skin-side down and cook until the skin is golden brown. Discard the fat and place chicken in the oven. Continue to cook approximately 10 minutes until the chicken loses all its pinkness but is still juicy. Roast in the oven for 30 minutes making sure to cook on both sides.

5. In another large sauté pan, cook the bacon until the fat is three-quarters rendered. Add the onions, cooking over low heat until the onion is soft. Add the mushrooms and thyme and cook until the mushrooms have released all their liquid.

6. Make the mushroom hash: In another saucepan, place the potatoes, add the chicken stock to cover the potatoes, and reduce the liquid by half. Add the mushroom mixture and, if desired, pour in the heavy cream and cook until the hash is just barely moist. Correct the seasonings and add fresh herbs. If not using cream, finish with a tablespoon of butter.

7. In a medium sauté pan, melt the remaining tablespoon of butter and sauté the spinach for a few minutes until cooked *al dente*. Season to taste with salt.

8. To serve, place the hash off-center on a dinner plate and top with the chicken. Arrange the spinach alongside the mushroom hash.

SERVES: 6

CHEF'S HINTS: The mushroom hash can be made in advance and reheated when ready to serve.

Duck Confit Empanadas with Wild Mushrooms, Golden Raisins, and Kalamata Olives

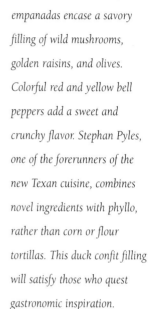

2 tablespoons golden raisins

1/2 cup Marsala wine

1 tablespoon olive oil, plus extra for brushing

1 tablespoon diced yellow bell pepper

1 tablespoon diced red bell pepper

2 garlic cloves, peeled and minced

2 tablespoons diced onion

1/4 cup chopped mixed wild mushrooms, such as shiitakes, chanterelles, and pleurottes (oyster mushrooms)

1/2 ounce prosciutto (or Smithfield ham), julienned

2 tablespoons diced Kalamata olives

1 teaspoon orange zest

1 1/3 tablespoons chopped marjoram

1 teaspoon chopped chives

1/4 teaspoon chopped rosemary

2 tablespoons goat cheese, crumbled

1/2 cup diced or shredded duck confit (see page 193)

salt

4 sheets phyllo pastry dough

1/4 cup dried breadcrumbs

3 cups chicken stock (see page 190)

GARNISH:

4 marjoram sprigs

These light phyllo dough empanadas encase a savory filling of wild mushrooms, golden raisins, and olives. Colorful red and yellow bell peppers add a sweet and crunchy flavor. Stephan Pyles, one of the forerunners of the new Texan cuisine, combines novel ingredients with phyllo, rather than corn or flour tortillas. This duck confit filling will satisfy those who quest gastronomic inspiration.

1. Soak the raisins in the Marsala. Heat 1 tablespoon of olive oil over medium heat until lightly smoking. In a sauté pan, sauté the bell peppers, garlic, and onion for 1 minute. Add the wild mushrooms and prosciutto and cook for an additional minute. Add the raisins, Marsala, and olives, and cook until the Marsala evaporates. Add the orange zest, 1 teaspoon marjoram, chives, rosemary, goat cheese, and duck confit. Season with salt to taste; combine thoroughly.

2. Preheat the oven to 450°F.

3. Make the empanadas: Place a sheet of phyllo dough on a work surface with the long side facing you. Lightly brush the dough with olive oil. Evenly sprinkle 1 tablespoon of the dried breadcrumbs over the phyllo. Fold one-third of the phyllo pastry from the top edge and fold the bottom edge up over the two folded layers to form a third layer. Spoon a quarter of the duck mixture in the left-hand corner of the pastry. Begin folding the pastry triangularly (as if folding a flag) to encase the duck mixture. Trim any remaining phyllo dough. Repeat the procedure for the other empanadas with the remaining 3 sheets of phyllo dough.

4. Place the empanadas on a baking sheet and brush with olive oil. Bake until golden brown for 8 to 10 minutes.

5. In a saucepan, bring the chicken stock to a boil and reduce to 3/4 cup for about 15 minutes. Add the remaining marjoram and infuse at a simmer for 3 minutes.

6. To serve, ladle 3 tablespoons of stock onto each plate and serve the empanadas on top of the stock. Garnish with fresh marjoram sprigs.

SERVES: 4

Goat Cheese and Olive-Stuffed Chicken Wrapped in Swiss Chard with Balsamic Butter and Grilled Polenta

*S*wiss chard with a rosette of light green leaves and large textured white ribs envelop a sumptuous combination of goat cheese-stuffed chicken. These luscious pockets of chicken slices showcase the plump tomatoes enriched with balsamic vinegar and are served with a Parmesan-flavored polenta triangle.

POLENTA:

 7 cups water

 1 teaspoon coarse salt

 2 cups coarse yellow polenta (Golden Pheasant brand)

 1 tablespoon unsalted butter

¹/2 cup grated Parmesan cheese
    kosher salt and freshly ground white pepper

 8 large Swiss chard leaves, ribs removed and blanched

 4 chicken thighs, skinless and boneless
    freshly ground black pepper and kosher salt

 1 tablespoon fresh thyme, stemmed and chopped

 6 tablespoons goat cheese

 2 tablespoons chopped kalamata olives, pitted, and roughly chopped

 1 garlic clove, peeled, chopped, and diced

 2 tablespoons canola oil

BALSAMIC BUTTER SAUCE:

¹/2 tablespoon olive oil

 1 shallot, peeled and chopped

 1 garlic clove, peeled and chopped

¹/2 cup water

¹/2 cup balsamic vinegar

 2 plum tomatoes, quartered and seeded

 5 whole black peppercorns

 1 sprig fresh thyme

 1 bay leaf

¹/4 pound (1 stick) unsalted butter

 8 slices pancetta (Italian bacon), sliced on the round

 1 cup all-purpose flour, for dusting

    olive oil or unsalted butter, for brushing

1. Prepare a small sheet or aluminum baking pan approximately 15 inches by 10 inches in size by brushing with olive oil or softened butter.

2. Make the polenta: Bring the water and salt to a boil. Gradually whisk in the polenta to remove the lumps. Continue to stir occasionally with a wooden spoon for approximately 20 minutes, depending on the brand of polenta. During the last 5 minutes of cooking the polenta, whisk in the butter and Parmesan cheese and season to taste with salt and pepper. Pour into the sheet pan and cool in refrigerator until hard, at least 30 minutes. Remove from the refrigerator and cut with a knife into approximately twelve 4-inch triangles.

3. Blanch the chard leaves in boiling salted water and pat dry.

4. With a meat mallet or heavy skillet, flatten chicken thighs to even thickness. Season with pepper and thyme. In small bowl, mix the cheese with a wooden spoon, breaking up the cheese and smoothing it out with the spoon. Add the olives and garlic, and with the back of a spoon smooth the mixture onto the flattened thighs, leaving a $^1/_2$-inch border around the edges so that, when you roll it, the goat cheese won't seep out. Roll up and tie with a string to secure. Season rolled thighs with salt and pepper.

5. In large skillet over medium-high heat, heat the oil until it is almost smoking. Add the rolled thighs and cook 5 minutes or until browned on all sides, turning often. Remove from the heat. Let cool in skillet and remove string.

6. Make the balsamic butter sauce: In a medium saucepan over medium heat, heat the oil. Add shallots and garlic; sweat 5 minutes or until translucent, stirring often. Add the water, vinegar, tomatoes, peppercorns, thyme, and bay leaf; bring to a boil. Cook 5 to 10 minutes or until the liquid is reduced to $^1/_2$ cup. Remove the bay leaf. Whisk in the butter, bit by bit, until all is incorporated. (Do not boil or sauce will separate.) Season to taste with salt and pepper. The sauce should have a syrupy consistency and coat the back of a spoon. Pass sauce through a fine strainer, pressing down with the back of a spoon.

7. Heat the grill over medium coals or use a hot sauté pan. Wrap one or two slices of pancetta around the rolled thighs, and cook for 5 minutes. If using a sauté pan, remove the excess fat and use the same pan for the rest of this step. Cool and then roll in 1 or 2 pieces of chard leaf, covering the ends if the chard leaf is large enough. Brush with the olive oil if cooking on a grill and season with salt and pepper. Cook for 10 minutes longer, or until cooked through, turning often in the pancetta pan. Let it rest for 5 minutes. Slice thighs on the bias into 5 pieces.

8. Place the polenta triangles in your hands, dust with flour, and place into a 10-inch sauté pan heated with 3 tablespoons of olive oil. An oiled grill is preferable to obtain the grill marks and grilled flavor. Cook until golden on both sides.

9. To serve, fan out the chicken slices on a plate, surround with 2 pieces of grilled polenta, and drizzle plate with the balsamic butter sauce.

Serves: 4

Grilled Spiced Chicken with Tomato and Cilantro Salsa

This grilled chicken is elegant in its simplicity, highlighting flavors and textures of the freshest ingredients. Through the use of Michigan's agricultural bounty, Jimmy Schmidt pioneered simple cuisine and focused on the essence of the food, imparting natural flavors rather than fanciful artistry.

MARINADE:

1 tablespoon toasted coriander, ground
1 tablespoon toasted cumin, ground
1 1/2 tablespoons paprika
1 teaspoon freshly ground black pepper
1 tablespoon minced garlic
salt

4 large, thick chicken breasts, boneless and skinless, trimmed of all fatty tissues

SALSA:

2 tablespoons boiling water
2 fresh limes, juiced
2 tablespoons extra virgin olive oil (optional)
2 large, fresh, ripe tomatoes, peeled, seeded, and diced
1 medium sweet onion, peeled and diced
1/4 cup picked cilantro leaves, chopped

GARNISH:

8 cilantro or other green herb sprigs

1. Preheat the grill.

2. Make the marinade: In a food processor, combine the coriander, cumin, 1 tablespoon of the paprika, black pepper, garlic, and a pinch of salt. Pulse until the mixture is fine and homogenized. Lay the chicken breasts in a flat dish or pan. Rub the mixture over all surfaces of the chicken breasts. Refrigerate for at least 30 minutes to allow the flavors to combine.

3. Make the paprika mixture: In a small bowl, combine the remaining paprika with 2 tablespoons of boiling water, mixing well to combine. Cover and allow the flavor to develop for about 5 minutes. Stir in 3 tablespoons of the lime juice and the olive oil.

4. Make the salsa: In a medium bowl, combine the tomatoes, onion, and cilantro. Add the paprika mixture and stir to combine well. Season to taste with salt and additional freshly ground pepper. Refrigerate covered with plastic wrap until serving.

5. Raise the grill to the highest setting. Brush the grill grate to insure it is clean. With a tightly rolled piece of paper toweling dipped in olive oil, carefully brush the grill grates to "season." Place the chicken breasts on the grill for about 4 minutes, cooking until golden. Turn the chicken over and close the grill or cover with an ovenproof lid or pan to allow the heat to intensify and penetrate. Cook until done, about 3 minutes, depending on the thickness of the chicken. Transfer to a clean plate and sprinkle with the remaining lime juice. Slice chicken into 1-inch pieces on the bias and finish at 350°F for 5 minutes.

6. To serve, position the chicken breast in the center of each serving plate. Place small mounds of salsa on the plate. Garnish with 2 herb sprigs and serve.

SERVES: 4

Grilled Prime Rib Steak and Cannellini Beans in Red Wine Sauce

CANNELLINI BEANS:

1 ½ cups (³/4 pound) cannellini beans, rinsed (if unavailable, substitute great northern or other white bean)

2 tablespoons olive oil

½ medium (¼ pound) white onion, peeled and diced

4 garlic cloves, peeled and smashed

1 teaspoon chopped fresh rosemary

1 teaspooon chopped fresh thyme

1 bay leaf

¼ pound thick slab of bacon

2 tablespoons balsamic vinegar

8–9 cups chicken stock (see page 190) or half stock and half water

kosher salt and freshly ground white pepper

SAUCE:

1 tablespoon unsalted butter

2 (4 tablespoons) shallots, peeled and chopped

1 teaspoon cracked black pepper

½ cup dry red wine

½ cup port

2 cups brown veal stock (see chicken stock page 190)

cracked black pepper

10- to 12-ounce rib-eye steaks (Black Angus)

1 cup tapenade (see page 64)

½ pound bitter greens, such as mustard greens

This hearty, well-seasoned Black Angus steak is coated with a tapenade of olives, capers, and anchovies, and bathed in a luxurious red wine and port sauce. Served with flavorful white beans simmered in bacon, thyme, and rosemary, this bewitching dish is eminently satisfying.

1. Cover the beans in cold water and soak overnight. When ready to cook, drain well.

2. In a heavy 3-quart saucepan, heat the olive oil. Over low heat, sweat the onion with the garlic, rosemary, thyme, and bay leaf until the onion is translucent. This should take approximately 3 to 4 minutes. Add the beans and toss to coat with the oil. Add the bacon, vinegar, and 5 cups of stock, and bring to a boil. Lower the heat and simmer very gently for 1½ to 2 hours, until the beans are tender, adding stock as needed to keep beans "simmering" in the stock. Stir often to prevent sticking. Season with salt and pepper to taste. Remove the bacon and bay leaf.

3. Make the sauce: In a sauté pan, melt the butter. Over medium heat, sweat the shallots with the pepper 2 to 3 minutes until the shallots are translucent. Add the red wine and port and reduce to a glaze (until the sauce coats the back of the spoon). Pour in the stock and reduce until the sauce thinly coats the back of a spoon. This should take approximately 30 minutes altogether. Strain into a clean pan and season with salt to taste. Keep warm.

4. Make the steak: Season the steaks well with kosher salt and cracked black pepper. Preheat the grill for 30 minutes. Grill the steaks to desired degree of doneness, about 3 to 4 minutes on each side for medium-rare. Let rest in a warm spot 5 to 10 minutes for perfect results. Spread a thin layer of tapenade over each cooked steak and cut the steaks into slices.

5. In a medium saucepan, heat the beans with the bitter greens over low heat.

6. To serve, spoon some of the cannellini beans in a few greens in the center of each of 4 heated plates. Arrange the steak slices on the beans and serve immediately.

SERVES: 4

Grilled Venison Chop with Wild Mushroom Strudel and Blueberry Grappa Sauce

From the heart of America comes this marriage of a tender venison chop with a flaky wild mushroom strudel. A classic sauce made with grappa becomes contemporary and "Americanized" with fresh and dried blueberries. In Italy, grappa is a celebratory drink, a sign of camaraderie and vivacity. Packed with flavor, this venison and mushroom strudel paired with the blueberry grappa sauce tantalizes the senses.

STRUDEL:

- 1 tablespoon unsalted butter
- 1/4 cup extra virgin olive oil
- 1 shallot, peeled and minced
- 2 garlic cloves, peeled and minced
- 1 pound assorted wild mushrooms, cleaned and sliced (morels, shiitake, black trumpets, oyster, porcinis)
  kosher salt and freshly ground white pepper
- 1/2 ounce each finely chopped thyme, tarragon, Italian parsley, chives
- 2 eggs, plus 1 egg yolk, mixed together
- 2 sheets phyllo dough (usually 15" x 26"), cut in half
- 1/4 cup clarified butter

SAUCE:

- 1/2 cup dried blueberries
- 1 cup fresh blueberries
- 1 thyme sprig
- 1 cup blueberry-flavored wine or brandy
- 1 tablespoon sugar
- 2 tablespoons unsalted butter
- 3 tablespoons Muscato grappa

VENISON CHOP:

- 4 center-cut venison rib chops cut about 1 3/4-inch thick, frenched by the butcher like lamb chops
  kosher salt and freshly ground black pepper
- 1 1/2 ounces fresh chopped thyme
  olive oil for rubbing

1. Preheat oven to 350°F.

2. Cook the mushrooms: In medium size sauté pan, melt together the butter and olive oil. When the mixture is just beginning to get hot, add the shallot and garlic. Cook for a few seconds, and then add assorted mushrooms. Season with salt and pepper. Sauté over low heat until the mushrooms are tender. Continue to cook until all the juices have been reduced and stir in three-fourths of the chopped mixed herbs. Transfer the mushrooms to a wire rack to cool and drain. When the mushrooms reach room temperature, transfer to a bowl, and mix with the egg mixture.

3. Make the strudel: Lay out 1 phyllo sheet on a hard surface, placing it so that the 15-inch side is horizontal. Always cover the sheets that are not in use with a damp cloth to avoid drying out. Lightly brush the sheet with warm clarified butter. Sprinkle with 2 teaspoons of mixed herbs. Spread the mushrooms over three-fourths of the phyllo sheet, leaving a 1-inch border on all sides. Tuck the ends up over the filling, as if wrapping a package, and roll carefully. Place on a baking pan, seam side down. Brush the outsides of the strudel, including the ends, with clarified butter. Repeat with the 3 remaining sheets. The strudels can be refrigerated, rolled in plastic wrap, until ready to use.

4. Make the sauce: In a small saucepan, combine all the berries with the thyme and brandy (add more brandy by increments of a teaspoon, if desired) and sprinkle with sugar. Simmer together until the berries are soft and the alcohol from the brandy has cooked off. Transfer to a blender, add butter, and blend until smooth. Balance the flavor with sugar and grappa, and

strain twice through a medium-fine sieve, pressing down with a spoon. If the sauce is too thick, thin with a neutral-flavored stock (vegetable or chicken). Cover and keep warm; do not boil.

5. Bake the strudel on a baking sheet until golden brown on all sides, approximately 12 to 15 minutes. After removing from the oven, wait 2 minutes before slicing.

6. Allow the chops to come to room temperature. Pat dry, and season lightly with salt, heavily with pepper and thyme. (Reserve a few pinches of thyme for garnish.) Brush with oil and grill over very hot coals on a clean, hot grill. Mark the chops evenly on both sides, grilling approximately 2 to 3 minutes per side for rare or longer to desired doneness. Grill the sides also. Instead of grilling, the chops may be pan-seared in 1 tablespoon olive oil and 1 tablespoon butter.

7. Transfer the chops to a warm serving plate. To serve, spoon a pool of blueberry-grappa sauce onto one side of the plate. Arrange 3 slices of mushroom strudel, overlapping, on the other side of the plate, and sprinkle the entire plate with the remaining thyme. Place each chop in the puddle of sauce.

SERVES: 4

CHEF'S HINTS: The meat cooks better if allowed to warm up after being refrigerated. Season it and let it sit until it reaches room temperature.

If fresh blueberries are unavailable, use all dried blueberries increasing the amount by 1 cup and adding ³/4 cup brandy or cognac diluted with ¹/4 cup water.

Black pepper is preferable to white with game. Granulated salt provides uniform flakes that dissolve more evenly than sea salt. Be careful not to over-season at any point.

An easy way to roll strudel is to place the initial layer of dough on a piece of waxed paper or parchment, which allows you to roll without handling the dough and may result in a tighter strudel and a better presentation. Please note that this recipe is based upon a standard phyllo sheet, which is 15 inches by 26 inches. Cut the 2 sheets in half to yield four 15-inch by 13-inch pieces.

Herb-Crusted Lamb with Ratatouille Risotto

*T*his bold herb-crusted lamb was inspired by Alain Ducasse's Monaco kitchen. While this recipe may seem daunting for the novice, it is just right when taste and style count. The flavorful ratatouille risotto has a creamy underpinning that showcases our agricultural bounty. This is truly "a garden of earthly delights."

4 racks of lamb (frenched to the bone)

LAMB MARINADE:

4 teaspoons chopped rosemary

2 garlic cloves, peeled and finely chopped kosher salt and freshly ground black pepper

1 cup pure olive oil juice of 1 orange

RATATOUILLE:

2 cups olive oil

8 garlic cloves, peeled and minced

4 small Spanish onions, peeled and finely diced

2 eggplants, unpeeled, finely diced, lightly salted for 20 minutes to draw out water (remove water with paper towels)

2 yellow zucchini, diced

2 green zucchini, diced

2 each red and yellow bell peppers, seeded and diced

3 cups white wine

2 cups chicken stock (see page 190)

1 cup tomato paste

1 can plum tomatoes, seeded, roughly chopped, reserving liquid

1 teaspoon thyme, stemmed and finely chopped

2 bay leaves

1 teaspoon fresh oregano, minced

HERB CRUST FOR LAMB:

4 cups brioche (see page 190) or substitute bread crumbs

1/2 cup hazelnuts, peeled

4 garlic cloves, peeled

2 shallots, peeled

1/2 orange rind, grated (zest, no white)

1/4 cup extra virgin olive oil

1 teaspoon olive oil

1/4 cup hazelnut oil

1 bunch parsley, stemmed and minced

1/4 bunch fresh basil, stemmed

LAMB SAUCE: (Yield: 1 1/2 gallons)

1 tablespoon olive oil

1 Spanish onion, peeled and diced

1 carrot, peeled and diced

3 celery stalks, leaves removed and diced

2 shallots, peeled and minced

3 garlic cloves, peeled and minced

1 tablespoon fresh thyme, picked and chopped fine

4 tablespoons fresh rosemary, stemmed and chopped

1 teaspoon whole black peppercorns, crushed

6 button mushrooms, roughly chopped

1 cup white wine

2 cups lamb stock (see page 197)

2 tablespoons unsalted butter salt and freshly ground pepper

2 tablespoons Dijon mustard

GARNISH:

4 rosemary sprigs

1. Make the lamb marinade: Combine all but 1 teaspoon of olive oil of the marinade ingredients in a bowl, pour over the lamb, and cover with plastic wrap. Marinate for 24 hours in the refrigerator.

2. Make the ratatouille: In a large saucepan, heat the olive oil, add the garlic and diced onions, and sweat until translucent. Add the eggplant and cook for 4 minutes, stirring with a wooden spoon. Add zucchini and peppers and cook for another 5 minutes. Deglaze with the wine for about 3 minutes. Add the chicken stock and tomato products and stew for 15 minutes until the rest of the vegetables are cooked. Add the herbs and cook for another 5 minutes. Season to taste with salt and pepper, remove the bay leaf, and reserve covered with buttered parchment paper.

3. Preheat the oven to 250°F.

4. Make the herb crust: Cut the brioche and lay on a sheet pan. Toast in the oven with the hazelnuts approximately 6 to 7 minutes until the brioche is dry and the hazelnuts are toasted. Cool the hazelnuts and set aside. Let the brioche cool. Crumble brioche with hands. Set aside.

5. Mix the garlic cloves, shallots, and orange rind, and pulse in a food processor for 1 minute. Then add the extra virgin olive oil and the olive and hazelnut oils until the mixture absorbs the oil, lightly holding itself together. Season with salt and pepper to taste. Add the hazelnuts and process for 2 minutes until finely chopped. Combine the parsley, basil, and the brioche crumbs, and process for 1 minute.

6. Make the lamb sauce: In a saucepan, add the olive oil and sweat the onion, carrot, celery, shallots, and garlic until the onions and shallots are translucent. Add the thyme and the rosemary, peppercorns, mushrooms, and white wine, and reduce by one-quarter to make a glaze. Add the lamb stock and simmer over medium heat for about 15 minutes. Strain into a small saucepan and whisk in the butter over medium heat until the sauce barely coats the spoon. Season to taste with salt and pepper.

7. Preheat the oven to 400°F.

8. Remove the lamb from the marinade. Season lamb with salt and pepper. In a saucepan, with 1 teaspoon of olive oil, sauté the lamb meat-side down and sear approximately 5 minutes until golden brown on both sides. Let rest for 1 minute.

9. Generously spread the Dijon mustard on both sides of the seared rack. Spread the brioche crumbs on a sheet pan or place in a mixing bowl. Then dip the lamb into the crumbs, packing with your hands to cover well.

10. Place the racks on a roasting tray and cook in oven for 7 to 10 minutes until medium-rare or desired doneness. Let rest for 2 to 3 minutes. Heat the ratatouille and sauce until hot.

11. To serve, divide the ratatouille among 4 dinner plates. Carve lamb rack into 4 chops and place the lamb with the bones in a pinwheel, resting on the ratatouille and the meat resting on the plate. Spoon the sauce over the lamb.

12. Garnish center of ratatouille with one fresh rosemary sprig.

SERVES: 4

Lamb Shanks with Wheat Berries and Lentils

This earthy dish is bistro home-cooking at its best. The same braising principle can be used for other dishes such as pot roast and osso buco, and similarly the wheat berry-lentil vinaigrette makes a satisfying accompaniment to salad. The tender lamb shanks sitting in a lusty pool of red wine sauce make hearty fare for a Saturday night at home by the hearth.

4 lamb shanks
1 cup wheat berries

SAUCE:

4 cups chicken stock (see page 190)
1/2 medium white onion, peeled and diced
2 bay leaves
1 thyme sprig
1/4 pound raw bacon, chopped
1 cup tiny green lentils

2 parsnips, peeled
1/4 cup olive oil
1 cup peanut or canola oil
   salt and freshly ground white pepper

MIREPOIX:

2 carrots, peeled and diced
1/2 medium white onion, peeled and diced
2 celery stalks, peeled and diced
6 garlic cloves, peeled and smashed
2 cups red wine
2 cups lamb or chicken stock
   (see page 190)
4 tomatoes, blanched, seeded, and coarsely
   chopped
1 thyme sprig
2 rosemary sprigs
   pinch of cracked pepper
1 basil sprig
2 tablespoons unsalted butter

GARNISH:

   field salad of red leaf, la rosa, frisée, and
   green leaf lettuce
1 small bunch chives, chopped
1 tomato, seeded, skinned, and diced

1. In water to cover, soak wheat berries overnight. Drain the water from the wheat berries.

2. Make the sauce: In a heavy saucepan, place 2 cups of stock, onion, 1 bay leaf, thyme sprig, and half of the bacon. Cover and cook over medium heat for 2 hours. Strain and reserve.

3. Meanwhile, in another saucepan, cover and cook the green lentils over medium heat with the remaining stock and bacon for approximately 1 hour, until tender. Strain and reserve.

4. Make the parsnip chips: On a sharp mandoline, slice parsnips into 1/8-inch-thick strips. Cook in hot olive oil (350°F) for 2 to 3 minutes, turning strips with tongs. Drain on paper towels. Season with sea salt and freshly ground white pepper.

5. Season the lamb shanks with salt and pepper.

6. In a roasting pan, heat the canola oil and sear lamb on both sides approximately 5 minutes until it reaches a nice brown color. Drain excess oil and return to pan.

7. Preheat the oven to 350°F.

8. In the same pan, slowly cook the diced vegetables ("mirepoix") and garlic on top of the stove. Add the red wine and stock. Then add the tomato, remaining bay leaf, thyme sprig, 2 rosemary sprigs, cracked pepper, and basil, and cook in the oven about 2 1/2 hours until tender. Remove, strain stock, and reduce over high heat to make the liquid a little syrupy. When the stock thickens after approximately 30 minutes to a consistency that slightly coats the back of a spoon, whisk in the butter. Season to taste.

9. To serve, reheat the lentils and wheat berries in the lamb sauce and serve over lamb in large plates. Season to taste. Garnish with fried parsnip and a field salad of red leaf, la rosa, frisée, and green leaf lettuce. Top with chopped chives and tomato dices.

SERVES: 4

AUTHOR'S NOTE: Wheat berries are available from Middle Eastern shops. Bread flour is the most well-known by-product of wheat berries. Also made from wheat berries are bulgur (partially cooked and cracked) and semolina (the purified middle part).

Mahogany Quails on Tender Snow Pea Vines with Drunken Sour Cherries

Chef Martin Kouprie, a devoted oenophile, adds just the right amount of liqueur to heighten the gustatory appeal of these sesame soy marinated quail. He dubs his cooking style "cuisine vitale," since the flavors, colors, and textures are vibrant, while the preservatives are natural and retain the essence of the food.

9 extra large quails

3/4 cup soy sauce, natural

2 tablespoons toasted sesame oil (pure)

1/3 cup sugar

2 garlic cloves, peeled and minced

1/2 cup sun-dried sour cherries

1/3 cup brandy

1 cup game sauce (see page 196)

1 bunch tender snow pea vines and shoots (about 3 cups)

1. With a sharp knife, carefully divide the quail in half. Leaving the leg attached to the breast, remove the meat from the rib cage. Free the leg and wing from the cavity at the joints. Pinch the bottom of the larger leg bone, push up the meat to the first joint, and remove with a twisting action, leaving the smaller bone still in the leg. Cut off wing tips. Cover and reserve boned quail in refrigerator.

2. In a saucepan combine the soy sauce, sesame oil, sugar, and garlic. Place over medium-high heat and, once the marinade has boiled, set aside to cool. Add the marinade to the quail and refrigerate for at least 2 hours and up to 24 hours.

3. In a small bowl, combine the sour cherries and brandy, and set aside.

4. Heat the game sauce and keep warm.

5. Grill the quails for about 2 minutes per side or until the skin is a mahogany color.

6. To serve, arrange bouquets of the snow pea vines, gathered at their bases, on 6 serving plates; place 3 quail halves on each, spoon over the game sauce, and sprinkle evenly with the brandy-marinated cherries.

SERVES: 6

Pheasant with Basil, Sauternes, and Polenta

Four 2-pound aged pheasants (female is more tender), reserving carcass and bones for stock, clipped breasts and boned thighs

POLENTA:

3 *cups milk*

2 *tablespoons clarified butter*

3/4 *cup cornmeal*

1 *cup grated Vermont cheddar cheese salt and freshly ground white pepper nutmeg*

4 *shallots, peeled and finely diced*

1 1/2 *cups Vermouth*

1/4 *cup sauternes (or sweet white wine)*

1 *teaspoon star anise*

1/4 *teaspoon chopped orange rind*

3 *tablespoons basil, stemmed and julienned*

3 *tablespoons shiitake mushrooms, reserving stems*

3 *tablespoons oyster mushrooms, reserving stems*

1/4 *cup morel mushrooms, reserving stems, cleaned well*

4 *cups unsalted pheasant or chicken stock (see page 190)*

1/4 *teaspoon cornstarch*

1/8 *cup water*

1/2 *cup olive oil*

1/4 *cup diced tomatoes*

1/4 *cup cooked peas*

GARNISH:

8 *basil sprigs*

This juicy pheasant perfumed with sauternes, vermouth, and star anise is the ultimate fall or winter indulgence. In addition to farm-raised Vermont pheasant, indigenous cheddar cheese distinguishes this polenta timbale. Wild mushrooms, crunched peas, and tomato dice accent the dish with color and flavor.

1. Make the polenta: In a saucepan, place the milk and butter into a pot and bring to a boil. Sift the cornmeal into the milk, whisking vigorously. Stir for 10 minutes over low flame. Remove from heat and stir in the cheddar cheese. Season with salt, pepper, and nutmeg to taste.

2. While the mixture is still warm, pour into eight 4-ounce (3-inch diameter) buttered ramekins. Refrigerate about 2 hours or until the cornmeal sets.

3. In a saucepan, bring the shallots, Vermouth, sauternes, star anise, orange rind, basil, and mushroom stems to a boil and reduce by one-half. Add the pheasant broth and reduce by half. While simmering, whisk in the cornstarch dissolved in water. Strain the sauce.

4. Preheat the oven to 375°F.

5. Season the pheasant breasts and thighs with salt and pepper. In a sauté pan, add the olive oil and, when hot, sauté the pheasant pieces, skin-side down. Cook the breasts 2 to 3 minutes on each side until pink. Continue cooking the thighs in the oven for 6 to 7 minutes until cooked throughout. Remove to a warm plate and reserve the oil in the pan to sauté the mushrooms.

6. Reheat the oil and sauté the mushrooms until tender. Place in a warming bowl and toss with fresh tomato and warm peas. Recheck the seasoning.

7. Unmold the polenta timbales on a buttered sheet pan. Cook for 1 minute in the broiler to make golden on top.

8. When ready to serve, slice the pheasant breasts and thighs and fan out on the plates. Arrange on each plate with the sauce and unmold the polenta. Ladle the mushroom mixture over the polenta. Garnish the polenta with a basil sprig.

SERVES: 8

Pan Roasted Guinea Hen with Cauliflower Purée and Bean Ragout

This classic combination of tomato, tarragon, onions, and earthy beans complement the richness of the guinea hen. The mellow texture of the cauliflower and braised onions are a contrast for the crisply roasted breast. Served slightly pink, guinea hen, a full-flavored bird, is exceptionally moist and tender, and compared to other game birds has the highest quality of protein.

2 guinea hens

TARRAGON OIL:

1 bunch tarragon, stemmed and roughly chopped
1 cup extra virgin olive oil

1 cup pencil pod beans (black), soaked overnight and rinsed
1 cup butter beans (white Peruvian lima beans), soaked overnight and rinsed
1 cup fresh lima or fava beans, shelled from pod
3 large vine-ripened red tomatoes, cored
12 white boiling onions, tops snipped and peeled
1½ cups game stock (see page 196)
7 tablespoons unsalted butter

AROMATICS:

pinch celery seed
3 parsley stems
1 tablespoon black peppercorns

1 cauliflower head, cored and stems removed except for 2 inches
2 cups milk or water
kosher salt and freshly ground black pepper
2 tablespoons chicken stock (see page 190) (optional))
6 tablespoons crème fraîche (see page 191)
pinch celery seed

GARNISH:

4 tarragon sprigs

1. Make the tarragon oil: Add tarragon and the oil to a small bowl and infuse for several hours.

2. In two separate pots of boiling salted water, simmer pencil pods and butter beans over medium heat until tender, approximately 40 minutes. Cool them in their cooking liquid.

3. In 2 quarts of boiling salted water, cook the fava or lima beans for 5 minutes or until tender. Refresh in salted ice water.

4. Preheat the oven to 400°F.

5. Purée tomatoes in a food processor, pass through a sieve, and press down with a large spoon to obtain liquid.

6. Braise the onions: In a small casserole or sauté pan, place the onions and add the game stock, 1 tablespoon butter, and aromatics. Cover with aluminum foil. Cook until very tender, for approximately 20 minutes in the oven. Remove onions from pan.

7. In a medium pot, place the cauliflower and milk and cook approximately 10 minutes until tender. Drain and wring dry in a clean cloth. Purée in a food processor approximately 2 minutes until smooth.

8. Clean the hen and separate breasts and legs from carcass. Season the hen with salt and pepper and place skin-side down in a hot saucepan with a thin coat of neutral oil. Sear for 7 minutes. Remove from the heat, turn over in pan, and let sit for 1 minute. Remove from the pan.

9. In a medium saucepan, melt 4 tablespoons of the butter, add the onions, chicken stock (optional), pencil pod beans, and fava or lima beans. Season with salt and pepper and warm.

10. Place the cauliflower purée in a saucepan and add the crème fraîche, butter, and celery seed. Whisk together and place over medium heat until warm. Season with salt and pepper.

11. In a medium saucepan, add 6 ounces of the tomato liquid to 10 ounces of game stock and the butter beans. Heat. Add the remaining tablespoon of butter and swirl the pan.

12. Thinly slice the guinea hen breast at an angle with a serrated knife.

13. To serve, place a 4-inch diameter $^3/4$-inch metal ring in the center of a large dinner plate. Place cauliflower purée in the center to the height of the ring. Fan out guinea hen slices like a flower over the purée. Place the onions, pencil pods, and fava beans in one area. Spoon the tomato and game stock and randomly scatter the butter beans. Streak the tarragon oil around the plate. Place a tarragon sprig in the center of the meat.

SERVES: 4

CHEF'S HINT: The legs are somewhat firmer than the breast meat, and can be removed them from the bird and cooked them separately, usually by braising.

Pork Loin and Honey Mustard Sauce with Cheddar Cheese Spoonbread

This Southern dish from Washington D.C.'s Victorian Morrison-Clark Inn represents vintage glamour. The historic landmark building housing the Morrison-Clark Inn supplied grain during the Civil War. One can imagine the soft, creamy-textured spoonbread as the hallmark of any turn-of-the-century Southern table. These traditional favorites have been reconstituted in an attractive freestanding form. The cuisines of such Southern states as South Carolina and Virginia prefer the yellow cornmeal, as used here. The honey mustard sauce is a sweet, tart complement for the succulent pork and the perfect dip for the spoonbread.

2 pounds trimmed, boneless pork loin
kosher salt and freshly ground white pepper
1 tablespoon peanut oil

CHEDDAR CHEESE SPOONBREAD:

4 cups water
1/2 tablespoon kosher salt
2 tablespoons unsalted butter
1/4 cup course ground yellow cornmeal
1/4 cup fine ground yellow cornmeal
2 tablespoons course ground grits
1 egg yolk
1/2 cup half-and-half cream
1 cup grated white cheddar cheese
1 egg white

HONEY MUSTARD SAUCE:

6 tablespoons honey
1/2 cup plus 2 tablespoons Dijon mustard
1/4 cup chicken stock (see page 190)
2 tablespoons unsalted butter

VEGETABLES:

1 tablespoon peanut oil
1/2 pound fresh green beans
1/2 pound blanched pearl onions

1 tablespoon chopped fresh tarragon
1 tablespoon chopped fresh thyme
1 tablespoon chopped fresh chives

1. Preheat the oven to 350°F.

2. Make the cheddar cheese spoonbread: Bring the water, salt, and butter to a boil in a medium saucepan. Slowly stir cornmeals and grits into the mixture. Reduce heat and cook, stirring for 15 to 20 minutes until the grains are swollen and soft. If mixture dries out and becomes difficult to stir, add enough water to loosen mixture. Remove from the heat. Add egg yolk, half-and-half, and cheese. Mix well. Beat egg white to a soft-peak stage and fold into the mixture. Divide the mixture among six 6-ounce (3-inch diameter) buttered ramekins, filling to the top (you will have 2 extras). Bake in the oven in a water bath for approximately 25 to 30 minutes until light brown and just barely set. Keep the oven on for the pork. To serve, unmold from ramekins and, if making in advance, reheat on a greased baking sheet.

3. Make the honey mustard sauce: In a bowl, whisk together the honey and mustard until well-blended. In a small saucepan, add the chicken stock. When the stock comes to a boil, stir in the honey mustard sauce and the butter. Season with salt and pepper.

4. Season the pork loins well with kosher salt and pepper. In a medium sauté pan, add the peanut oil. When the oil is almost smoking, sear the pork loins on all sides until nicely browned. Place the meat on a rack within a roasting pan, and roast for 45 to 55 minutes until cooked to medium. Let rest for 10 minutes prior to slicing.

5. Make the vegetables: Add 1 tablespoon of peanut oil to a hot saucepan and, when the oil is hot, add vegetables. Season well with kosher salt and quickly sauté. When ready to serve, gently reheat the sauce, adding additional chicken stock if the sauce requires thinning. Stir in the herbs.

6. To serve, slice the pork loin and arrange 5 slices per plate. Spoon the honey mustard sauce over the sliced pork. Unmold the spoonbread onto the plate and artfully surround with sautéed vegetables.

SERVES: 4

Roasted Rack of Lamb with Black Olive Sauce and Garlic Mashed Potatoes

Wolfgang Puck presents this exciting rendition of roasted rack of lamb with a rich, densely flavored Madeira wine sauce. While reminiscent of my childhood, these mashed potatoes are heightened in flavor with roasted garlic and are today's highly sought comfort food.

BLACK OLIVE SAUCE:

- 1/2 pound unsalted butter
- 8 garlic cloves, peeled and crushed
- 8 shallots, peeled and chopped
- 1 tablespoon black peppercorns
- 2 cups Madeira wine
- 2 cups red wine
- 2 rosemary sprigs
- 1 tomato, medium, seeds squeezed out and diced
- 1 cup demiglace (game or veal stock recipe reduced until syrupy) (see page 196)
- 1/2 cup pitted Niçoise olives (about 1 1/4 cups unpitted)
- salt and freshly ground black pepper

GARLIC MASHED POTATOES:

- 8 large baking potatoes, peeled, cut into 5 pieces
- 1 cup heavy cream, to taste
- 8 peeled garlic cloves
- kosher salt and freshly ground white pepper
- 2 tablespoons unsalted butter

LAMB:

- 2 lamb racks, chine and fat cap removed, room temperature
- 4 tablespoons virgin olive oil
- 2 rosemary sprigs, stemmed and chopped

1. Make the sauce: In a heated sauté pan, melt 1 tablespoon of butter. Sauté the garlic, shallots, and peppercorns until lightly browned.

2. Add the Madeira and red wine, rosemary, and tomato, and simmer until reduced by two-thirds (about 1 cup total). Add the demiglace and return to a boil. Off the heat, slowly whisk the remaining butter until incorporated.

3. Strain the sauce through a fine strainer and then transfer to a blender. Add half of the olives and purée until almost smooth. Roughly chop the remaining olives and combine with the sauce. Season with salt and black pepper to taste. Reserve in a warm place until ready to serve.

4. Make the potatoes. Place the potatoes in a medium pot covered with water and 1/4 teaspoon salt. Bring to a boil and simmer until the potatoes are tender. Drain the potatoes.

5. Add most of the cream to the pot that the potatoes were cooked in and bring to a boil. Return the potatoes along with the garlic, salt and pepper to taste, and butter to the pot. Stir well and heat through.

6. Purée the potato mixture through a food mill. Adjust the consistency with warm cream as desired and season to taste with salt and white pepper. Keep warm until serving.

7. Preheat the oven to 400°F.

8. Make the lamb racks: Rub well with the olive oil and season generously with salt, pepper, and rosemary. Heat a roasting pan until very hot. Add a few drops of oil and sear the lamb racks on all sides until brown. Place the lamb racks, bone-side down, into the hot pan, and roast until medium-rare or to desired doneness. (Medium-rare takes about 10 minutes).

9. Allow the lamb to rest at room temperature, then slice the lamb into 8 chops per rack.

10. To serve, spoon the mashed potatoes onto the center of each plate. Ladle the sauce around the potatoes. Place the lamb chops, 4 to a plate, around the potatoes. Garnish with lightly cooked vegetables of your choice.

SERVES: 4

Grilled Squab with Grits

An aromatic marinade of maple syrup, thyme, and pepper perfumes the squab, and the grits provide a burst of energy. Stoneground grits are recommended since they have more texture and are a little rougher than ordinary grits. Typically American ingredients—grits, tomatoes, and maple syrup—are combined with the European touch of a delicate game sauce.

Four 1-pound squabs
2 tablespoons olive oil
1 large white onion, peeled, quartered
1/2 head garlic with skin
1 tomato, cored and quartered
2 cups water
4 cups chicken stock (see page 190)
3 parsley sprigs
3 basil sprigs

MARINADE:
1 cup extra virgin olive oil
3 tablespoon maple syrup or Grade A honey
1 tablespoon thyme, stemmed and chopped

2 garlic cloves, peeled and pressed
1 tablespoon freshly ground black pepper

2 tomatoes, blanched, cored and peeled
coarse salt or kosher salt and freshly
ground black pepper
1 cup grits, stone-ground
3 tablespoons milk
1 tablespoon unsalted butter

GARNISH:
20 black Niçoise olives (pitted)
4 fresh thyme sprigs

1. Preheat the oven to 450°F.

2. Make the squab stock: Remove the breast and detach second joint of the wing. Reserve. Roughly chop the rest of the carcass. Add to a lightly oiled roasting pan the onion, garlic, and tomato. Roast all the items approximately 45 minutes until golden brown. Remove the bones, garlic, tomato, and onion to a stockpot, remove excess grease from the pan, and deglaze with 2 cups of water over a low flame by taking a metal spatula and scraping the brown bits. Place the liquid and everything in the stockpot with chicken stock and bring to a boil. Simmer for about 2 hours, skimming the scum from time to time. Add the parsley and basil and continue simmering for an additional half hour, then strain through a fine mesh strainer.

3. In a saucepan over medium heat, reduce the liquid by half until it coats the back of a wooden spoon.

4. While the stock is simmering, make the marinade: In a bowl, whisk the olive oil, maple syrup, thyme, garlic, and black pepper. Mix the squab breasts with the marinade and let stand for 1/2 hour.

5. Lower the oven to 250°F. Cut the tomatoes in half and season with salt and pepper. Roast in the oven for 1 hour on a sheet pan lined with parchment paper.

6. In a medium saucepan, whisk the grits into 2 cups of boiling salted water. Cook uncovered for 20 minutes, stirring occasionally to prevent sticking and lumps. Add the milk and butter and stir to incorporate.

7. Raise the oven temperature to 450°F. Season squab with salt and grill the squab breast to medium-rare, or sear it in a hot pan with a thin coating of olive oil (2 tablespoons) until brown on both sides. Finish in the oven for 7 minutes until medium-rare or desired doneness.

8. To serve, spoon the grits in the center of each plate. Place the squab breasts on both sides of the grits with wings on either side. Place the roasted tomato on the side and spoon the juice over and around the squab. Garnish with olives next to the tomato and a thyme sprig positioned vertically in the grits.

SERVES: 4

Sautéed Squab with Figs, Foie Gras, and Ginger Port Vinaigrette

GINGER PORT VINAIGRETTE:

- 1 pint fresh Black Mission figs
- 1/2 cup ruby-red port
- 1/2 cup champagne vinegar
- 1 teaspoon finely chopped ginger
- 1 teaspoon sugar
- 1/2 teaspoon mango pickle (if unavailable, substitute chili paste)

- 4 squabs, deboned to remove breast and legs (intact)
  kosher salt and freshly ground black pepper

- 1/2 cup corn oil
- 4 medium Yukon gold potatoes, sliced into thin rounds
- 3 endives, cored and julienned
- 3 tablespoons sugar
- 1/4 cup champagne wine vinegar
- 8 Black Mission figs, stemmed and quartered
- 1 small knob of ginger, peeled and julienned
- 1 small bunch of chives, finely cut
- 1 small bunch of tarragon, stemmed and minced
- 10 ounces foie gras, cut into 4 even pieces

The velvety Sonoma Valley foie gras is the perfect foil for California's intensely flavored, plump Black Mission figs. The 17th century Spaniards brought figs to the New World. These were cultivated at the missions of the Franciscan monks. The carmelized endives sautéed with ginger, tarragon, and Yukon gold potatoes are enlivened by the intensity of the port vinaigrette, which imparts a butterscotch flavor to the sauce.

1. Make the ginger port vinaigrette: Purée the figs in a blender. Add the rest of the ginger-port ingredients and purée the mixture until smooth.

2. Season the squabs with salt and pepper. Heat a sauté pan and add half of the corn oil. Place the squab skin-side down and cook approximately 2 minutes until the skin is golden brown. Turn squabs over with tongs and cook an additional 3 to 4 minutes until medium-rare. Remove the squabs and keep warm.

3. Blanch the potatoes in salted boiling water approximately 3 minutes until tender. Remove and then lay flat on a sheet pan to dry.

4. In a second sauté pan, add the rest of the corn oil and sauté the blanched potatoes for 1 minute. Add the endives and toss to coat with oil. Add the sugar and toss to coat the potatoes and endives. Cook briefly to lightly caramelize the sugar. Deglaze with the vinegar. Reduce until the sauce is almost dry. Add the figs, ginger, chives, and tarragon, and toss. Season with salt and pepper.

5. Score the foie gras to release the fat and tenderize it by making diagonal knife cuts on both sides with a knife. Season with salt and pepper. Place the foie gras in a hot skillet. Cook on both sides until seared on the outside and rare inside. (This should take approximately 2 minutes altogether.)

6. In the skillet, cook the squab until desired doneness. Remove the excess fat and heat until almost smoking.

7. To serve: Dress the potato-endive mixture with 1/2 cup of the vinaigrette around the edges of the plate. Arrange 3 squab breasts interconnecting the legs on top of the breasts and foie gras on top of the potato and endives.

SERVES: 4

Seared Beef with Boniato Purée and Black Bean Broth

Douglas Rodriguez puts his nuevo Latino twist on the classic Cuban vaca frita (literally "fried cow"). The seared beef is enhanced by the boniato purée, which imparts a slightly richer flavor than sweet potato. The bell peppers, onions, and garlic enliven a refreshing black bean broth.

BLACK BEAN BROTH:

- 1 bag dry black beans (12 ounces)
- 2 bay leaves
- 1 teaspoon cumin
- 1 teaspoon fresh oregano
- 2 quarts water
- 6 red bell peppers, seeded
- 2 white onions, peeled
- 10 garlic cloves, peeled

BONIATO PURÉE:

- 2 pounds boniato, peeled and diced (if unavailable, use sweet potato or yam)
- 4 cups plus milk
- 2 cups water
- 1 stick unsalted butter, cubed
  salt

SEARED BEEF:

- 3 pounds skirt steak
- 12–15 fresh garlic cloves, peeled
- 2 tablespoons dry oregano
- 4–6 bay leaves
- 3 tablespoons salt
- 3 tablespoons black peppercorns
- 1 tablespoon crushed red pepper flakes
- 1 small bunch fresh thyme
- 2 medium red onions, peeled and julienned
- 1 teaspoon diced garlic
- 6 parsley sprigs, stems removed, coarsely chopped
- 3 cilantro sprigs, stems removed, coarsely chopped
- 4 limes, juiced
- 4 tablespoons olive oil for pan searing
  salt and pepper

1. Make the black bean broth: Place the beans, bay leaves, cumin, fresh oregano, and water in a large pot and simmer for 2 hours. Place the peppers, onions, and garlic through a juice extractor (if a juice extractor is unavailable, process in a blender until smooth and then strain through a fine sieve) into a bowl. Add this to the bean pot and cook an additional 30 minutes. When the beans are tender, season with salt and pepper to taste. Strain out the beans. Reduce the broth for another 20 minutes. (Refrigerate or freeze until ready to use.)

2. Make the boniato purée: In a large pot, place the boniato, milk, and water. Bring to a boil and simmer for 1 hour or until tender. Drain and mash the boniato, adding enough milk to keep it moist. Whisk in the butter 1 cube at a time, then season with salt to taste.

3. Make the skirt steak: Place the steak, garlic, oregano, bay leaves, salt, peppercorns, red pepper flakes, and thyme in a medium stockpot, cover with water, and bring to a boil. Reduce to a simmer, cover, and simmer for 1 hour. Remove from the heat and cool in its liquid. Remove the meat from the liquid and trim off any excess fat, and finely shred on a flat surface using 2 forks.

4. In a bowl, place the meat, onions, garlic, parsley, cilantro, and lime juice and toss. Heat an 11-inch skillet, then the olive oil until very hot, and add the tossed meat. Sear the meat mixture well on one side, then flip and sear on the other side about 5 minutes until crispy and nicely browned.

5. To serve, place a 4-inch ring mold on individual serving dishes. Press in some boniato purée remove the ring mold, and top with seared beef frita. Spoon some black bean broth around the beef and serve immediately.

SERVES: 6

Venison with Sour Cherries and Hickory Nuts

1¹/2 cups game stock (see page 196)

2 pounds venison loin, cut into 6 medallions, ¹/4 inch thick

salt and freshly ground black pepper

all-purpose flour, for dusting

3 tablespoons peanut oil

¹/4 cup hickory (or pecan) nuts

¹/2 cup canned sour cherries, pitted and
drained

1 cup red pinto bean and bulgur salad
(see page 89)

1. In medium saucepan, reduce the stock by half over medium heat to a demiglace.

2. Season the venison medallions with salt and black pepper. Dust with all-purpose flour. Pat off excess.

3. Heat the peanut oil in a heavy pan until the oil is smoking. Place the venison in the pan and sear in the juices over a high flame until deep brown. Turn, add hickory nuts, and continue cooking on the other side until deep brown. Remove the excess fat, add the cherries, brown demiglace, and reduce to syrupy consistency. (Venison will be medium-rare).

4. To serve, place a venison medallion in the center of each plate. Spoon the cherry sauce around and serve with red pinto bean and bulgur salad.

SERVES: 6

Farm-raised organic free-range venison is as tender and velvety as the finest "plume de veau." This Appalachian specialty is heightened in flavor by smoky hickory nuts and the sweet-sour addition of cherries. Cherries have been known to symbolize glory and truth ever since George Washington confessed to cutting down his father's cherry tree. They infuse this game sauce with a beguiling flavor.

CHAPTER 7

Fish

"Fish is held out to be
one of the greatest luxuries of the table
and not only necessary, but even indispensable
at a dinner where there is any pretense
to excellence or fashion."

MADAME ISABELLA BEETON
Mrs Beeton's Book of Household Management

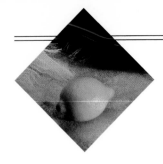

Barbecued Salmon with Crispy Yams

Four 7-ounce salmon filets, with skin

A marinade of apple cider, soy sauce, and garlic distinguish this moist salmon barbecue. The dark hue of the crispy julienned yams adds a dash of textural contrast to the plate.

BARBECUE SAUCE:

4 cups apple cider

1²/3 cups soy sauce

8 tablespoons unsalted butter

1 teaspoon chopped garlic

2 tablespoons arrowroot, diluted in 3 tablespoons water

2 yams, peeled and julienned

1 quart vegetable oil

1. Make the barbecue sauce: In a medium saucepan, combine the apple cider, soy, butter, and garlic, and simmer for a few minutes. Bring to a boil. Reserve a third for the marinade and thicken the remaining with arrowroot by whisking over the simmering heat. Strain through a fine strainer over a small saucepan and reserve.

2. Marinate the salmon filets with half of the barbecue sauce, skin-side up, in a flat glass dish covered with plastic wrap. Refrigerate overnight or up to 2 days.

3. Soak julienned yams in water for 2 to 3 minutes.

4. Heat the vegetable oil for approximately 20 minutes to read 350°F and fry the yams until golden brown. Remove and drain on paper towels.

5. Remove salmon filets from the marinade. Heat and oil a grill and cook salmon for approximately 5 minutes to desired doneness.

6. To serve, with a ladle, make a pool of barbecue sauce in the middle of each dish. Place the salmon filet on top, leaning at an angle. Place the yams behind the sauce using prongs to create height. As a side dish, serve each person 1/2 cup of steamed vegetables such as broccoli, cauliflower, julienned carrots, and pea pods.

AUTHOR'S NOTE: Arrowroot has more protein and is a more effective thickening agent than cornstarch.

SERVES: 4

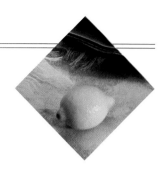

Coriander Crusted Salmon with Winter Ratatouille in a Ginger-Butter Sauce

Four 6-ounce salmon filets, skinned and
blood line removed

1/2 cup coriander seeds, crushed with the
bottom of a pan or in a food processor

1 tablespoon olive oil

RATATOUILLE:

1 tablespoon olive oil

1 tablespoon chopped garlic

1/2 yellow onion, peeled and diced

1/2 zucchini, peeled and diced

1/2 squash, peeled and diced

1 tomato, peeled and diced

1/2 small eggplant, peeled and diced

1 1/2 cups white wine

1 tablespoon tomato paste
salt and freshly ground white pepper

GARNISH:

2 cups vegetable oil

1 bunch dill, stemmed

GINGER-BUTTER SAUCE:

1 cup fish stock (see page 194)

1 tablespoon chopped fresh ginger

1 teaspoon chopped shallots

1/2 cup heavy cream

2 tablespoons whole soft butter

2 tablespoons chopped chives

Walking through Philadelphia's charming Center City, where many cobblestone and brick streets are reminiscent of its Revolutionary past, you reach the famed Rittenhouse Square, which offers striking culinary fare. The crunchy coriander crust is easier to digest than peppercorns and, when cooked, is a tender contrast to the flaky salmon filet.

1. Make the ratatouille: In a medium, hot sauté pan, place 1 tablespoon of olive oil. Sweat the garlic for 2 minutes and then add the onion. Sauté until translucent, then add the rest of the vegetables and cook for 5 minutes. Deglaze with 1/2 cup of white wine. Fold in the tomato paste with a plastic spatula. Season with salt and pepper to taste and set aside.

2. Make the garnish: In a medium saucepan, heat the oil until it reaches 275°F. This should take approximately 20 minutes. Fry the dill for 20 seconds until lightly crisp. Remove with a slotted spoon and pat dry on paper towels.

3. Make the ginger-butter sauce: In a large saucepan, add the remaining wine, fish stock, ginger, and shallots. Reduce approximately 7 to 10 minutes until dry. Add the heavy cream; reduce by half. Finish the sauce by whisking in whole butter and chives to a consistency that coats the back of a spoon.

4. Preheat the oven to 375°F.

5. Meanwhile, place the crushed coriander in a bowl. Lightly dust the top of the salmon filet with coriander. In a medium, hot sauté pan, add 1 tablespoon of olive oil and, over medium heat, sauté the salmon until crispy on both sides. (The coriander will start getting brown.) Flip over and cook until the bottom is caramelized. Cook in the oven for 3 minutes for medium-rare or until desired doneness.

6. To serve, place a bed of the ratatouille in the center of the dinner plate, the salmon filet on top, and lightly drizzle the sauce around the edge and over the salmon. Artfully place dill sprigs equidistant from each other around the plate with leaves pointing outward.

SERVES: 4

CHEF'S HINT: If preparing sauce in advance, increase the cream quantity to 1 1/2 cups so that cream will be more stable and not break down.

Black Bass in Herb Broth with Artichokes

*G*ray Kunz was at the fore-front of popularizing emulsified stock infusions in America. He elevates the concept of steaming with this challenging black bass in herb broth. The broth, infused with stock, creates a light, yet assertive, herb-scented signature dish. The baby arti-chokes, with their soft, fern-like stalks add drama to this firm yet delicately flaked fish.

1/2   pound baby artichokes
1   fresh lemon, halved

2   tablespoons unsalted butter
1 1/2   pounds black bass, fileted with skin coarse salt and freshly ground white pepper

TOPPING:
1   tablespoon finely chopped shallots
1   teaspoon lemon thyme
1   teaspoon finely chopped chives
1   teaspoon lemon zest, finely chopped

1   tablespoon olive oil
1   red ripe tomato, blanched, peeled, cored, seeded, and diced

HERB BROTH:
2   teaspoons unsalted butter
1   teaspoon chopped shallots
1/2   teaspoon minced garlic
3/4   cup chicken, fish, or vegetable stock (see pages 190, 194)
1   teaspoon thyme leaves
1   teaspoon fresh chervil
1   teaspoon chopped basil
1   teaspoon finely chopped chives

VEGETABLE GARNISH:
1   tablespoon diced carrot
1   tablespoon finely diced celery
1   tablespoon finely diced red pepper

GARNISH:
4   chervil sprigs (or chives)
1   lemon zest, julienned

1. Prepare the baby artichokes: Remove the top outer leaves with a small paring knife and flatten the top with the knife. Shave the stem a little. Dip the artichokes in a small bowl of water and squeeze a fresh lemon over them to prevent discoloration. In a medium saucepan filled halfway with salted water, cook the artichokes over medium heat. Bring to a boil and then simmer slowly over low to medium heat approximately 20 minutes. Test with a knife to make sure they are tender. Drain the artichokes, slice in half, and reserve.

2. Prepare the bass: Brush with 2 tablespoons of butter and place on a buttered tray to fit your steamer. Season with salt and pepper and top each filet with a mixture of chopped shallots, lemon thyme, chives, and lemon zest, and reserve for steaming. Refrigerate covered with plastic wrap until ready to use.

3. Cook the vegetables: In a hot sauté pan, heat the olive oil and sauté the artichokes, turning until crispy, then add the tomato and season to taste with salt and pepper.

4. Make the herb broth: Warm the saucepan and sweat the shallots and garlic in 1 teaspoon of butter. Add the chicken stock and bring to a boil. Simmer and reduce by one-third for approximately 5 minutes. Add the herbs, vegetable garnish, and remaining butter, and blend with a hand blender or whisk until foamy.

5. Steam the fish in a steamer approximately 3 to 6 minutes until tender. The time may vary depending on the thickness of the fish.

6. To serve, divide the sauce among 4 large soup plates. Place the artichokes in the center. Top with the fish and garnish with a chervil sprig and lemon zest.

    SERVES: 4

Grilled Filet of Red Snapper with Marinade of Vegetables in Lemon Herb Vinaigrette

2 tablespoons green beans

2 tablespoons baby artichoke hearts, halved

1 red tomato

2 tablespoons fennel

2 tablespoons cucumber, peeled and finely diced

2 tablespoons red bell pepper, seeded and finely diced

2 tablespoons red onion, peeled and finely diced

2 tablespoons scallions, peeled and finely diced

2 teaspoons chives, chopped

2 teaspoons Italian parsley, stemmed and chopped

coarse salt and freshly cracked white pepper

1/4 cup freshly squeezed lemon juice

4 teaspoons plus 5 tablespoons olive oil

1 pound red snapper filets, with skin

2 tablespoons fish glaze (available at Oriental markets)

GARNISH:

1 bunch parsley, roughly chopped

2 lemons, thinly sliced

In addition to Saguaro cactus, Christian missions, and desert flora and fauna, the Grand Canyon State is ablaze with culinary talent. The crispy filet and the crunchy vegetable marinade provide soothing lightness for the hot Arizona desert climate.

1. Make the marinade of vegetables: Blanch the green beans, artichoke hearts, tomato, and fennel in a gallon of salted boiling water for 3 minutes. Plunge into a bowl of ice water. Cut into small dice, except cut the artichoke hearts in half and thinly slice. Place vegetables in a medium bowl.

2. Add the cucumber, red bell pepper, onion, and scallion dice to the bowl along with the chives and parsley. Season to taste with salt and white pepper. Add the lemon juice and 4 teaspoons of the olive oil. Cover with plastic wrap and refrigerate until ready to serve at room temperature.

3. Cut openings vertically along both sides of the fish in a diagonal pattern, 1 inch apart. Place in a glass dish and brush with fish glaze. Marinate for 1 hour, covered with plastic wrap.

4. Preheat the oven to 500°F.

5. In a sauté pan, heat 5 tablespoons of the oil and, when very hot, sear the snapper on both sides for a few minutes and then place in the oven or hot grill or broiler for 5 to 7 minutes.

6. To serve, place a spoonful of the marinated vegetables on each warm place. Top with a fish filet meeting at a point in the center. Garnish with parsley and 3 lemon slices.

SERVES: 4

135

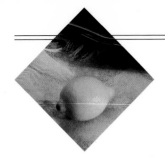

Grilled Tuna Steak with Nectarine-Red Onion Relish

Auguste Escoffier, the founder of classic French cuisine, noted that "grilling is the remote starting point, the very genesis of our art." Chris Schlesinger believes that such direct cooking by conduction concentrates the tuna's flavor on the outside and the juiciness inside. Once available only regionally, tuna has become one of the darlings of today's American chefs. The savory red pepper and juicy nectarines add a sweet flavor to the relish while the fresh citrus juices heighten the tenderness of the tuna steaks. The addition of red wine vinegar, olive oil, garlic, and basil to the nectarine-red onion relish adds a distinctively Mediterranean slant.

Four 10-ounce boneless tuna steaks, skinless, 1 inch thick

1/4 cup vegetable oil

RELISH: (3 cups)

1 red bell pepper, seeded and cut into thin 1 1/2-inch strips

6 ripe but firm nectarines, pitted, peeled and cut into 8 slices each

1 medium red onion, peeled and sliced into 1 1/2-inch strips

1 teaspoon minced garlic

1/4 cup julienned fresh basil

1/4 cup red wine vinegar

1/4 cup fresh orange juice

2 tablespoons lime juice (about 1 lime)

1/4 cup virgin olive oil

salt and freshly ground white pepper

GARNISH:

4 lemon wedges

8 basil sprigs

1. Make the relish: Combine all the ingredients in a stainless-steel bowl, and toss gently. Chill covered with plastic wrap until ready to serve.

2. Rub the tuna steaks lightly with oil and season to taste with salt and pepper. Grill the tuna steaks 4 to 5 minutes per side over a medium fire. (Check for doneness by bending steak gently and peering inside, looking for a slight translucence in the center.) Remove the steaks from the grill. If cooking in the oven, cook under the broiler for 2 minutes on each side or until the crust forms, then place on the lower rack for a few minutes on each side.

3. To serve, place the relish in the middle of each plate with the relish sticking out and top with tuna steak. Place a lemon wedge on each plate and a basil sprig crisscrossed on top of the tuna.

SERVES: 4

Half-Seared Peppered Tuna in Fragrant Cilantro Lime Essence

CILANTRO LIME ESSENCE:

- 1/2 cup cold water
- 1/2 cup Vietnamese fish sauce
- 2 tablespoons sugar
- 2 tablespoons fresh cilantro, stemmed and minced
- 1 tablespoon rice wine vinegar
- 1 tablespoon very fine julienned carrots
- 1 large garlic clove, peeled and minced
- 1 jalapeño pepper, finely chopped
  juice of 1/2 lime

TUNA MARINADE:

- 1 cup soy sauce
- 1/2 cup sugar
  juice of one lemon
- 1/4 cup dry sherry
- 2 tablespoons minced ginger
- 1/4 cup chopped scallions
- 1 tablespoon chopped garlic (2 garlic cloves)
- 1/4 teaspoon cayenne pepper
- 1 tablespoon freshly ground black pepper

- 1 pound tuna loin

VEGETABLES:

- 1 red bell pepper, seeded and finely julienned
- 1 yellow bell pepper, seeded and finely julienned
- 2 leeks with greens, finely julienned
- 3 carrots, peeled and finely julienned

  salt and freshly cracked black pepper
  vegetable oil, for rubbing

Nestled in the hills of the Blue Ridge Mountains, The Inn at Little Washington has frequently been named the best inn in America. It is well worth "carrying Me back to Ole Virginia" to sing its praises. Cilantro and lime essence enliven the character of the tuna, while the julienned vegetables add a light and colorful crunch.

1. Make the cilantro lime essence: In a medium bowl, combine all ingredients.

2. Make the tuna marinade: Combine the marinade ingredients in a medium bowl and marinate the tuna for ten minutes. Remove the tuna from the marinade.

3. In a medium saucepan of boiling salted water, blanch each vegetable separately using a strainer to remove the vegetables. Combine in a bowl.

4. Season the tuna with salt and cracked black pepper to taste and lightly rub with vegetable oil.

5. Rewarm the vegetables together in sauté pan when ready to serve.

6. In a hot smoking ridged skillet, sear the tuna quickly until it is charred on all sides but rare in the center or cooked to your desired doneness. Slice the tuna into thin pieces.

7. To serve, place fine julienne of peppers, leeks, and carrots in the center of a dinner plate. Place 5 tuna slices on top of vegetables and drizzle with the cilantro lime essence.

SERVES: 4

Jalapeño Ginger Crusted Salmon with Soba Noodles and Spicy Peanut Sauce

The balance of hot and cool flavors produces this visually arresting East-meets-West symphony. The spicy crust of moist salmon flakes and the nutty-flavored soba noodles tossed with piquant peanut sauce make an irresistible combination.

Four 5 ounce salmon filets, with skin
   kosher salt
1 bunch scallions, cut on the diagonal into
   1-inch pieces

TOPPING:

2 jalapeños, seeded, very finely chopped
   1-inch piece ginger, peeled and very finely
   chopped
3 garlic cloves, peeled and very finely
   chopped
1 bunch scallions, with greens, very finely
   chopped
1 egg white, lightly beaten

SPICY PEANUT SAUCE:

1/2 pound unsalted peanuts
1/4 cup saki
1/4 cup rice vinegar
2 tablespoons chili oil
2 tablespoons sesame oil

SOY VINAIGRETTE:

1/4 cup soy sauce
1/4 cup rice wine vinegar
1/4 cup saki
1 teaspoon coarsely ground black pepper
1/8 cup sesame oil
1 cup salad oil

2 English cucumbers, with skin, thinly
   sliced

2 tablespoons canola or peanut oil

1 package soba noodles

6 shiitake mushrooms, stemmed and
   quartered
   salt and freshly ground black pepper

GARNISH:

1 tablespoon black sesame seeds

1. Soak scallions in a bowl of cold water for up to 3 hours.

2. Preheat oven to 375°F.

3. Season both sides of the salmon generously with kosher salt.

4. In a small bowl, mix the jalapeños, ginger, garlic, and scallions with the egg white. Dip the skin side of the salmon into the mixture to thinly coat.

5. Blend the spicy peanut sauce ingredients for 3 minutes in a food processor. Reserve.

6. In a glass jar with a top, blend soy vinaigrette ingredients. Drizzle the vinaigrette over the cucumbers.

7. In a very hot nonstick pan, add 1 tablespoon of oil and, when very hot, brown the salmon, skin-side down, for 3 minutes. Turn over and cook for another 3 minutes. Cook in the oven for 5 minutes or until desired doneness.

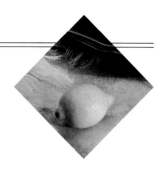

8. Bring 1 quart of salted water to a boil. Add the soba noodles and cook for 3 to 5 minutes until *al dente*. Drain.

9. In a medium sauté pan, heat the oil, add the mushrooms, and sauté for 5 minutes, seasoning with salt and pepper to taste.

10. In a bowl, mix the spicy peanut sauce with the hot noodles.

11. To serve, place a heap of noodles in the center of each plate. Top with salmon, herb-side up. Make a circle around the center with cucumbers. On every other cucumber, place a mushroom. Garnish plate with black sesame seeds.

SERVES: 4

AUTHOR'S NOTE: Soba noodles are available in Korean fruit and vegetable stores and many supermarkets such as Pathmark.

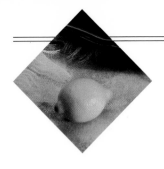

Nori-Wrapped Tempura Ahi with a Soy Mustard Sauce and Tomato-Ginger Relish

This nori-wrapped ahi, or yellow-fin tuna, enables you to contemplate Hawaii's natural habitat while retreating to palm trees, turquoise lagoons, and friendly alohas. Warm and crispy on the outside, this tasty seared Pacific Rim tuna is cool and rare inside. The bold-flavored soy mustard sauce adds a lusty pungency to the fish and tomato-ginger relish— a Chinese-Filipino inspiration, a cultural blending that works beautifully.

BATTER:

1 large egg

1³/4 cups ice water

2 cups low-gluten flour

Four 3-ounce ahi (tuna) filets, cut into 6-inch-by-1-inch rectangular logs

coarse salt

4 tablespoons wasabi paste

2 sheets nori seaweed, halved to make 4 pieces

shoyu (soy sauce), for dipping

low gluten flour, for dusting

3 cups vegetable oil for frying

Tomato-ginger relish (see page 202)

Soy mustard sauce (see page 201)

GARNISH:

¹/4 teaspoon black sesame seeds

1. Prepare the batter: In large bowl, beat the egg. Using a wire whisk, mix in the ice water. Stir in the flour until smooth.

2. Prepare the tempura ahi: Season the ahi filets with salt. With a plastic spatula, spread an equal amount of wasabi paste on each of the 4 nori sheets. On each piece of nori, place the ahi and roll. Dip the roll lightly in shoyu and then in the flour.

3. In a large saucepan or a fryer, if possible, heat the oil for approximately 10 to 15 minutes until it is smoking or, preferably, has reached 400°F. Dip the ahi roll into the tempura batter and fry in the hot oil until the outside is crisp and the fish is rare. This should only take a few minutes. Remove the roll from the oil and slice into 1-inch pieces.

4. To serve, place the tomato-ginger relish in the center of the plate. Place the ahi roll slices in a pyramid on top of the relish. Sprinkle with black sesame seeds. Surround with a pool of soy mustard sauce.

SERVES: 4

AUTHOR'S NOTE: Low-gluten flour is recommended, since the elasticity of all-purpose flour is unnecessary for a tempura batter.

Pecan and Bran-Crusted Catfish with Apple-Braised Cabbage

APPLE-BRAISED CABBAGE:

2 heads red cabbage, cored and thinly sliced

4 Granny Smith apples, cored, peeled, and diced

1 yellow onion, peeled and sliced

1/3 cup raspberry vinegar

2 tablespoons crushed peppercorns

2 tablespoons olive oil

1/3 cup Parma ham, diced

1 cup chicken stock (see page 190)

5 tablespoons lingonberries (or red current jelly)

MARINADE:

2 tablespoons teriyaki sauce

2 tablespoons chopped basil

2 shallots, peeled and minced

2 garlic cloves, peeled and minced

1 tablespoon snipped cilantro

1 teaspoon minced ginger root

Six 6-ounce farm-raised catfish filets

PECAN MIXTURE:

1 cup bran flakes cereal, crushed

3/4 cup pecan crumbs

3/4 cup brioche crumbs

1 tablespoon freshly cracked white pepper

flour, for dusting

3 eggs, lightly beaten

3 tablespoons clarified butter or virgin olive oil

GARNISH:

6 basil sprigs

While Texas conjures up rodeos, state fairs, barbecue ribs, and the Dallas Cowboys, this catfish specialty embedded with a combination of bran, pecan, and brioche crumbs gives the fish a wonderfully crunchy texture. The apple-braised cabbage perfumed with vinegar and onions contrasts well with the nutty crust.

1. Make the apple-braised cabbage: In a bowl, combine the cabbage, apples, onion, vinegar, and peppercorns. Toss and marinate overnight, refrigerated.

2. In a large saucepan, heat the olive oil and cook the Parma ham over low heat until crispy.

3. Add the cabbage mixture and stock, and cook slowly over low heat for 40 minutes, stirring frequently. Add the lingonberries, season with salt and pepper to taste, and simmer for 20 minutes. Reheat when ready to serve.

4. Make the marinade: In a medium bowl, combine teriyaki, basil, shallots, garlic, cilantro, and ginger root. Marinate the catfish refrigerated for 2 hours.

5. Make the pecan mixture: Mix the bran flakes, pecans, brioche crumbs, and pepper.

6. Remove catfish from the marinade. Dust fish with flour, dip in beaten eggs and coat with the pecan mixture.

7. Preheat oven to 350°F.

8. Heat the butter or virgin olive oil in a sauté pan and sauté the catfish until golden brown. Finish in the oven for 5 minutes.

9. To serve, place the cabbage mixture in the center of the plate. Then place the fish with the nicer crusted side showing, abutting the cabbage mixture. Garnish with a basil sprig.

SERVES: 6

Pepper-Crusted Red Snapper

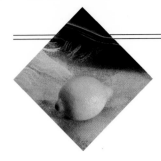

Reflecting both its Creole heritage and its antebellum past, New Orleans' Commander's Palace commands a totally American respectability. Mark Twain and Jefferson Davis both graced the gardens of this splendid landmark. This crisply seared Gulf Coast red snapper, encrusted with pungent black peppercorns and served in a light fennel tomato sauce, ignites an incendiary reaction.

RED WINE FENNEL FUMET:

- 1 pound fish bones, cleaned
- 1 small onion, peeled and diced
- 3 celery ribs, diced
- 3 tomatoes, cored and roughly chopped
- 1 fennel bulb, sliced
- 1 cup red wine
- 3 cups water

BRAISED FENNEL:

- 1 fennel bulb

FENNEL SAUCE:

- 1 tablespoon olive oil
- 1/8 cup finely diced red onion
- 1/8 cup finely diced carrots
- 1/8 cup finely diced celery
- 2 cups red wine fennel fumet (save remaining 1/2 cup for another use)
- 1/8 cup diced tomatoes, blanched and peeled
- 1/8 bunch tarragon, stems removed and diced
- salt and freshly ground white pepper
- 1 tablespoon unsalted butter

PEPPER CRUST:

- 1 egg white
- 1 cup lowfat milk
- 1/4 cup black peppercorns, rough-cracked
- 1/4 cup corn starch
- 1 cup flour
- 1 small red onion, peeled and finely diced
- 3 teaspoons kosher salt

- 1 pound red snapper, 4 filets with skin, cut in half horizontally
- coarse salt
- 1 tablespoon olive oil

GARNISH:

- 1/2 bunch chopped chives

1. Make the red wine fennel fumet: In a medium soup pot, place the fish bones, vegetables, and red wine. Over low heat, reduce the wine by half. Add the water and simmer for 1/2 hour, skimming the scum from time to time. Strain the soup into a bowl.

2. Preheat the oven to 325°F.

3. Make the braised fennel: Place the fennel in an oiled baking pan and roast in the oven for 40 minutes or until tender. Dice the fennel and set aside for the fennel sauce.

4. Make the fennel sauce: In a sauté pan, heat the oil and sauté all the vegetables, except for the tomato and tarragon. Add 2 cups of the fumet and cook, reducing by half for approximately 5 minutes. Stir in the tomato and then the tarragon. Add the diced fennel to the sauce, and cook for a few minutes to pick up the flavor. When ready to serve, reheat, season to taste with salt and pepper, and finish by whisking in the butter.

5. Make the pepper crust: Mix the egg and milk in a medium bowl for the egg wash. In another bowl, combine the rest of the pepper crust ingredients, and spread on a small flat pan.

6. Season skin side of the fish with salt. First dip the skin side only in the egg wash, and then into the pepper crust mixture. To secure the coating press the mixture with your hands.

7. In a sauté pan, heat the olive oil over medium heat until the oil is almost smoking. Gently position the fish skin-side down and steam the fish by covering the pan with a lid or another pan, cooking for 3 to 4 minutes, depending upon the thickness of the fish.

8. To serve, divide the fennel sauce in the center of the plates. Place on top 2 pieces of fish per person with the fish overlapping one another, skin-side up. Garnish the top of the fish with a tablespoon of the vegetables and sprinkle with chopped chives.

SERVES: 4

Pompano with Potato Crust and Roasted Red Pepper Sauce

The Bayous have spawned a refreshing modern interpretation of Creole tradition that inherited its gastronomic lore from France and Spain. Pompano, seasonal fresh-water fish found along the Gulf Coast and Florida, has a delicacy of flavor not found in many fish. Encrusted with potato sticks and sitting in a pool of well-seasoned roasted red pepper sauce, this pompano has all the color, freshness, and taste of the Old South.

Four 6–8-ounce filets, pompano, snapper, catfish, sea bass, grouper, or lemonfish

EMERIL'S CREOLE SEASONING:

2^1/$_2$ *tablespoons paprika*

2 *tablespoons kosher salt*

2 *tablespoons garlic powder*

1 *tablespoon black pepper*

1 *tablespoon onion powder*

1 *tablespoon cayenne pepper*

1 *tablespoon dried oregano*

1 *tablespoon dried thyme*

ROASTED RED PEPPER SAUCE:

2 *tablespoons olive oil*

3 *medium–large red bell peppers*

^{1}/$_4$ *cup coarsely chopped onions*

2 *teaspoons minced fresh garlic*

1 *teaspoon chopped fresh basil*

1 *teaspoon coarse salt*

^{1}/$_8$ *teaspoon cayenne pepper*

^{1}/$_2$ *teaspoon freshly ground black pepper*

2 *cups chicken stock (see page 190)*

^{1}/$_8$ *cup heavy cream*

4 *teaspoons Dijon mustard*

2 *cups coarsely grated potatoes*

1 *teaspoon salt*

8 *turns freshly ground black pepper*

^{1}/$_2$ *cup olive oil*

GARNISH:

4 *tablespoons snipped 1-inch fresh chives*

1. Make the Creole seasoning: Combine all of the Creole seasoning ingredients and store in an airtight container.

2. Make the roasted red pepper sauce: With tongs over high heated burners, place the peppers and char evenly. When the skin cracks and chars, instantly submerge in a bowl of ice water. Remove the skins, seed the peppers, and chop coarsely.

3. Heat a medium saucepan, add the olive oil, and, when the oil is smoking lightly, sauté the roasted peppers, onions, garlic, basil, salt, cayenne, and black pepper over high heat for 3 minutes. Add the stock and the cream and bring to a rapid boil. Reduce the heat to medium and simmer approximately 8 minutes stirring occasionally. Remove to a food processor and purée about 2 minutes. Check the seasoning and strain through a sieve. Reheat when ready to serve.

4. Season each filet with ^{1}/$_2$ teaspoon of the Creole seasoning. (Save the remainder for use at another time.) Then coat with 1 teaspoon of the mustard and top with ^{1}/$_2$ cup of the grated potatoes, pressing them down with a spatula. Season each filet with ^{1}/$_4$ teaspoon salt and 2 turns of pepper.

5. Divide the olive oil between 2 medium iron skillets and, when hot, gently place 2 filets coated-side up. Sauté for 2 minutes, gently flip the filets quickly with a spatula and continue with crust-side down until golden brown, about 2 to 3 minutes.

6. To serve, coat each dinner plate with approximately ⅛ cup of the warm roasted red pepper sauce. (Save the remainder for use at another time.) Place each filet crust-side up and sprinkle generously with the chives.

SERVES: 4

AUTHOR'S NOTE: If using a substitute fish, note that pompano is thinner than a fish such as grouper. Thicker fish requires a few more minutes of cooking.

Salmon in Woven Potatoes with Herbed Parsley Sauce

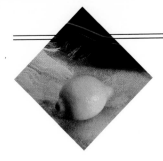

This masterful presentation of fish enveloped in crispy potato sticks makes a stunning conversation piece. The aromatic bright-green parsley sauce enlivens the presentation. Waldy Malouf features the growers in the Hudson Valley, known for fertile farmlands, dazzling orchards, and an inspiring 19th-century school of landscape painting.

HERB PARSLEY SAUCE:

- 1/2 cup dry white wine
- 1 tablespoon white wine vinegar
- 2 shallots, peeled and thinly sliced
- 2 mushrooms, wiped clean and thinly sliced
- 1 garlic clove, smashed and peeled
- pinch dried thyme
- 1 bay leaf
- 1/2 pound cold unsalted butter, cut into large dice
- 2 tablespoons fresh lemon juice
- 1 tablespoon finely chopped parsley
- 2 tablespoons finely chopped dill, chervil, or tarragon (or mixture)
- coarse salt and freshly ground white pepper

FISH:

- 1 1/2 pounds fresh salmon filet from head end, skinned and cut into 4 equal pieces
- salt and freshly ground white pepper
- 2 large shallots, peeled and minced

POTATO BASKET:

- Four 10-ounce Idaho potatoes, peeled and submerged in cold water (to prevent browning)
- 1 cup olive or vegetable oil

VEGETABLES:

- 1 carrot, peeled, julienned
- 1 leek, peeled, washed thoroughly and julienned
- 1 turnip, peeled and julienned
- 1 celery, finely julienned
- 1 tablespoon minced shallots
- 1 tablespoon finely chopped fine herbs (parsley, dill, chervil, and/or tarragon)

1. Make the herb sauce: In a small nonreactive saucepan, bring the wine, vinegar, shallots, mushrooms, garlic, thyme, and bay leaf to a simmer over medium heat until almost dry. (Approximately 2 tablespoons should remain.) Remove the bay leaf.

2. Over very low heat, heat the wine mixture. Whisk in the cold butter piece by piece for approximately 4 to 5 minutes until thoroughly mixed, never allowing the pan to get too hot or the sauce will break. Pour in the lemon juice and whisk until incorporated. Season with salt and pepper to taste. Remove from the stove and strain the sauce through a fine strainer or chinois and pour into a bowl. Then stir in the chopped herbs and keep warm in the bowl over hot water sitting in a double boiler. Off the flame, whisk the mixture from time to time.

3. Season the salmon filets lightly with salt and pepper and place the shallots evenly on top of the fish.

4. Make the potato baskets: Using a mandolin with a hard motion or food processor, coarsely shred the potatoes. Season with salt and pepper and immediately place on a cloth towel and squeeze out the liquid. Make 8 mounds.

5. In an 8-inch sauté or crêpe pan, heat the pan, and heat half the oil until it is just smoking. Add 1 potato mound, spreading with a metal spatula so that the potatoes evenly coat the bottom of the pan. When the rim is golden brown after approximately 2 to 3 minutes, place the

salmon filet skinned-side up (no skin will be on the fish) and then sprinkle loosely with another potato mound over the fish to cover the entire surface.

6. Cook an additional 2 to 3 minutes until the bottom of the potatoes are golden brown. Shake the pan a little and, using a metal slotted spatula, flip the potato basket over and cook for 3 to 4 minutes until golden brown. Continue the procedure, making 3 more baskets in the same pan with the remaining oil.

7. Preheat the oven to 300°F.

8. In heavily salted boiling water, blanch each julienned vegetable separately until the color is very bright. Cook the turnip approximately 5 to 6 minutes until soft. With a slotted spoon, immediately remove and refresh in ice water. Once cool, drain well.

9. Heat the fish in the oven for approximately 10 minutes. With a sharp knife, cut each basket in half along the length of the fish, splitting the baskets evenly down the middle.

10. In a small sauté pan, toss the vegetables, shallots, and herbs in a small amount of heated sauce or melted butter.

11. To serve, spoon approximately 3 tablespoons of the herb-parsley sauce on each dinner plate. Arrange 2 halves of the salmon in potatoes at a diagonal on top of one another, creating some height on the plate. Place approximately 3 tablespoons of the vegetables pinched to a tepee on top of the highest salmon piece and garnish with chopped herbs.

SERVES: 4

AUTHOR'S NOTE: If preparing in advance, set the baskets on a metal oven rack covered with paper towels. All the vegetables and herbs can be cut and stored well-wrapped in the refrigerator up to 1 day in advance.

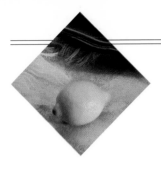

Sautéed Soft-Shelled Crabs with Scallion Butter and Spaghetti Vegetables

Noted for his fresh seafood and architecturally stunning culinary dishes, Edward Brown obtains the choicest ingredients from purveyors and fishermen. Soft-shelled crabs called by author James Mitchener "the tastiest morsels in the [Chesapeake] bay," are presented here in a pool of scallion butter.

SCALLION BUTTER:

1 bunch scallions, green part only, roughly chopped

1 stick unsalted butter

   juice of $1/2$ lemon

$1/2$ bunch fresh Italian parsley, stemmed and roughly chopped

$1/2$ cup pine nuts

1 tablespoon water

   salt and freshly ground black pepper

1 teaspoon freshly squeezed juice of lemon

1 small zucchini

1 small yellow squash, seeded

2 small carrots, peeled

2 tablespoons olive oil

2 tablespoons fresh thyme, chopped

12 soft-shelled crabs, cleaned, with tabs, gills, and eyes removed

2 cups milk

3 cups flour, for dredging

4 tablespoons unsalted butter

4 tablespoons olive oil

GARNISH:

$1/4$ bunch scallions, chopped

1 red bell pepper, cored, seeded, and finely diced

8 chive sticks

1. Make the scallion butter: Combine the scallions, butter, lemon juice, and Italian parsley in food processor for approximately 45 seconds to 1 minute, until well-blended. Scrape the butter into a log in a sheet of foil, wrap and refrigerate.

2. Preheat the oven to 400°F.

3. On a medium baking sheet, spread the pine nuts evenly. Brown in the oven for 6 to 8 minutes, shaking the pan every few minutes. Remove to a small bowl.

4. In a small nonreactive saucepan, bring water to a boil. Whisk in the scallion butter away from heat. Season with salt and pepper. Add lemon juice if needed.

5. With a sharp knife or mandoline, julienne each vegetable, making strips the length of the vegetable.

6. In a medium sauté pan, heat the oil over medium heat. Sauté the vegetables about 3 minutes until tender. Season with salt and pepper. Sprinkle with thyme.

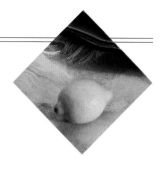

7. Soak the crabs in milk for 5 minutes. Remove and pat dry with a cloth towel. Dredge crabs in flour. Season with salt and pepper.

8. In a well-heated heavy iron skillet, add butter and oil. When sizzling, add crabs shell-side up. Brown on one side for 2 minutes, the other side a little less. Remove to a cloth towel. Place the crabs in the oven for 3 minutes.

9. To serve, place the spaghetti vegetables in the center of the plate, creating some height. Add the soft-shelled crabs by placing one and then the other with the leg side up. Drizzle the scallion butter around the plate and on top of the soft-shelled crabs. Sprinkle chopped scallions, diced red pepper, and toasted pine nuts to finish the garnish. Add chive sticks to form a tent around the crabs.

SERVES: 4

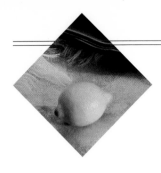

Steamed Black Bass in a Bamboo Leaf with Kaffir Lime Broth

*P*art of the key to Gray Kunz's challenging culinary genius is the infusion of exotic ingredients into a fish broth. The technique of preparing and finishing the broth can be adapted to a wide range of seafood broths and court bouillons. This citrus zest topping with a sauce of turnips, lime leaf, red pepper, and lemongrass creates a haunting and seductively complex flavor, beautifully adorning the steamed black bass nestled in a bamboo leaf.

Four 6-ounce black bass filets, with skin

4 pieces bamboo leaf

4 pieces kaffir (lime leaf) or lemongrass

2 teaspoons olive oil

salt and freshly ground white pepper

KAFFIR BROTH:

3 tablespoons minced shallots

4 tablespoon unsalted butter

3/4 cup turnip slices, quartered

1/2 cup English seedless cucumbers, peeled, thinly sliced

1 cup chicken stock (see page 190)

1 chopped lime leaf or lime zest

6 tablespoons very finely chopped red peppers

TOPPING:

3/4 cup finely chopped shallots

2 tablespoons unsalted butter

zest of 1 orange, finely chopped

zest of 1 lemon, finely chopped

2 tablespoons finely chopped chives

VEGETABLES:

10 tablespoons unsalted butter (8 tablespoons cut into cold bits)

1/2 cup English seedless cucumbers, peeled, thinly sliced, halved

1/2 cup papaya, peeled and diced

2 tablespoons rice wine or white wine vinegar

1/2 teaspoon sugar

1. Soak the bamboo leaves in cold water overnight. Peel 1 or 2 leaves from the kaffir or lemongrass and cut them into four 2-inch strips. Make 2 small vertical inserts approximately 1/2 inch in length in the bamboo leaves, and weave the lemongrass through the bamboo leaf. (If the lemongrass does not hold the leaf together, also tie ends with lemongrass strips.)

2. Marinate the remaining kaffir or lemon grass in 2 teaspoons of olive oil overnight. Drain and chop finely, and reserve for use in the broth.

3. Prepare the bass: Lightly butter the fish tray and the bass. Season with salt and pepper. Refrigerate covered with plastic wrap. Prepare a steamer or a pot of rapidly boiling water.

4. Make the broth: In a medium saucepan, sweat the shallots in 2 tablespoons of butter for 1 or 2 minutes. Add the turnips and 1/2 cup of cucumber slices and a pinch of salt and sauté briefly. Deglaze the pan with chicken stock, bring to a boil, and then reduce for 3 minutes. Add 2 tablespoons of the butter, the reserved chopped kaffir, and red pepper, and season to taste with salt and pepper. Use a hand blender to make frothy.

5. Make the topping: Fry the shallots in 1 tablespoon of butter for approximately 15 minutes until crisp. When the butter starts to foam and the shallots are golden, strain the shallots into a bowl sitting in a *bain-marie*. Finish with 1 tablespoon of butter.

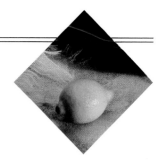

6. In a small nonstick saucepan, mix the orange and lemon zest and chives, and heat for a few minutes. Stir into the topping.

7. Cook the vegetables: In a medium saucepan, slowly melt 2 tablespoons of the butter and sweat the ½ cup of cucumber half-moon slices for 1 to 2 minutes. Add the papaya and let stew for an additional minute. Add vinegar and reduce by a small amount. Add sugar to taste, ½ teaspoon of salt, and white pepper. Add the cold bits of butter and move around in the pan to glaze.

8. Steam the fish in the bamboo leaves for 3 to 5 minutes. Remove from the steamer and place some topping on each filet to cover.

9. To serve, spoon the sauce into large soup plates. Place the bamboo leaf with the fish on the sauce and the vegetables beside it. Serve immediately.

SERVES: 4

AUTHOR'S NOTE: Bamboo leaf, lime leaf, and lemongrass can be purchased at Oriental markets. Lemongrass is often available at major supermarkets.

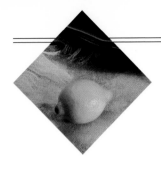

Stir-Fried Maine Lobster with Spiced Chinese Cabbage and Curried Kaffir Lime Sauce

The combination of exhilarating spices makes this succulent Maine lobster a culinary masterpiece. The curried sauce dotted with coconut flakes balances the spicy Oriental stir-fry. The leafy Chinese cabbage creates a seductive crunchiness and assertive flavor.

Four 1¹/2 pound Maine lobsters, parboiled for 6 to 7 minutes, shelled

CURRIED KAFFIR LIME SAUCE:
- ¹/2 medium white onion, peeled and finely diced
- ¹/2 garlic clove, peeled and chopped
- ¹/2 teaspoon finely diced ginger
- 1 tablespoon canola oil
- 2 tablespoons yellow curry powder
- ¹/8 cup coconut flakes
- ¹/8 cup rice vinegar
- 1 pint heavy cream
- 1 kaffir (lime leaf) chopped

STIR-FRY SAUCE:
- ¹/2 cup Chinese black vinegar
- 1 tablespoon Asian chili oil
- ¹/4 cup sake
- ¹/4 cup rice vinegar

- 1 head bok choy, shredded
- 1 head napa cabbage, shredded
- 1 bunch scallions, cut in 1-inch sections
- 5 Chinese long beans, cut in 2-inch pieces (if unavailable, use 10 haricot verts)

- 3 tablespoons canola oil

1. Make the curry sauce: In a saucepan, combine the onion, garlic, and ginger with the canola oil and cook slowly for 15 minutes. Then add the curry powder and cook an additional 5 minutes. Add coconut flakes and rice vinegar and cook until the liquid evaporates. Add the cream and lime leaf, bring to a boil, and simmer for 15 minutes. Mix the ingredients together in a blender until smooth.

2. Combine all ingredients for the stir-fry sauce in a bowl. Mix in the bok choy, napa cabbage, scallions, and Chinese long beans.

3. Heat a wok or a large, heavy-bottomed sauté pan. Add the canola oil to the pan. When the oil is smoking, add the lobster and lightly brown on both sides. Then add all the vegetables. Stir rapidly and quickly. Add the stir-fry sauce, continuing to stir.

4. Divide the vegetables among 4 dinner plates. Add the lobster to each plate. Drizzle each plate with the curried kaffir lime sauce.

SERVES: 4

AUTHOR'S NOTE: Chinese black vinegar is made with Asian vinegar and molasses. If unavailable in your Chinatown, whisk together in a bowl 4 tablespoons of molasses and 1 cup of red wine vinegar and use as needed.

Swordfish with Arugula, Potatoes, and Rosemary Vinaigrette

1½ pounds swordfish, sliced into 4 pieces

ROSEMARY VINAIGRETTE:

4 tablespoons cider vinegar

1 tablespoon honey, more to taste

¾ cup olive oil

2 tablespoons shallots, peeled and finely minced

1 teaspoon rosemary, stemmed and chopped

   salt and freshly ground white pepper

1 pound potatoes, peeled and thinly sliced into chips

¾ pound arugula, stemmed

¾ pound tomatoes, cored and thinly sliced

1½ tablespoons clarified butter

Arugula and swordfish have a natural affinity for each other. The salad greens tossed with garlic, shallot, and rosemary vinaigrette accent the swordfish with an aromatic perfume. The floral quality of the honey adds a complexity and sweetness to the vinaigrette. Elka Gilmore's Asian aesthetic is evident here in the circular presentation of the tomato-potato slices and the angling of the swordfish.

1. Make the vinaigrette: In a small bowl, whisk the cider vinegar, honey, and olive oil. Add the shallots and rosemary. Adjust seasoning with additional honey, salt, and pepper.

2. In a pan of boiling salted water, cook the potato slices approximately 7 minutes until tender. Drain and place in a medium size bowl.

3. Mix the warm potatoes with the arugula. Add ½ cup of the vinaigrette and toss.

4. In a small sauté pan, season the tomatoes with salt and pepper. Quickly heat the clarified butter and sauté the tomatoes.

5. Starting at the inner rim of the plate, arrange the potatoes in a circular pattern alternating with the tomatoes. Place the arugula in the center, giving it some height. Drizzle with the vinaigrette.

6. Season the swordfish with salt and pepper. Grill the swordfish approximately 5 minutes on both sides to desired consistency on an oiled grill.

7. To serve, place the grilled swordfish on the arugula salad sitting on the tomatoes and potatoes and drizzle with the remaining vinaigrette.

SERVES: 4

CHAPTER 8

Desserts

"Oh cakes and friends
We should choose with care,
Not always the fanciest cake that's there
Is the best to eat! And the plainest friend
Is sometimes the finest one in the end."

FRENCH PASTRY BY MARGARET SANGSTER

"The dessert is said to be to the dinner
what the Madrigal is to literature.
It is the light poetry of the kitchen."

GEORGE ELLWANGER

"If the people have no bread, let them eat cake."

MARIE ANTOINETTE

"The only emperor is the emperor of ice cream."

WALLACE STEVENS

"Friends of the present day are like the melon.
You must try 50 before you find a good one."

UNKNOWN

Apple and Vidalia Upside Down Cake

While onions may appear to be a cacophonous note in a fruit dessert, the combination dates back to the 1500s. The caramelization of the onions and the sweetness of the baked Granny Smith apples makes a moist composition which defies expectation.

1 cup Vidalia onions, peeled and cut into 1-inch strips

2 tablespoons vegetable oil

6 Granny Smith apples, cored, peeled, halved, and cut into 1/8-inch slices (maintaining the apple's form)

1/2 cup butter

3/4 cup brown sugar

BATTER:

2 large eggs

3/4 cup plus 2 tablespoons all-purpose flour, sifted

1 1/2 teaspoon double-acting baking powder

5 ounces whole milk

1/4 teaspoon vanilla extract

3/4 cup plus 2 tablespoons granulated sugar

GARNISH:

1 cup confectioners' sugar, for dusting

1. Preheat the oven to 350°F.

2. Caramelize the onions by cooking them for 1 hour on a sheet pan greased with vegetable oil. Remove.

3. Bake the apples in the oven for 4 to 5 minutes on a greased sheet pan. Remove.

4. Melt the butter in a 10-inch skillet and add the brown sugar. Stir with a wooden spoon until dissolved. Remove the pan from the heat and add the caramelized Vidalia onions.

5. Make the batter: In the bowl of an electric mixer, beat the eggs with the flour, baking powder, milk, vanilla extract, and sugar until well incorporated.

6. Line a 9-inch greased bundt or cake pan with parchment paper. Make a layer of butter-brown sugar mixture with caramelized onions. Place the apple slices with the core side up to cover the onions. Press the onions down between the apples to fill in the gaps. Cover with the batter. Bake approximately 45 minutes.

7. Remove from the oven and, when the cake reaches room temperature, reverse the pan onto a serving tray. Place the confectioners' sugar in a sifter and lightly dust the top of the cake.

SERVES: 8

Banana Macadamia Nut Phyllo Tart

CRUST:

    8 tablespoons (1 stick) unsalted butter
    8 sheets phyllo or strudel dough
    3 tablespoons confectioners' sugar

FILLING:

    8 tablespoons (1 stick) unsalted butter
    4 large eggs
    1 cup light corn syrup
    1 cup firmly packed light brown sugar
    2 teaspoons vanilla extract
    1/2 teaspoon salt

    1 cup whole unsalted macadamia nuts,
       lightly chopped
    1 large ripe banana

GARNISH:

    3 tablespoons confectioners' sugar, for
       dusting
    1 cup heavy cream, whipped, or banana or
       macadamia brittle ice cream

Although Ponce de Leon failed to find the mythical Fountain of Youth, Floridians discovered their pot of gold in Chef Mark Miletello. Here, he dazzles us with this hedonist's tart similar in texture to a traditional pecan pie. The tart is a precious tropical confection of creamy sweetened banana and macadamia nuts.

1. Make the crust: In a small saucepan, melt the butter and cool. Lightly butter a 10-inch round springform pan and gently line with a sheet of phyllo dough with some of the phyllo dough folding over the sides. Brush the dough with melted butter. Sprinkle the dough with confectioners' sugar.

2. Place a second sheet of phyllo dough on top, perpendicular to the first. Brush with melted butter and sprinkle lightly with confectioners' sugar. Continue assembling the crust according to this process until all the sheets are used up. Trim crust with scissors, leaving a 1-inch rim hanging over the sides. Reserve. Save the remaining melted butter.

3. Preheat the oven to 325°F.

4. Make the filling: In a small saucepan, melt the butter and cool to room temperature. In a large bowl, combine the eggs, corn syrup, brown sugar, vanilla, and salt, and mix. Whisk in the cooled butter.

5. Arrange the nuts over the bottom of the crust. Peel the banana and cut into 1/4-inch slices. Arrange on top. Pour the filling over the nuts and bananas. Gently fold the phyllo dough over the filling. Brush the top with the butter remaining from the crust and sprinkle with confectioners' sugar.

6. Bake the tart for approximately 1 1/2 hours so the filling is set but still soft inside. If the dough starts burning, cover with aluminum foil and pinch around the springform pan. Cool to room temperature and remove the bottom of the pan. Lightly dust the top with confectioners' sugar.

7. To serve, cut the tart into wedges. Serve with a dollop of cream or banana or macadamia brittle ice cream.

SERVES: 8

AUTHOR'S NOTE: Phyllo dough must be covered with a damp cloth, and you must work quickly or it will dry out and become brittle.

B-52 Cake

For someone mad about chocolate, this unadulterated chocolate heaven laced with Grand Marnier, Kahlua, and whiskey is irresistible. Named after the B-52 bomber, these three fudgy layers are an explosion in taste. This dessert is as big in flavor as its name-sake and is as potent as the cocktail of the same name.

GRAND MARNIER LAYER:

$10^1/2$ ounces semisweet fine chocolate

$1^1/3$ ounces Grand Marnier

$5^1/4$ ounces cream

KAHLUA LAYER:

$10^1/2$ ounces milk chocolate

$5^1/3$ ounces plus 2 tablespoons unsalted butter

$3^1/3$ ounces Kahlua

1 egg yolk

WHISKEY LAYER:

$1/4$ pound milk chocolate

$1/2$ pound white chocolate

2 tablespoons bourbon whiskey

$2^1/2$ ounces cream

CRÈME ANGLAISE FLORENTINE:

4 Florentine cookies

2 cups crème anglaise (see page 191)

$1/4$ cup pistachios, shelled and powdered

1. Line the bottom of an 8-inch springform pan with parchment paper.

2. Make the Grand Marnier layer: In the top of a double boiler, melt the chocolate and Grand Marnier. Bring the cream to a boil and add to the chocolate. Pour the mixture into the spring-form pan.

3. Make the Kahlua layer: In the top of a double boiler, melt the milk chocolate and $5^1/3$ ounces of the butter with the Kahlua. Cool to room temperature and whisk in the egg yolk. When cool, pour second layer into pan.

4. Make the whiskey layer: Over a double boiler, melt the chocolate and the remaining butter. Whisk in the whiskey and cream. Cool to room temperature and add third layer into pan.

5. Freeze overnight until hardened, covered with plastic wrap.

6. Make the crème anglaise Florentine: Pulverize the Florentine cookies to a paste. Whisk into the crème anglaise.

7. Unmold from the tin with a torch (or gas flame if torch is absolutely unavailable). Quickly place the cake onto an 8-inch cardboard circle. Clean up the sides with a hot spatula. Cut a strip of cellophane a bit larger than the cake and mold it around the cake.

8. Cover the cake top with powdered pistachios, pressing into the cake.

9. To serve, make a pool of crème anglaise Florentine on each plate and place a slice of the cake in the center.

SERVES: 10–12

AUTHOR'S NOTE: Keep the cake cold and work quickly with this product.

Banana Wild Rice Pudding

1 cup Japanese sticky rice (or Arborio rice)

1 cup water

1/2 cup milk

2 strips orange or lemon rind (cut into 1/3-inch strips, with a paring knife)

2 tablespoons wild rice

3/4 cup water

CRÈME ANGLAISE:

1/4 vanilla bean, split

1 cup cream

1 cup half-and-half

6 large yolks

1/2 cup granulated sugar

2 bananas, peeled

SAUCE:

1 overripe mango, peeled and pitted
   juice of 1/2 lime

3 teaspoons orange juice (optional)

GARNISH:

1/4 cup coarse sugar (sugar in the raw)

The Windy City of Chicago is howling with great food but in a country with a plethora of great rice pudding varieties, this elegant banana version filled with wild rice and sticky rice is in a class of its own. Sitting in a pool of a sweet mango sauce spiked with a zesty dash of lime juice, this creamy rice pudding is a truly sophisticated creation.

1. Make the sticky rice: Rinse the sticky rice with cold water until the water runs clear. Place the rice in a saucepan with 1 cup water, milk, and orange or lemon rind, and bring to a boil. Turn the heat to low, cover the pan tightly with foil pinched around the edges, and cook for 15 to 20 minutes until the liquid is absorbed. Remove from heat. Leave covered 5 extra minutes to steam after the rice is tender. Remove the foil and then the orange rind. Aerate the rice with a wooden spoon not longer than 30 seconds. (The steam should be released like sushi rice.) Spread on a small sheet or cookie sheet pan and fluff with a fork to cool.

2. Make the wild rice: Place wild rice in a sauce pan with 3/4 cup water and cook about 20 minutes until tender and the grains split open. Add more water if needed. Toss with the sticky rice.

3. Make the crème anglaise: Split the vanilla bean and place in a saucepan with its inner scrapings (remove with a paring knife). Add the cream and half-and-half and scald. Meanwhile, in a separate bowl, whisk the yolks with the sugar. Gradually whisk in the scalded cream mixture. Return the mixture to the saucepan and cook over medium heat until it reaches 180°F. The custard will thicken; stir constantly with a wooden spoon. Strain through a chinois or fine sieve into a metal container surrounded by ice cubes in a bowl. Chill, stirring from time to time.

4. Stir the custard into the rice mixture until the consistency is creamy and slightly loose. (You may not use all the custard.) Let the mixture sit for 20 minutes refrigerated to pull in the moisture. Slice the bananas. Fold banana slices into the wild rice mixture and spoon into eight 1/2-cup ramekins (3 inches in diameter) or baking dishes, leveling off the top with a knife. Refrigerate covered with plastic wrap for at least 1 hour.

5. Make the mango sauce: In a food processor, purée the mango with the lime juice and blend until smooth. Strain through a fine sieve. If the purée is very thick, thin with a few teaspoons of orange juice and sweeten with a little sugar if necessary.

6. Lightly sprinkle the purée with coarse sugar and caramelize with a blowtorch or by placing the purée under a broiler.

7. To serve, immediately place the ramekins on a dinner plate lined with a doily. Serve with sauce.

SERVES: 8

AUTHOR'S NOTE: Other satisfying combinations for the pudding include raspberries with sticky rice and saffron sticky rice with golden raisins.

Boysenberry Soup with Vanilla Ice Cream and Peaches

SOUP:

- 3 half-pint baskets of ripe boysenberries (if unavailable, substitute blackberries)
- 3/4 cup water
- 3 tablespoons granulated sugar
- 1/2 teaspoon kirsch

- 6 ripe juicy peaches, halved, pitted, and thinly sliced
- 6 tablespoons granulated sugar

GARNISH:

- 1 1/2 pints good vanilla ice cream, preferably homemade
- 5 mint sprigs

Prepare yourself for an epiphany. Lindsey Shere is the consummate fruit dessert craftsman. This rhapsody in blue relies on the pure essence of the boysenberries, heightened with a spike of cherry-flavored kirsch. The vanilla ice cream adds a luscious, creamy consistency to the fruitiness of the boysenberries.

1. Make the soup: In a noncorroding medium saucepan, heat the berries with the water and sugar until the sugar is dissolved. Remove from the heat and strain through a fine sieve into a bowl, pressing with the blade of a spoon to remove the seeds. Add additional sugar, if necessary, then add the kirsch to combine. Chill thoroughly, covered with plastic wrap.

2. In a bowl, toss the peach slices with the sugar, sweetening them to taste.

3. Divide the cold soup among the soup plates and place a scoop of vanilla ice cream in the center of each. Garnish with a mint sprig. Surround with the sliced peaches and serve immediately with a crisp cookie.

SERVES: 4–5

Bread Pudding Soufflé with Whiskey Sauce

Soufflés are my favorite desserts, and this version incorporates the finest of American bread puddings with France's temple of gastronomy, the soufflé. Laced with bourbon, made with corn and potatoes a-plenty in Louisiana, the whiskey sauce cuts the sweetness of the bread pudding soufflé. The recipe for bread pudding is a winner standing alone.

BREAD PUDDING:

- 4 cups sugar
- 1 tablespoon cinnamon
- 1/8 teaspoon nutmeg
- 6 eggs
- 1 quart heavy cream
  Three 18-inch loaves of French bread, very thinly sliced
- 1 cup raisins
- 1 tablespoon vanilla
  unsalted butter, for greasing

WHISKEY SAUCE:

- 1 cup heavy cream
- 2 tablespoons cornstarch
- 4 tablespoons water
- 1/2 cup sugar
- 1/2 cup bourbon whiskey

SOUFFLÉ:

- 6 egg yolks
- 1/2 cup granulated sugar
- 2 1/2 cups bread pudding
- 6 egg whites
- 1/2 cup confectioners' sugar

  confectioners' sugar, for coating

1. Preheat the oven to 325°F.

2. In a large bowl, mix the sugar with the cinnamon and nutmeg. Whisk in the eggs and the cream. Add the bread, the raisins, and vanilla, and mix thoroughly so that the bread is completely broken up. (If the mix is too loose, add more bread. If too dry, add more cream.)

3. Pour the pudding mixture into an 8-inch-by-8-inch-by-2-inch buttered pan and bake for approximately 45 minutes or until browned. (Test the center with a toothpick for doneness.) Remove from the oven and set aside 2 1/2 cups of the bread pudding for the soufflé.

4. Make the whiskey sauce: Bring the cream to a boil in a large saucepan. In a bowl, whisk together the cornstarch and the cold water. Pour the cornstarch mixture into the boiling cream, whisking vigorously. Let the sauce return to a boil and remove from the heat.

5. Stir in most of the sugar and the bourbon. Add the rest according to your taste.

6. Increase the oven temperature to 375°F.

7. Make the soufflé: Place the egg yolks and sugar in the top of a double boiler. Whisk until frothy and shiny. Put the yolk mixture in a medium bowl with the reserved bread pudding and mix until smooth.

8. Beat the egg whites until frothy. Gradually add the confectioners' sugar, beating constantly until the resulting meringue reaches stiff peaks. Gently fold the egg whites into the bread pudding mixture.

9. Butter and lightly sugar a 1^1/$_2$-quart soufflé dish (or ten 3-ounce individual cups). Pour the soufflé mixture into the dish until it is three-quarters full. Clean the lip of the soufflé dish and bake 20 to 30 minutes. During the last 15 minutes of cooking, heat the whiskey sauce so that it is served piping hot.

10. To serve, remove soufflé from the oven, dust with confectioners' sugar through a fine sieve. Present the sauce in a separate bowl. Serve immediately.

SERVES: 10

Caramelized Apple and Currant Upside Down Walnut Brioche Pudding

Besides beers and bratwurst, Milwaukee brags about Sandy D'Amato, who presents an inspired confection of apple, currant, and walnut brioche pudding. An original twist to a traditional upside down cake, the brioche pudding is the grand finale to any satisfying meal.

1 cup unsalted butter
1 cup sugar
8 Granny Smith apples, peeled, cored, and quartered

BRIOCHE PUDDING:

1 pound loaf brioche (see page 190) (crust removed, sliced into 3 triangles) (If unavailable, use challah)
1/2 cup melted butter
1/2 cup currants, soaked overnight in 3 tablespoons applejack brandy
1/2 cup chopped toasted walnuts, with skin
1/2 cup sugar
2 large eggs

1 egg yolk
1 cup milk
1 cup heavy cream
1/4 teaspoon nutmeg
1/2 teaspoon cinnamon

SPICED WHIPPED CREAM:

1 1/2 cups heavy cream
2 tablespoons sugar
1 teaspoon ground cinnamon
1/2 teaspoon ground nutmeg
1/2 teaspoon ground cardamom
1/2 teaspoon ground cloves
2 tablespoons bourbon

1. Preheat oven to 400°F.

2. For the caramel and apples: Melt the butter in a sauté pan, add the sugar, and stir with a wooden spoon. Bring to a boil and caramelize to a nice amber color. Pour the caramel into the bottom of a 10-inch-by-2-inch round cake pan. Place the apples on their sides, next to one another in a circle, with the larger end facing the outside edge of the pan. When the bottom of the pan is covered, arrange the rest of the apples between the cracks. Place the pan on a sheet tray and bake in the oven for 20 minutes.

3. Make the brioche pudding: Lightly brush the brioche with melted butter on each side and toast in the oven for about 5 to 7 minutes until golden. Place half of the brioche over the apples to fill in gaps in the pan. Sprinkle with the currants and any remaining brandy liquid and walnuts. Place the rest of the brioche over the top so the triangle toasts fit snugly into the cake pan.

4. In a bowl, mix together the sugar, eggs, yolk, milk, cream, nutmeg, and cinnamon, and pour evenly over the brioche. Place the pan in a water bath and bake in the oven for 30 minutes.

5. While the brioche pudding is cooking, make the spiced whipped cream: Whip the cream with the sugar and spices. When whipped to soft peaks, add the bourbon and whip until stiff. (Do not overwhip.)

6. Remove the pudding from the oven. Place a 10-inch round cardboard over the cake. Place the serving tray over the cardboard and turn over. Tap the top of the cake pan and slowly unmold.

7. Serve warm with spiced whipped cream. Place the cake slice on the center of each plate. Pipe the spiced whipped cream with a medium star tube #5 into the middle of the pudding and surrounding area, or spoon onto the side.

SERVES: 10

Chèvre Cheesecake with Pear Gratin

5 d'Anjou or Comice pears, peeled, cored, and sliced in half

3 cups port wine

1 cup granulated sugar
   salt and freshly ground black pepper

CHÈVRE CHEESECAKE:

3/4 pound goat cheese

6 tablespoons granulated sugar

3 tablespoons heavy cream

3 large eggs, lightly beaten

1 1/2 cups sabayon sauce (see page 200)

This rhapsodic presentation teases the palate with a creamy, light goat cheesecake flanked by pear wedges that are saturated with a full-flavored port wine.

1. Poach the pears: In a saucepan, combine the pears, port wine, sugar, and salt and pepper to taste, and cook for approximately 1/2 hour depending on the ripeness of the pears. Pierce with a paring knife to see if they are tender. Reserve the poaching liquid.

2. Preheat the oven to 325°F.

3. Make the cheesecakes: Brush ten 2-ounce timbale molds (preferably aluminum foil) lightly with butter and coat them with sugar. In an electric mixer, cream the cheese and sugar, cleaning the sides from time to time until the sugar dissolves. Add the cream and beat until smooth, making sure to remove the lumps. Whisk the eggs into the cheese mixture until smooth. Fill the timbale molds an eighth of an inch from the top.

4. Make a *bain marie* by filling a small roasting pan halfway up with water and place the timbales gently inside. Bake for approximately 25 minutes. Remove from the oven.

5. Slice each pear half into small slices and arrange on a plate in a pinwheel fashion, spooning 2 teaspoons per person of the poaching liquid onto them. Drizzle the sabayon over them. Place each plate under a broiler, watching carefully and turning the plates or use a propane torch in sweeping motions to lightly brown the sabayon.

6. To serve, unmold the cheesecakes onto the plates with a paring knife, saving some of the brittle in the bottom to encase the cheesecakes. Sprinkle some remaining brittle on top of the cheesecakes.

SERVES: 10

AUTHOR'S NOTE: When making the cheesecake mixture, make sure not to overmix any of the steps or the cheese will break. To unmold beautifully, tap the bottom with a knife to release suction and blow on it.

Chocolate Tower

The Valley of the Sun has reached culinary heights with this towering inferno of dark and white chocolate. Cacao trees, introduced in central Mexico in the 16th century, played a sacramental role in Mayan and Aztec religion. It is no wonder that Aztec ruler Montezuma became seriously addicted to ground cacao. This is the ultimate in "death by chocolate," the crowning glory of any meal. The smooth, seductive espresso sauce respectfully accompanies the deft chocolate artistry of Christopher Gross.

CHOCOLATE MOUSSE:

5^1/$_2$ ounces dark chocolate chips

3 tablespoons unsalted butter

^{1}/$_4$ cup heavy cream

10 large egg whites, room temperature

4 tablespoons superfine sugar

LATTICE:

8 pieces parchment paper

^{3}/$_4$ cup dark chocolate, melted (may be some left over)

5 ounces white chocolate chunks, melted

ESPRESSO SAUCE:

1 cup half-and-half (light cream)

^{1}/$_2$ vanilla bean and scrapings

12 espresso beans

4 egg yolks

3^1/$_2$ tablespoons sugar

GARNISH:

2 kiwis halved, peeled, sliced or figs

8 strawberry fans

12 blackberries, halved

2 cups raspberries

8 mint sprigs

1. Make the chocolate mousse: In the top of the double boiler, slowly melt the dark chocolate and the butter, stirring occasionally to remove all lumps. Remove the top pan from the heat and cool. In a stainless-steel bowl, whip the cold cream to stiff peaks. In another stainless steel or copper mixing bowl, whip the egg whites with the sugar until stiff peaks form.

2. Fold the melted chocolate and the butter mixture into the whipped cream with a plastic spatula. Fold in the stiff egg whites until fully incorporated. (This can be made a day in advance.)

3. Make the towers: Cut 8 parchment paper strips 3^1/$_2$ inches wide by 5 inches long. Roll the strips into tubes 1^1/$_2$ inches in diameter and fasten with tape. Cover with a plastic wrap and stand them up. Using a pastry bag without a tip, fill them with the chocolate mousse, leaving ^{1}/$_2$ inch unfilled at the top. Place them in the freezer for 3 to 4 hours until frozen well.

4. Make the lattice decoration: Cut 8 parchment paper strips 5 inches high and 5 inches wide and lay them on baking sheets. Place the melted dark chocolate in a small cone made of parchment paper and drizzle a crisscrossed pattern on these strips. The crisscrosses should be a quarter-inch apart. Allow the drizzled dark chocolate to set slightly, then freeze for at least 5 minutes to set firmly. Carefully pour approximately 3 tablespoons of the melted white chocolate over each chocolate lattice square, leaving 1 inch on top with the dark chocolate lattice (i.e., the white chocolate should be poured only over a 3 ^{1}/$_2$-inch by 5-inch area). Pour white choco-

late over the crisscrossed pattern of the dark to create a basket effect on the top of the choco-late tower. Unwrap each frozen mousse tower and lay these onto the white-chocolate-coated portion of the lattice square. Immediately wrap a lattice strip around the chocolate mousse. While still pliable, wrap the parchment paper around the lattice strip. Refrigerate and remove the paper after 5 minutes. Refrigerate again for a minimum of 6 hours making sure the frozen mousse is soft before serving. (Otherwise freeze and defrost for at least 1/2 hour.)

5. Make the espresso sauce: In a saucepan, bring the half-and-half, vanilla bean and scrap-ings, and the espresso beans to a simmer. Remove from the heat. In a stainless-steel bowl, beat the egg yolks and the sugar. Temper the egg yolk and sugar mixture by adding one quarter of the warmed half-and-half. Stir well and pour in the remaining half-and-half, and cook gently over the top of a double boiler, stirring constantly so that the egg yolks don't get lumpy. When the sauce is thick enough to coat the back of a spoon, strain the liquid over a bowl and cool. Discard the beans.

6. To serve, rim the inside edge of each plate with a line of espresso sauce, bringing the tip of a small knife through each drop to create the heart-shaped pattern. Stand each of the chocolate towers up in the center of the plates and garnish the plates with the kiwis or fresh figs and berries. Fill the basket top of the towers with raspberries and top with a mint sprig.

SERVES: 8

Falling Chocolate Cake with Raspberry Sauce and Vanilla Ice Cream

RASPBERRY SAUCE:

2 pints frozen or fresh raspberries

1/2 cup granulated sugar

juice of 1/2 lemon

CHOCOLATE CAKE:

3/4 pound semisweet chocolate

2 sticks (1/2 pound) unsalted butter

1 cup sugar

1/2 cup all-purpose flour

6 large eggs

GARNISH:

confectioners' sugar, for dusting

1 1/2 pints vanilla ice cream

10 mint sprigs

1/2 pint red raspberries

This sensual chocolate treasure with a soupy liquid center is a heavenly confection for any chocolate lover. Sitting in a pool of raspberry purée, this dazzling hot chocolate cake with confectioners' sugar craves the soothing cold vanilla bean ice cream gracing the plate.

1. Make the raspberry sauce: In a small saucepan, mix raspberries, sugar, and lemon juice together. Boil until the sugar dissolves. Let cool. Purée half of the sauce in the blender. Then add the remaining sauce to the puréed mixture. Chill covered in the refrigerator until ready to use.

2. Preheat the oven to 350°F.

3. In the top part of a double boiler, over simmering water, melt the chocolate and unsalted butter. Let cool.

4. In the bowl of an electric mixer, place the sugar, flour, and eggs. Beat with its wire whisk for 5 minutes or until very thick and fluffy. Fold in the cooled chocolate. Refrigerate covered with plastic wrap until ready to use. Pour the mixture into buttered individual ramekins (3 inches by 2 inches).

5. Bake in the oven for 15 minutes or until the edges are firm and the center loose.

6. To serve, spoon a 4-inch circle of sauce onto each plate. Remove the cakes from the ramekins and place on top of raspberry sauce. Dust the cakes with confectioners' sugar. Place 1 scoop of vanilla ice cream next to the cake. Garnish the cake with mint and raspberries.

SERVES: 8–10

AUTHOR'S HINT: If using 5-inch-by-2-inch soufflé dishes or ramekins, the yield will be 6 and the cooking time will be 20 to 25 minutes.

Gingersnap Cannoli with Wisconsin Dried Cherry and Mascarpone Cream

This innovative gingersnap cannoli filled with dried Door County cherries provides a lighter and more balanced dessert than the traditional Italian version. Wisconsin, one of the cherry baskets of the nation, also boasts of other flavorful indigenous ingredients such as currants and mascarpone.

GINGERSNAP:

4 tablespoons sugar

4 tablespoons unsalted butter

1 teaspoon ground ginger

1/2 teaspoon lemon juice

4 tablespoons all-purpose flour

FILLING: *(Keep cold before mixing)*

2 tablespoons bourbon
fine zest of 1/2 orange

1 tablespoon sugar

2 tablespoons dried currants

2 tablespoons coarsely chopped dried cherries

1/2 cup Wisconsin mascarpone

1/4 cup softened pastry cream (see page 198)

1 1/2 teaspoons Grand Marnier

1/4 cup chilled heavy cream, whipped

GARNISH:

3 tablespoons roasted chopped pistachios
confectioners' sugar, for dusting

1/4 pound dried cherries

1. Make the gingersnap cookie: Combine all ingredients except flour in small stainless-steel bowl. Place the bowl in the top part of a double boiler, and melt the ingredients slowly at a low simmer. Whisk periodically. When blended and warm, stir in the flour with a spatula. (Yields 8 cookies in case of breakage.)

2. Preheat the oven to 375°F.

3. Place the warm mixture into a pastry bag with a #2 round tip. Before filling, push part of the pastry bag into the tip to prevent the mixture from running out when filling. Pipe the mixture onto a parchment-paper-lined cookie sheet, placing a dab of the mixture under each corner to hold down the paper. Pipe the mixture in 4-inch circles in a spiral motion toward the center. Hold the tip a quarter of an inch off the paper to control the thickness, and leave quarter of an inch open spaces between the spirals.

4. Bake for two minutes. Turn the cookie sheet around and bake an additional three minutes or until golden brown. Remove from the oven. After about 45 to 60 seconds, while they are still warm, form them around a 20-inch-by-1 1/4-inch thick wooden dowel in a tube shape or other rolling pin (dowel should be suspended from work surface in some fashion—have this ready prior to baking). If the cookies are too hard to form into cannolis, place them back in the oven for 30 seconds and repeat the process. Carefully remove the cannoli shells from the dowel—they will be fragile. Shells can be made ahead and stored in a covered container in a cool and dry place.

5. Make the filling: Reduce the bourbon, zest, sugar, currants, and cherries in a nonstick pan, stirring until almost dry. Cool in the refrigerator. When cold, add the mascarpone and mix with a rubber spatula. Add the pastry cream, mix, and then add the Grand Marnier and mix again. Fold in the whipped cream, making sure not to overmix.

6. Place the mixture in the pastry bag with a round tip, approximately #18, and fill the cannoli shells.

7. Dip the ends of the filled shells in the pistachios and dust the exterior with confectioners' sugar. Garnish the plates with dried cherries.

SERVES: 4

Grapefruit and Grapefruit Sorbet with Coriander in Gin Syrup

This citrus maceration provides a subtle surprise for even the most sophisticated palate. Wayne Nish concocts a warm syrup infused with cracked coriander that he finishes with a shot of gin. The majesty of this sweet and sour composition rests in its simplicity.

SORBET:

- 1/4 cup sugar
- 1/2 cup water
- 3 cups freshly squeezed grapefruit juice, including fruit pulp
- 1/4 cup Campari
- 1 teaspoon egg white
   pinch of kosher salt

GRAPEFRUIT AND SYRUP:

- 6 large ruby red grapefruits, skin and pith removed
- 1 cup sugar
- 1/2 cup coriander seeds, cracked in a blender and tied in a cheesecloth
- 1/4 cup gin

GARNISH:

- 10 tablespoons black currants in syrup (Vavel or Krakus)
- 10 fresh mint sprigs

1. Make the sugar syrup: In a small saucepan, bring the sugar and water to a rapid boil, stirring constantly. Cool the syrup and cover with plastic wrap.

2. Finish the sorbet in a large mixing bowl by combining grapefruit juice and pulp, sugar syrup, Campari, egg white, and salt. Pour the mixture into an ice-cream maker and freeze according to manufacturer's directions.

3. Section the grapefruits, removing membranes, and squeezing the remaining membrane with your hands, saving 1 cup of the juice.

4. Make the grapefruit syrup: In a small saucepan, combine the sugar and grapefruit juice and boil over low heat, stirring, until the sugar dissolves. Cool to room temperature.

5. Place in a bowl the coriander seeds wrapped in cheese cloth and grapefruit sections. Add the syrup and infuse for 20 minutes at room temperature. Then add the gin and combine.

6. To serve, fan into a circle some macerated grapefruit sections on the bottom of a soup plate, pour some syrup over the sections, garnish each with a spoonful of black currants without syrup and a scoop of grapefruit sorbet, then top with a sprig of fresh mint.

SERVES: 10

Icky Sticky Coconut Pudding with Warm Macadamia Nut Rum Toffee Sauce

1/4 cup pitted dates, soaked in water for 15 minutes, then skins removed and finely chopped

1/2 cup shredded fresh or dry coconut

1 cup water

1 teaspoon baking soda

4 tablespoons unsalted butter (at room temperature), plus 1 tablespoon butter for the molds

3/4 cup sugar, plus sugar for the molds

2 large eggs

3/4 cup all-purpose flour

2 teaspoons baking powder

1/2 teaspoon vanilla extract

1/4 cup coarsely chopped macadamia nuts

WARM RUM TOFFEE SAUCE:

7 ounces light brown sugar

6 tablespoons heavy cream

8 tablespoons unsalted butter

1/2 teaspoon vanilla

3 tablespoons dark rum

1 pint tropical-flavored ice cream

One of the hallmarks of new Floridian cooking is its playfulness. In Southeast and Southern Florida, such food is frequently laced with rum or bourbon. Local tropical ingredients make this ambrosial pudding a perfect dessert to enjoy on the promenades and outdoor cafes of Miami Beach or at home on the patio. Eat your heart out with Miami's latest vice.

1. In a saucepan, combine the dates, coconut, and water, and bring to a boil. Remove from the heat; stir in the baking soda and reserve.

2. Preheat the oven to 350°F.

3. In an electric mixer, cream the butter with the sugar, little by little, until it is light and fluffy. Beat in the eggs, one by one. Gently fold in the flour and baking powder and then stir in the coconut mixture and vanilla.

4. Butter and then dust with sugar 12 small timbale molds (2-ounce, 2-inch diameter) or ramekins, or use one 7-inch bowl or souffle dish thickly buttered and sprinkled with sugar. Add the mixture and cover with buttered foil. Bake the puddings for approximately 20 minutes on a sheet pan until an inserted knife comes out clean.

5. While the puddings come to room temperature, increase the oven to 400°F. Lightly toast the macadamia nuts in a roasting pan for 6 to 8 minutes, or until golden brown.

6. Make the warm rum toffee sauce: Combine the ingredients for the sauce in a heavy pan and boil for 3 minutes.

7. To serve, unmold puddings onto each dessert plate, spoon the sauce over them, and cover with the macadamia nuts. Top with any tropical-flavored ice cream such as macadamia brittle, coconut, or banana.

SERVES: 6

Lemon Buttermilk Tart

This sweet-sour tart with candied lemon slices in the shape of a flower and creamy buttermilk filling is a soothing refresher for a hot summer day. The rich lemon color of the tart dotted with mint sprigs will dazzle any buffet table.

CRUST:

1¹/₃ cups all-purpose flour

2 tablespoons sugar

¹/₄ teaspoon salt

¹/₂ cup (1 stick) unsalted butter, cut into pieces

1 large egg yolk

1¹/₂ tablespoons cold water

POACHED LEMONS:

¹/₂ cup sugar

1 cup water

2 large lemons, (3 medium) sliced paper thin

FILLING:

³/₄ cup buttermilk

¹/₂ cup sugar

2 large eggs

5 tablespoons freshly squeezed lemon juice

¹/₂ teaspoon grated lemon peel

2 tablespoons all-purpose flour

GARNISH:

8 mint sprigs

1. Make the crust: In the bowl of an electric mixer, mix the flour, sugar, and salt. Add the butter until the dough looks like coarse meal. In a separate small bowl, whisk the yolk and the cold water to blend. Pour yolk mixture over the flour mixture and blend with a fork. Form the dough into a ball and flatten into a disk. Cover in plastic wrap and refrigerate for 1 hour.

2. Remove the dough from the refrigerator and roll on a lightly floured hard surface into an ¹/₈-inch-thick round piece, approximately 10 inches in diameter. Place the dough in a buttered and floured 9-inch-round tart pan with a removable bottom. Trim the edges, reserving the remaining dough. Freeze the crust for approximately 30 minutes until firm.

3. Preheat the oven to 350°F.

4. Make the poached lemons: In a saucepan, bring the sugar and water to a boil and poach the lemon slices for 2 minutes. Remove from the liquid to dry on a rack for several hours. Gently remove the pits.

5. Weight the pie crust with aluminum foil and dry beans or something comparable. Bake for approximately 12 minutes until the crust is golden. Cool and use the dough trimmings to fill in any cracked areas.

6. Make the filling: In a large stainless-steel bowl, whisk the buttermilk, sugar, eggs, lemon juice, and peel to blend. Then stir in the flour, pour the filling into the crust, and bake for 25 to 30 minutes or until the filling sets. Cool.

7. To serve, arrange the lemon slices, starting from the outside of the crust in a circular motion until you reach the center. Slice the tart into 8 pieces and place each mint sprig in the upper-left portion of the slice.

SERVES: 8

Lemon Poppyseed Minis

11 ounces cake flour

11 ounces sugar

1 1/2 teaspoons baking powder

2 teaspoons poppy seeds

2 teaspoons lemon zest

3 ounces milk

13 ounces unsalted butter, softened

6 large eggs

3 teaspoons vanilla extract

SYRUP:

1/2 cup freshly squeezed lemon juice

5 ounces sugar

1. In a bowl, mix the flour, sugar, baking powder, poppy seeds, and lemon zest. Reserve. In the bowl of an electric mixer, mix the milk, butter, eggs, and vanilla. Beat for 1 1/2 minutes on medium speed. To the dry ingredients, add 1/2 of the milk mixture, scraping the bottom of the bowl to avoid lumps. Then incorporate the remaining milk mixture.

2. Preheat the oven to 325°F.

3. Fill twenty-four 1 1/2-inch buttered muffin tins a third of the way full with the batter. Bake for approximately 25 minutes or until the cake pulls away from the side of the tin. (There will be enough batter left for a 9-inch cake, or for 48 more minis.)

4. While the minis are baking, make the syrup by placing the lemon juice and sugar in a saucepan and cooking over medium heat until all the sugar is dissolved and the mixture is hot. Stir with a wooden spoon.

5. Remove the cakes from the oven and brush with lemon syrup while the cakes are in the tin.

6. Let cool a little. Remove from tin and finish cooling on a wire rack.

YIELD: 72 minis or 24 minis plus one 9-inch cake

AUTHOR'S NOTE: If making a cake also, coat the bottom of a springform pan with butter, pour in the mixture, and cook at 325°F for approximately 50 minutes.

Lemon and poppyseeds have a natural affinity for one another. Refreshingly light, these moist, golden miniatures will be the hit of any dessert tray. The eggs and the cake flour—a low-gluten, soft wheat flour sifted to an extra-fine texture—make these minis irresistibly delicate.

Maple Charlotte in Charlotte's Web

MAPLE MOUSSE:

3/4 teaspoon powdered gelatin

1/4 cup cold water

3/4 cup Vermont maple syrup, Grade B

2 cups heavy cream

1/3 cup chopped walnuts

2 tablespoons unsalted butter

30 ladyfingers (see page 198)

1/4 cup apple jam

SAUCE:

2 1/4 cups milk

1 cup granulated sugar

3 tablespoons ground espresso coffee

9 egg yolks

RASPBERRY PURÉE:

1 cup fresh raspberries

up to 1 cup granulated sugar

GARNISH:

1/2 cup whipped cream

8 mint leaves

8 raspberries

4 walnuts, shelled and halved, crystallized with sugar (optional)

Set in a restored 1860 house at the foot of Vermont's Killington Mountain, Hemingway's makes dessert charlottes all year around. Drizzled with raspberry and espresso sauces, this charlotte incorporates maple syrup, which is plentiful throughout New England, where horse teams still bring maple sap to sugar shacks for processing. Maple charlotte is a worthy indulgence of which even E. B. White, author of the children's classic, Charlotte's Web, *would be proud.*

1. Make the maple mousse: Dissolve the gelatin in the cold water. In a saucepan, bring the maple syrup to a boil. Remove from heat and add the gelatin mixture to it. Stir and then cool to room temperature. Whip the cream and fold into the maple mixture until well blended. Fold in the nuts.

2. Butter 8 individual ramekins (3 inches in diameter). Vertically line with ladyfingers around the ramekin to the height of the rim. Spread apple jam between the ladyfingers for a styled design. Ladle the maple mousse into the lined ramekins and refrigerate for 2 hours. Even out the top with a knife.

3. Make the sauce: In a saucepan, place the milk and half of the sugar and bring to a boil. Add espresso grounds and cover. Steep for 10 minutes. Place the egg yolks and remaining sugar in a bowl and whisk until fluffy. Add the coffee infusion and return all into saucepan, stirring over low heat until the sauce coats the back of a spoon. Strain and immediately set the pan into a bowl of ice and water. Stir until cool.

4. Make the raspberry purée: In a blender, mix the raspberries and sugar until smooth. Strain through a sieve and pour into a squeeze bottle.

5. Place a few spoons of espresso sauce on a dinner plate and lightly coat the inside rim. Beginning from the center of the plate, drizzle a spiral pattern with the raspberry pureé on top of the espresso sauce. With the tip of a knife, make 8 straight lines from the center of the sauce toward the outside of the plate, to create a "spoked wheel" effect. Between each "spoke" make new lines from the outside to the center of the plate to create a web.

6. Invert the charlotte from the ramekin and place in a corner of the web pattern. Garnish with the whipped cream, the mint leaf, a raspberry on top of the charlotte, and a walnut half on the web to look like a spider.

SERVES: 8

Milk Chocolate Caramel Crème Brûlée

The inspiration for this dessert derives from the dual American love of milk chocolate and crème brûlée. Milk chocolate complements caramel well, as evidenced by the American population's other great affection: chocolate-covered caramels.

1½ cups milk
1⅓ cups heavy cream
½ cup granulated sugar
¼ cup water
¾ pound milk chocolate, chopped
4 large egg yolks

TOPPING:
½ cup light brown sugar
½ cup pure cane sugar

1. Preheat the oven to 325°F.

2. In a saucepan over medium heat, bring the milk, cream, and 2 tablespoons of the sugar to a boil. Reserve in the pan.

3. Make the caramel base: In a separate saucepan, mix the remaining sugar with ¼ cup water and cook over medium heat until the sugar becomes golden caramel, approximately 20 minutes.

4. Slowly temper by adding ⅓ of the milk mixture and carefully whisking into the caramel until well mixed. Return all into the milk mixture and boil again.

5. Place the milk chocolate in a metal or stainless-steel bowl. Pour the milk mixture over the chocolate and whisk until the chocolate is dissolved. Cool approximately 45 minutes over a bowl filled with ice water.

6. In a stainless-steel bowl, whisk the egg yolks and then add a small amount of the chocolate mixture to the egg yolks. Whisk slightly and return to the mixture. Strain through a fine sieve and pour halfway into 6 shallow 4½-inch-wide Pyrex or ceramic round ramekins.

7. Bake the custard in the oven for approximately 1¼ hours in a hot water bath, poured halfway up the ramekins until the custard jiggles. Remove the ramekins from the water bath and cool at room temperature. Refrigerate for at least 1 hour covered with saran wrap.

8. Mix the light brown and pure cane sugar in a bowl and sprinkle with a shaker or sifter to create a medium coating over the custard. Spread evenly or the sugar will burn on top. Glaze under a broiler for 1½ to 2 minutes or use a propane torch to caramelize the sugar to a dark golden color.

SERVES: 6 (6-ounce portions)

AUTHOR'S NOTE: When you temper the caramel with the milk, an explosive reaction can occur. Whisk carefully. Use a heavy-bottomed pot for the caramel to prevent scorching. It prevents direct contact with heat. Use a stainless-steel bowl since, when cooling, stainless steel transfers the heat better, while glass and plastic insulate.

Pear "Tatin" Gratin

2 tablespoons unsalted butter

1/2 cup granulated sugar

8 Bosc pears, cored, peeled, halved lengthwise

2 teaspoons minced candied ginger

CUSTARD:

2 large egg yolks, room temperature

1/2 cup granulated sugar

1/4 cup unbleached all-purpose flour

1 cup milk, scalded

3/4 cup heavy cream

1 teaspoon pure vanilla extract

1/2 cup mascarpone

GARNISH:

confectioners' sugar for dusting

This wonderfully paper-thin caramelization on top of a crustless pear tatin is heaven on earth. The mascarpone cream adds a light custard taste that blends well with the mellow tender pear.

1. Make the caramel: In a large cast-iron skillet, melt the butter over medium heat. Add the sugar and stir constantly with a wooden spoon until the sugar melts. Lower the heat and continue stirring while the butter and sugar gradually darken to a rich brown color (approximately 10 to 15 minutes). Remove from the heat and continue to stir for a few minutes.

2. Arrange the pear halves, cut sides down, on top of the caramel. Sprinkle the minced ginger over the pears, cover with aluminum foil, and bake until the pears are soft, about 20 minutes for ripe pears and about 45 minutes for hard ones. Cool and bring to room temperature until ready to serve.

3. Preheat the oven to 475°F.

4. Make the custard: In the bowl of an electric mixer, whisk the egg yolks approximately 5 minutes at a medium speed until the yolks turn light and pale. Add the sugar gradually, beating well after each addition. Fold in the flour and beat until smooth.

5. Pour the hot milk into the yolk mixture in a slow, steady stream, beating constantly until smooth. Place the mixture in a saucepan over medium heat and cook, stirring until the mixture comes to a boil. Boil for 2 minutes, then remove from the heat and transfer to a mixing bowl. Bring to room temperature and refrigerate, covered, until well chilled, for at least 1 hour.

6. In a separate bowl, whisk the cream and vanilla until thick.

7. Whisk the chilled yolk mixture until smooth. Place the mascarpone in a large bowl, add in the yolk mixture, and then gently fold in the whipped cream. Chill covered with plastic wrap until ready to use. The custard will keep for up to 2 days.

8. Place 1 heaping tablespoon of mascarpone custard in 8 individual 4-inches-round and 1 1/2- inch-deep shallow, ceramic dishes. Top with 2 pear halves each, 1 to 2 tablespoons of the caramel, and an additional 2 to 3 tablespoons of mascarpone custard to cover the pears.

9. Place the gratin dishes on a baking sheet and bake on a middle rack in the oven for approximately 5 to 7 minutes, until the custard is heated through. Remove from the oven.

10. Caramelize the gratins for about 1 to 1 1/2 minutes under the broiler. Serve at once dusted with confectioners' sugar.

SERVES: 8

Pineapple-Banana Napoleon with Bitter Orange Relish

NAPOLEON SHEETS:

1/2 cup water

1/4 teaspoon salt

7 tablespoons unsalted butter

1/2 cup all-purpose flour

4 eggs plus 1 beaten for egg wash

SYRUP:

1 cup water

1 cup sugar

1 cup vanilla bean and scrapings

FRUIT SORBET:

1/2 pineapple, peeled and cored

1 banana

3 oranges, juiced

1 1/2 lemons, juiced

ORANGE RELISH:

4 navel oranges, pith removed, rind finely chopped

4 cups water

1/2 cup sugar

Acclaimed American chef Alessandro Stratta presents this delicate construction of pastry layered with an ambrosial combination of fruit sorbet and orange relish. Although the classic French napoleon dessert consists of flaky sheets of puff pastry and cream, this lighter version, lower in fat, is a noble inspiration worthy of an emperor's table.

1. Preheat oven to 350°F.

2. Make the Napoleon sheets: Bring salted water and butter to a boil. Over low heat, whisk in the flour until the moisture rolls off the bottom of the pan. Whisk in the eggs one at a time until incorporated by placing in the bowl of an electric mixer. Line 3 sheet pans with parchment paper and pipe out (with a small #3 tip) 24 Napoleon designs, 5 inches by 3 inches, in a zigzag pattern. Brush with an egg wash. Bake approximately 15 minutes. Remove with a metal spatula to another flat surface.

3. Make the syrup: In a saucepan, boil the water, sugar, and vanilla bean and its scrapings. Remove from heat and discard the vanilla bean.

4. Make the sorbet: In a food processor, purée the fruit and add the orange and lemon juices and the syrup mixture. It will take approximately 5 minutes to achieve a liquid consistency. Freeze in an ice cream maker. If unavailable, chill and freeze in the metal tray without the dividers. Remove from freezer after the mixture hardens. This will take approximately 30 minutes. Take a fork and move back and forth. Return to freezer and repeat the procedure three times.

5. Make the orange relish: In a medium saucepan, bring the orange rind and water to a boil; remove from the heat and strain out the water. Return the orange to the saucepan and repeat the process two times. Cover with the remaining cup of water and sugar. Cook on very low heat approximately 1/2 hour until the orange rind softens. Add the water as needed due to evaporation. (Relish is finished when rind is chewy and candied. It will remain bitter, but should also have a hint of sweetness. Mixture will be dense, with a slight amount of liquid.)

6. To serve: Take 3 of the Napoleon sheets and sandwich two 4-ounce scoops of sorbet between them. Place on a plate with 4 teaspoons of orange relish drizzled around each Napoleon.

SERVES: 8

Souffléed Lemon Custard

1/2 cup unsalted butter

1 1/2 cups sugar

6 large eggs, separated

1 cup fresh lemon juice

2/3 cup all-purpose flour, sifted

1/8 lemon, zest, finely chopped

2 cups milk

1 cup cream

pinch kosher salt

GARNISH:

1/2 pint raspberries

8–10 mint sprigs

This lemony dessert has a soupy consistency on the bottom and a luscious cake on top. Garnished with a sprig of mint surrounded by a bed of raspberries, this custard has enticed and satisfied Bostonians for years.

1. Preheat the oven to 350°F.

2. In the bowl of an electric mixer, cream the butter and sugar approximately 8 to 10 minutes until fluffy. Add the egg yolks one at a time and continue to mix. Add the lemon juice, flour, and zest until just barely combined. Stir in the milk and cream until smooth. Add a pinch of salt.

3. Beat the egg whites in the bowl of an electric mixer until soft-medium peaks are formed. Fold into the custard mixture. Pour the custard mixture into a greased 10-inch square cake pan. Bake in a *bain marie* for 50 minutes to 1 hour or until the custard is just set. Cool to room temperature.

4. Place a heaping spoonful of the souffléed lemon custard in the middle of a plate, surrounded with a few raspberries. Top with a mint sprig.

SERVES: 8–10

Stareos

COOKIES:

1 cup cold unsalted butter

1/2 cup sugar

11/2 cups all-purpose flour

    pinch of salt

1/2 cup cocoa powder, sifted

FILLING:

1 cup mascarpone

1 tablespoon granulated sugar

1/4 teaspoon vanilla extract

A star-studded gourmet Oreo with a luscious mascarpone cream is snuggled between two delicate chocolate shortbread cookies. This sophisticated cookie represents America's particular affection for its heritage and reverence for chocolate.

1. Make the chocolate shortbread: In the bowl of an electric mixer, combine the butter and sugar using the paddle attachment. Mix on a low speed for 15 seconds. Add the flour, salt, and cocoa powder, and continue mixing on a low speed for 3 to 5 minutes, until the dough attaches. It will look dry just before it comes together.

2. On a lightly floured work surface, roll out the dough a quarter-inch thick. With a 2-inch star cutter, cut out 36 cookies and place on a baking sheet lined with parchment paper. Chill them in the freezer for 1 hour.

3. Preheat the oven to 250°F.

4. Bake the shortbread for about 1 hour, until firm. Remove with a spatula when cool.

5. Make the filling: In a small bowl, combine the mascarpone, sugar, and vanilla extract.

6. To assemble: Spread 1 tablespoon of the mascarpone cream filling in the center of each of the 18 cookies. (For a neater presentation, place filling in a pastry bag and pipe out.) Put the remaining uncoated cookies on top of the creamed cookies, making a sandwich.

YIELDS: 18 cookies

Summer Fruit Gratin

This tangy champagne gratin is meticulously crafted with a colorful display of baked fruits, including deep purple boysenberries and majestic magenta raspberries, which are larger and softer than the red variety. Any appealing combination of similiar fruits will work as long as they are ripe. The foamy sabayon sauce adds an ineluctable smoothness to this ambrosial dessert.

CHAMPAGNE SABAYON:

5	large egg yolks
5	tablespoons granulated sugar
1/2	cup plus 2 tablespoons champagne
7/8	cup whipping cream

FRUITS:

3	peaches, peeled, pitted, and thinly sliced into 1/4-inch pieces
6	apricots, with skin, pitted and sliced
1	basket boysenberries
1/2	basket raspberries
1/2	basket black raspberries
2	tablespoons granulated sugar, depending on the sweetness of the fruit
1 1/2	teaspoons kirsch

1. Make the champagne sabayon: Prepare a water bath by half-filling a medium bowl with ice. Place the eggs, sugar, and champagne in the bowl of an electric mixer over a pan half-filled with boiling water. Whisk until the bubbles are very fine and the mixture holds a shape when a spoon is drawn through it. Immediately place the bowl in the water bath and chill, whisking occasionally. Whip the cream in a separate electric mixer bowl until soft peaks form, and fold into the sabayon. Chill.

2. In 6 gratin dishes sized 5 3/4 inches wide by 1 inch high, arrange a layer of peaches and then the apricots. Divide the berries among the dishes and sprinkle with the sugar and kirsch.

3. Preheat the oven to 350°F.

4. To serve, place gratin dishes in the oven on a sheet pan and cook 10 minutes or until the fruit is heated through. Remove from the oven and divide the sabayon among the dishes, spreading to cover the fruits as evenly as possible. Place under broiler approximately 2 minutes to brown the top. Serve hot.

SERVES: 6

White Chocolate Truffles with Pistachio

1¹/₂ pounds white chocolate, cut into small chunks

8 tablespoons unsalted butter, cut into small chunks

³/₄ cup heavy cream

¹/₄ cup orange liqueur

4 cups pistachios, shelled and unsalted

2 cups chopped bittersweet chocolate

*O*nce the closely guarded secret of French confectioners, these pistachio-studded white chocolate truffles can now be the crown jewels of any after-dinner repast. White chocolate is high in butterfat and does not require the addition of much cream. Pistachios provide a crunchy contrast to the silky-smooth center.

1. Place the white chocolate and butter in a large stainless-steel bowl.

2. In a medium heavy-bottomed saucepan, place the cream and liqueur and bring to a boil. Pour over the chocolate and butter and mix with a plastic spatula until smooth. Place the mixture through a strainer, pressing through any chocolate that does not dissolve. Cover with plastic wrap and refrigerate for a few hours until cool but not hardened. Remove from refrigerator and beat on medium speed approximately 10 minutes until light and fluffy.

3. Place the mixture in a pastry bag and using a medium-sized tip, pipe 1-inch truffles onto a baking sheet lined with parchment paper. Refrigerate until firm, approximately 2 hours.

4. Preheat the oven to 325°F.

5. Place the pistachios on a sheet pan lined with parchment paper and bake in the oven until toasted, approximately 10 to 15 minutes. Cool and place in a food processor until medium chopped. (Do not chop to a paste.)

6. Place the chopped bittersweet chocolate in a large stainless-steel bowl. Place the bowl over the bottom pan of a double boiler, stirring occasionally until the lumps have been removed. Do not let the mixture get too hot. Cool a little.

7. When the truffles are firm, remove from the refrigerator and, with a fork, roll in the melted bittersweet chocolate. Then roll each with your hands in the chopped pistachios until coated. Place each truffle on a tray lined with parchment paper and refrigerate for at least 20 minutes until the chocolate hardens.

YIELD: 50 truffles

185

Vanilla Wafer Cookies with Zinfandel-Marinated Raspberries

VANILLA WAFER COOKIES:

  2 egg whites

  1/2 cup plus 1 tablespoon sugar

  3/4 stick sweet butter, melted

  1/2 teaspoon vanilla extract

  1/2 cup plus 1 tablespoon all-purpose flour

ZINFANDEL-MARINATED RASPBERRIES:

  1 1/2 cups fruity zinfandel

  7 tablespoons sugar

    Three 1/4-inch orange rind strips

    Two 1/4-inch lemon rind strips

    pinch ground cinnamon

  3/4 cup water

  4 black peppercorns

  6 cups raspberries

CHANTILLY CREAM: (Yield: 4 1/2 cups)

  2 1/4 cups heavy whipping cream (not ultra-pasteurized)

  1 teaspoon vanilla extract

  1 1/2 tablespoons sugar

    small pinch of salt

Exciting textural combinations are exhibited here with a fruity zinfandel sauce spiced with sweetened orange and lemon rinds and raspberries. This European tradition of combining black pepper and red wine creates the perfect counterpoint to the vanilla wafer. The crunchy wafer also contrasts well with the fruit and velvety cream.

1. Preheat the oven to 350°F.

2. Make the vanilla wafers: In a stainless-steel bowl, whisk the egg whites and sugar until just blended. Whisk in the melted butter, vanilla extract, and then the flour until well incorporated.

3. Line two baking sheets with parchment paper. Using the back of a tablespoon, spread 1 tablespoon of batter in thin, even circles 4 inches in diameter (use a 4-inch metal ring as a guide). Repeat the procedure, making 8 circles on each papered sheet pan. (Make a few extra wafers, since they break easily.)

4. Bake the wafers in the oven's middle rack for about 5–8 minutes until golden brown. (The wafers burn quickly.) Cool, remove with a thin flat metal spatula, and wrap them airtight.

5. In a small saucepot over high heat, combine the zinfandel, sugar, orange and lemon rinds, cinnamon, water, and peppercorns. Bring the liquid to a boil, lower heat, and simmer for 20 minutes. Remove from the heat, cool, and strain the liquid. Pour the sauce over the raspberries and marinate for 30 minutes.

6. Make the chantilly cream: In the bowl of an electric mixer, place the cream, vanilla extract, sugar, and salt, and whisk the cream on a high speed until the cream holds its shape. Refrigerate, covered, until ready to use. (If it separates, whisk again when ready to use.)

7. To serve: Place a wafer on each plate, top with raspberries (8 to 10 each), a few tablespoons of the zinfandel liquid, some chantilly cream, and top with another wafer.

SERVES: 8 (2 wafers per person)

AUTHOR'S NOTE: Be careful not to overwhip the cream. Keep it soft. Make sure to use granulated sugar to sweeten chantilly cream, otherwise the cornstarch in powdered sugar will give it a chalky taste.

Fundamentals

Brioche

2 tablespoons fresh cake yeast (or 1 table-spoon powdered)	1 tablespoon kosher salt
1/4 cup warm water	5 tablespoons white granulated sugar
2 1/4 pounds bread flour (half all-purpose and half high-gluten flour)	10 large eggs
	1 1/3 pounds European sweet butter (Plugra) cut into bits

This buttery brioche can be baked in either a loaf pan or in brioche molds and is highly versatile. It can be used for French toast, bread and butter pudding, hors d'oeuvres, grilled vegetable club sandwiches, and feasts of artistic improvisation.

1. In a small bowl, dissolve the yeast by stirring in warm water.

2. In an electric mixer, blend together the flour, salt, sugar, eggs, and dissolved yeast with a dough hook. This should take about 4 minutes.

3. Add the cold butter and continue blending until the lumps are removed. Place the dough in a plastic container twice as large as the dough with an airtight lid. Chill overnight in the refrigerator.

4. Cut the dough in half. Place the dough on a flat work surface and roll into 2 logs the length of the loaf pans (3 1/2 inches high by 3 1/2 inches wide by 14 inches in length; or use a regular loaf pan). Cover with plastic wrap and let the dough proof in a warm spot in the bread pans, turning the pans once so they are evenly proofed. This should take approximately 2 hours.

5. Preheat the oven to 350°F.

6. Bake the breads for 30–40 minutes, turning once halfway through the cooking time, until the breads are golden brown all over. Remove the loaf pan from the oven or the loaves will lose their shape and retain too much moisture. Place on a cake rack, cool, slice, and serve.

YIELD: 2 loaves

SUSAN McCREIGHT LINDEBERG

Chicken Stock

3 1/2 pounds chicken bones	1 carrot, peeled and chopped
2 1/2 quarts water	1 garlic head, peeled
2 medium white onions, peeled and halved	2 bay leaves
4 celery stalks, chopped	8 black peppercorns

1. In a large stockpot, place chicken bones and cover with water. Add onions, celery stalks, carrot, garlic, bay leaves, and bring to a boil. Add the peppercorns, then simmer for 2 hours and strain. Cool the liquid for 1/2 hour. Skim off the fat. Refrigerate.

YIELD: 1 1/4 quarts

AUTHOR'S NOTE: This basic stock can be made in advance and frozen for soups and sauces.

Crème Anglaise

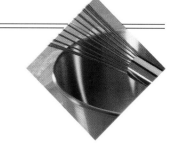

1 quart half-and-half cream
1 cup sugar

10 egg yolks
2 vanilla beans and scrapings

1. In a small pot, boil the cream. Whisk in the sugar, yolks, vanilla bean, and scrapings until the mixture coats the back of a wooden spoon. Strain.

2. Place sauce in an ice bath until ready to use.

YIELD: 2 cups

MARK MILLER

Crème Fraîche (Mexican Crema)

1 cup heavy cream (preferably unpasteurized)
1 cup buttermilk

1. Make 2 hours in advance: In a saucepan, heat the cream over low heat, but do not over-heat. Remove from the heat and pour into a container.

2. Add the buttermilk and stir, cover with cheesecloth, and place overnight in a warm location (75°F) to set to a loose consistency. (If any mold develops, discard the entire mixture.) Store refrigerated in a clean covered container. (It will keep for at least one week.)

YIELD: 1 cup

AUTHOR'S NOTE: The classic rich-flavored crème fraîche is made with unpasteurized cream. This American version requires the addition of buttermilk for the fermenting process to thicken the cream.

This heavy cream cultured with buttermilk has a slightly tangy and nutty flavor. Often used with Southwestern food, the crème fraîche cuts the spicy reaction from a dish with peppers. Whipped with a little sugar, it makes a satisfying topping for any chocolate cake.

Crêpes

3 large eggs

1/8 teaspoon salt

2 cups minus 2 tablespoons milk

2 teaspoons vegetable oil

1 cup all-purpose flour

1/2 cup melted butter, for the pan

1. Beat the eggs and salt with 1/2 of the milk. Add the oil and slowly add the flour while whisking constantly. Add the rest of the milk and whisk to combine.

2. Heat a flat 8-inch-bottomed skillet to medium heat. Cover the bottom of the pan with melted butter, removing any excess. When the butter is almost smoking, pour a scant 1/4-cup of batter to form thin pancakes, moving the pan around to cover the bottom. The batter should just coat the bottom of the pan. Cook approximately 1 minute, turn, and cook on the other side for 30 seconds until golden brown. If flipping the pancakes over, hit the pan against the stove to loosen. Remove to waxed paper sheets until ready to use.

YIELD: 15

ALLEN SUSSER

Dried Candied Orange and Lemon Zest

1 large orange

1 large lemon

1/2 cup sugar

1 cup water

1. Peel the orange and lemon rinds into long strips, preferably with a zester, excluding the white pith. If using a paring knife, cut the zest in very thin strips about 1/8 inch wide.

2. Place the zest in a small saucepan and cover with water. Bring to a boil and cook for 3 minutes. Drain in cold water and repeat the process.

3. Make the simple syrup: In a small heavy saucepan, combine sugar and 1 cup of water. Over low heat, dissolve sugar, stir occasionally. Increase the heat to high and bring to a boil. Submerge zest in the syrup. Poach uncovered over medium heat for 20 minutes until tender and syrup thickens. Cool the zest completely in the syrup.

4. Drain the zests on paper towels. Place loosely on a sheet pan, and cook at 150°F for 1 hour.

YIELD: 30 pieces

Duck Confit

One 4-pound duck

3 tablespoons coarse salt

1 teaspoon freshly ground black pepper

3 thyme sprigs

3 bay leaves, crumbled

4 cups olive oil

1. Cut the duck into 8 pieces. Reserve the neck, wings, and the backbone for stock.

2. Rub the duck with the salt and place in a roasting pan large enough to snugly fit the duck pieces in one layer. Sprinkle with pepper, the remaining salt, thyme, and bay leaves. Cover and refrigerate for 6–12 hours, turning the duck pieces occasionally.

3. When ready to cook, wipe the excess salt from the duck pieces. Heat the oven to 300°F. Place the duck pieces, skin-side down, back in the dish and cook on top of the stove over low heat for 15–20 minutes, or until the fat runs and the duck browns lightly.

4. Add enough olive oil to cover the browned duck, and cook in the oven for 2 hours, or until the duck is very tender and has rendered all its fat.

5. To preserve the duck, pour a layer of rendered duck fat in the base of a small terrine and set. Pack the pieces of duck on top and pour over enough fat to cover them completely; cover the terrine and refrigerate at least a week for the flavor to mellow.

6. To serve, remove all the fat and herbs from the duck and serve according to your specific recipe.

YIELD: 4–6 portions

This splendid and flavorful recipe originated in Gascony, a region in southwestern France known for such other delicacies as foie gras and magret, the chewy breast of fattened moulard duck. The tradition of cooking and storing duck in its own fat in earthenware pots derived from the Moors, who once passed through this part of France.

TODD ENGLISH

Egg Pasta Dough

2 cups all-purpose flour

1/4 teaspoon salt

3 large eggs, mixed

2 tablespoons oil (90% olive, 10% vegetable)

1. In a large mixing bowl, combine the flour and salt by hand.

2. In a separate bowl, lightly beat the eggs and then mix the eggs with the oil.

3. On a hard surface, place the flour and make a well in the center. Place the eggs into the center and, using your hands, work your way from the inside out until the eggs are fully incorporated with the flour to make a ball. In a stainless-steel bowl, place the dough, cover with plastic wrap, and rest for 20 minutes.

4. Use a pasta machine or knead the dough on a lightly floured work surface by hand until firm and smooth. Let the dough rest for 15 minutes.

5. Run the pasta through a pasta machine 4 times, making sure that the dough is very smooth and elastic and thin. If a machine is unavailable, make the pasta as thin as possible by rolling a floured rolling pin back and forth over the pasta on a floured work surface, turning the dough over from time to time.

YIELD: 1 pound

Fish Stock

5 pounds fish carcasses

1 cup celery, finely chopped

1 large white onion, peeled and chopped

2 bay leaves

1 fresh thyme sprig or $1/2$ teaspoon dried leaves

2 fresh parsley sprigs

1 fresh tarragon, rosemary, or chervil sprig, or $1/2$ teaspoon dried leaves

$1^1/2$ teaspoons salt

1 gallon water

1 cup dry white wine

1. Submerge the fish carcasses in cold water while removing the gills from the heads, scraping away any blood from the backbone. Rinse in water 2 or 3 times.

2. In a soup pot, place the celery, onion, bay leaves, herb sprigs, and salt. Add 1 cup of the water to cover, and sweat the mixture over low heat for 10 minutes.

3. Add the fish carcasses and remaining water and bring to a boil over high heat. Lower the heat to a bare simmer. Skim any scum off the surface, avoiding any floating vegetables or herbs. Simmer, uncovered, for 20 minutes. Add the wine and simmer another 20 minutes. Remove from the heat, let sit for 5 minutes, then carefully ladle all the stock into a fine strainer over a container. Do not press down on any fish in the strainer. Pour the remaining stock through the strainer into a bowl and discard the debris. Cover the stock with plastic wrap and refrigerate until ready to use.

YIELD: 1 gallon

Flour Tortillas

2 cups all-purpose flour	$^1/_2$ teaspoon sugar
1 teaspoon baking powder	1 tablespoon vegetable shortening, cold
$^1/_2$ teaspoon salt	$^1/_2$–$^3/_4$ cup warm water, approximately

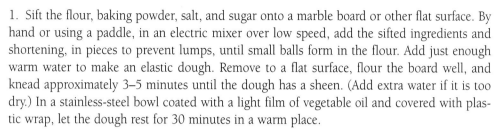

1. Sift the flour, baking powder, salt, and sugar onto a marble board or other flat surface. By hand or using a paddle, in an electric mixer over low speed, add the sifted ingredients and shortening, in pieces to prevent lumps, until small balls form in the flour. Add just enough warm water to make an elastic dough. Remove to a flat surface, flour the board well, and knead approximately 3–5 minutes until the dough has a sheen. (Add extra water if it is too dry.) In a stainless-steel bowl coated with a light film of vegetable oil and covered with plastic wrap, let the dough rest for 30 minutes in a warm place.

2. Cut the dough into 1-ounce balls approximately 2–2$^1/_2$ inches in diameter. Remove some flour from the board. Flatten the dough balls with a rolling pin, starting from the middle out into $^1/_8$ inch-thick round pieces. Separate the tortillas with waxed paper.

3. Cook the tortillas on a hot griddle about 2 minutes or until the edges are lightly browned. Turn and cook on the other side for about 1 minute or until the edges are browned. Tightly wrap in foil and keep warm if serving right away, or reheat, tightly wrapped in foil, at 300°F for about 10–15 minutes until heated through.

YIELD: 10–12 tortillas

Popular fare in Mexico and the Southwest, flour tortillas are most versatile and, when filled, are called tacos. *Fried into smaller wedges, they make excellent tortilla chips.*

Game Sauce

1 teaspoon unsalted butter	1 teaspoon garlic, minced
2 finely chopped shallots	1/4 cup brandy
1/2 teaspoon crushed black peppercorns	4 cups quail stock (see game stock below)
1/2 bay leaf	2 cups red wine
zest and juice of 1 orange	1/3 teaspoon finely chopped fresh rosemary
pinch ground clove	4 drops apple cider vinegar

1. In a saucepan set over medium heat, melt the butter and cook the shallots, crushed peppercorns, bay leaf, orange zest, ground clove, and garlic. Over medium-high heat, cook until the shallots are lightly caramelized. Deglaze with good brandy and reduce by half. Add 4 cups of quail stock (see game stock below), the red wine, and the orange juice, and reduce until the sauce is thick enough to lightly coat the back of a spoon, adding more stock, if necessary, to adjust the final consistency. Strain through a fine chinois or strainer. Season to taste and finish with finely chopped fresh rosemary and apple cider vinegar.

YIELD: 5 cups

AUTHOR'S NOTE: Serve with wild mushroom risotto (page 95).

Game Stock

This game stock recipe can be used to make veal, beef, or lamb stock by following the same procedure using the meat of your choice. For a richer stock, simply simmer the stock until it is reduced by two-thirds.

5 pounds game (duck, quail, pheasant, etc.) parts: carcass, backs, wings, feet, necks	3 celery stalks, washed, coarsely chopped
vegetable or olive oil	2 bay leaves
5 quarts water	2 fresh thyme sprigs or 1/2 tablespoon dried ground thyme
1 large white onion, peeled and coarsely chopped	4 parsley sprigs
1 medium carrot, peeled and coarsely chopped	1 teaspoon whole black peppercorns

1. Preheat the oven to 400°F.

2. Place game parts in a roasting pan coated with the oil. Roast for approximately 45 minutes, until they are crispy. Remove the bones to a large soup pot and drain off excess fat from the roasting pan. Add 1 cup of water to the roasting pan and remove the bits in the pan over the burner by moving the bits with a wooden spoon. Place this liquid and bits in the soup pot and then cover the bones with water.

3. Add the vegetables, herbs, and peppercorns and simmer, uncovered, for 3 hours. Strain the stock, cool, and then refrigerate, covered, until needed.

YIELD: 1 gallon

Lamb Stock

2¹/₂ pounds lamb bones

1 cup white wine

1 large yellow onion, peeled and chopped

2 carrots, peeled and chopped

¹/₂ bunch celery, chopped

1 small garlic bulb, cut in half, stemmed, and rough-chopped

1 tablespoon olive oil

¹/₂ cup tomato paste

1¹/₂ teaspoons black peppercorns

¹/₂ bay leaf

1 tablespoon fresh thyme

1 fresh rosemary sprig

2 gallons water

1. Preheat the oven to 425°F.

2. Roast the bones until well-browned. Remove the bones and place in a 1-quart stock pot. Discard the grease, pour the wine into the roasting pan, and heat to deglaze. Add this liquid to the stock pot.

3. Meanwhile, in the roasting pan, toss the onion, carrots, celery, and garlic in the olive oil and roast at 425°F until sweated. Stir in the tomato paste and continue cooking an additional 10 minutes. Place in the stockpot. Add the peppercorns, bay leaf, thyme, rosemary, and water. Cook on low to simmer for 5–8 hours (or for full flavor, 24 hours), skimming occasionally. Strain and return to heat and reduce by half, skimming occasionally.

4. Cool in an ice bath and refrigerate uncovered. When the fat layer forms, remove. Refrigerate covered until ready to use.

YIELD: 3 quarts

Lemon-Dill Pasta

1 pound all-purpose flour

4 large eggs

4 tablespoons olive oil

4 tablespoons chopped dill

pinch of salt

juice and zest of 1 lemon

1. In an electric mixer, using the dough hook, mix the flour, eggs, and olive oil for 5–7 minutes. Add the dill, salt, and lemon juice and zest to incorporate.

2. Wrap the ball of dough in plastic wrap and refrigerate for 6 hours.

3. Roll the dough on a floured surface with a rolling pin or bottle of wine and shape according to your recipe.

YIELD: 1 pound

Ladyfingers

5 large eggs
1/2 cup granulated sugar
1/2 cup all-purpose flour, sifted

This recipe is actually a "biscuit" recipe, meaning that the yolks and whites are whipped separately. In a genoise, the eggs and sugar are warmed and whipped together.

1. Preheat oven to 350°F.

2. Separate the yolks and whites of the eggs. Pour half of the sugar into the yolks and whisk in electric mixer until fluffy and ribbonized, approximately 5 minutes. Remove to a stainless-steel bowl.

3. In a clean bowl of an electric mixer, beat the egg whites on high speed until they form soft peaks. After they begin to fluff, sprinkle with the remaining sugar and whisk until stiff. Fold the egg yolks into the whites with a plastic spatula. Pour the sifted flour on top and incorporate gently by hand.

4. With a #4 tip, pipe onto parchment paper on cookie or baking sheet into 2-inch vertical strips approximately 1/2 inch thick.

5. Bake for 5 minutes or until golden. Remove from parchment paper with a spatula and serve.

YIELD: 30 ladyfingers

SANFORD D'AMATO

Pastry Cream

1/2 cup milk
2 tablespoons granulated sugar
1 egg yolk

1/2 tablespoon cornstarch
1/8 teaspoon vanilla

1. Bring the milk and 1 tablespoon of sugar to a boil in a small noncorrosive pot.

2. In a separate bowl, whip egg yolk with the rest of the sugar until lightly colored. Slowly whisk in the cornstarch, the hot milk sugar mixture, and the vanilla.

3. Return mixture to the pot and continue whipping while bringing it up to a boil so that the mixture does not stick to the bottom. Boil for 30 seconds and place in a clean bowl. Cool. Cover loosely with plastic wrap and refrigerate.

YIELD: generous 1/2 cup

Pico De Gallo (Spicy Red Salsa)

1/2 white onion, peeled, 1/4-inch dice	2 tablespoon cilantro, finely chopped
2 large red tomatoes, peeled, cored, seeded, and chopped	1 tablespoon lime juice
2 garlic cloves, peeled, finely chopped	1 tablespoon good quality olive oil
1 jalapeño pepper, finely chopped	kosher salt to taste

1. In a medium bowl, combine all the ingredients. Stir, marinate, and chill for at least 30 minutes. Cover with plastic wrap and refrigerate until ready to serve.

YIELD: 2 1/2 cups

Pizza Dough

CHILI AND GARLIC OIL: (or olive oil)

1 whole head garlic, peeled and cloves separated	1 package active dry or fresh yeast
2 cups olive oil	1 teaspoon honey or sugar
1 tablespoon chili flakes	3/4 cup warm water (105–115°F)
	2 3/4 cups all-purpose flour
	1 teaspoon salt

1. Make the chili and garlic oil: In a small saucepan, combine the garlic cloves and olive oil and bring to a boil. Reduce the heat and simmer approximately 10 to 15 minutes until the garlic turns golden brown. Cool and add the chili flakes. Place in a small bowl and infuse for at least 2 hours. Refrigerate until ready to use.

2. In a small bowl, dissolve the yeast and honey in 1/4 cup of the warm water. In a mixer fitted with a dough hook, combine the flour and the salt. On a low speed, add 2 tablespoons of the chili and garlic oil and, when absorbed, add the yeast. Add the remaining 1/2 cup of water and continue kneading for about 5 minutes. Remove the dough.

3. On a hard, lightly floured work surface, knead for an additional 2 or 3 minutes, until the dough is smooth and firm. Place in a stainless-steel bowl, cover with a damp towel, and let rise in a warm spot about 30 minutes. (Dough will stretch when lightly pulled.)

4. Cut the dough into 4 sections with a sharp knife and form 4 balls, about 6 ounces each. Work each ball by pulling down the sides and tucking under the bottom of the ball. Repeat 4 or 5 times. On a smooth unfloured surface, roll the ball under the palm of your hand for about 1 minute until the dough is smooth and firm. Cover with a damp towel and let rest 15 or 20 minutes. Then loosely cover with plastic wrap and refrigerate for 1–2 days.

5. Preheat the oven to 525°F. Place each dough ball on a lightly floured surface, pressing down in the center to spread the dough into a 7- or 8-inch circle with the edge a little thicker than the center. Arrange the pizzas on a baking stone and follow pizza recipe of your choice, baking for 15–20 minutes. Remove. Slice with a pizza cutter on a hard surface and serve immediately.

YIELD: 2 medium pizza shells

At last, we have the secret to Wolfgang Puck's crispy pizza crust with a chewy inside. Chef Puck has been so successful in achieving perfection in his pizzas that they are sold in supermarkets nationwide, to great acclaim.

Roast Tomato Purée

GARLIC CONFIT: *(1 tablespoon)*
1/4 cup extra virgin olive oil
3 garlic heads, cloves separated and peeled

8 plum tomatoes, cored and quartered lengthwise
1 teaspoon thyme leaves
  coarse salt and freshly ground black pepper

This wonderfully perfumed roast tomato purée is made with infused garlic oil. The process described for making the oil takes the bitterness out of the garlic.

1. Make the garlic confit: Place the garlic cloves in a small heavy saucepan with the virgin olive oil and a pinch of salt. Cook over low heat just beneath a simmer for 45 minutes to 1 hour until the garlic is soft and crushes easily with the back of a fork. (Store it refrigerated in the oil.)

2. Preheat the oven to 300°F.

3. Make the roast tomato purée: Place the tomatoes on an oiled baking sheet. Using a fork, smear the tomatoes with the garlic confit. Season with thyme, salt, and pepper. Roast in the oven for 1–1 1/2 hours until the tomatoes are dry and very intensely flavored.

4. Cool the sheet pan to room temperature and purée the roast tomato in a blender until smooth.

YIELD: 1 cup

CHARLIE TROTTER / ANDREW MCLAUGHLIN

Sabayon

1 large egg
1 egg white

1/4 cup granulated sugar
1 tablespoon brandy or cognac

Sabayon, or sweetened egg yolks flavored with wine or liqueur, is a provocative addition to a bowl of blueberries, strawberries, and raspberries.

1. In a bowl over a pan of rapidly boiling water, whisk the egg, egg white, and sugar for approximately 10 minutes.

2. Add the brandy or cognac and continue whisking for 2 minutes.

YIELD: 1 1/2 cups

AUTHOR'S NOTE: Either use immediately or cool, refrigerate covered, and serve within 1 hour.

Salsa Fresca

2 tablespoons diced onions

2 cups tomatoes, seeded and chopped into
  1/2-inch cubes

2 serrano chilies, stemmed and finely
  chopped

2 tablespoons chopped cilantro

2 teaspoons granulated sugar (add to taste
  if tomatoes are not ripe)

1/4 cup Mexican dark beer

2 teaspoons salt

  juice of 1 lime

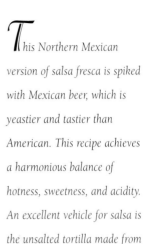

1. Place the diced onions in a strainer and rinse under hot water for 15–20 seconds to eliminate sharpness. Drain.

2. In a stainless-steel bowl, mix all the remaining ingredients with the diced onions. Macerate the salsa refrigerated for 30 minutes before serving.

YIELD: 2 cups

This Northern Mexican version of salsa fresca is spiked with Mexican beer, which is yeastier and tastier than American. This recipe achieves a harmonious balance of hotness, sweetness, and acidity. An excellent vehicle for salsa is the unsalted tortilla made from corn, cut into wedges, and fried.

Soy Mustard Sauce

SHOYU MUSTARD:

1/4 cup (hot) dry mustard

2 tablespoons warm water

5 tablespoons shoyu (Japanese soy sauce,
  preferably Yamasa)

BUTTER SAUCE: (beurre blanc)

1 cup white wine

1/4 cup white wine vinegar

3 tablespoons minced shallots

3 white peppercorns, crushed

1/2 cup heavy cream

1 pound cold unsalted butter, cut into 16
  pieces

  coarse salt and freshly ground white
  pepper

1. Make the shoyu mustard: Whisk the mustard into the warm water to make a smooth paste. Slowly stir in shoyu until mixture is smooth.

2. Make the butter sauce: In a heavy, nonreactive saucepan, combine the wine, vinegar, shallots, and peppercorns. Cook over medium-high heat until about 6 tablespoons of liquid remain. Add heavy cream and bring to a boil. Cook until the mixture is thick and coats the back of a wooden spoon. Remove from heat. Whisk in the butter, one piece at a time, adding each after the previous one is incorporated. Season to taste with salt and pepper. Strain through a fine-mesh sieve. Slowly add shoyu mustard to half of the butter sauce, adding just enough mustard to suit your taste. (Use the remaining butter sauce for another dish.)

YIELD: 1 cup

AUTHOR'S NOTE: Keep the butter sauce in a warm spot so it does not solidify.

Shellfish Essence

4 cups cooked lobster, crayfish, or shrimp
   shells

4 cups fish stock (see page 194)

1. Grind the shells in a food processor just enough to break them up. Place them in the bowl of an electric mixer fitted with the dough hook or paddle. Add 1 cup of the fish stock and mix on low speed until the shells are completely broken up into small pieces and the stock in the bowl is red, about 40 minutes.

2. Scrape out any remaining shells and the essence sticking in the bowl into a saucepan. Add the remaining fish stock, bring to a boil, and then simmer for 15 minutes. Strain completely, pressing down on the shells, reserving the liquid and discarding the shells.

YIELD: 3 cups

Tomato-Ginger Relish

1 cup red tomato, peeled, cored, seeded, and diced (3 large tomatoes)

1/2 cup minced scallions, green part only

1/4 cup minced Maui onion (may substitute Vidalia or Walla Walla)

1 tablespoon black sesame seeds

1 tablespoon white sesame seeds

1/2 tablespoon crushed black peppercorns

1/4 cup rice wine vinegar

1 tablespoon mirin (sweet sake)

1 teaspoon Hawaiian or other rock salt

1 teaspoon Thai fish sauce (nam pla, anchovy water)

2 tablespoons fresh minced ginger

1/4 cup peanut oil

*M*aui onions are sweet onions like Vidalias, indigenous to Hawaii, and Walla Walla onions are the sweet variety from Washington.

1. In a nonaluminum bowl, combine the tomatoes, 1/4 cup scallions, onions, black and white sesame seeds, black peppercorns, rice wine vinegar, mirin, salt, and Thai fish sauce.

2. Place the minced ginger and the remaining scallions in a small, heatproof bowl.

3. Heat the oil in a small frying pan over high heat until the oil is smoking. Pour the hot oil over the ginger mixture. Stir the mixture into the relish. Cool, cover, and refrigerate until ready to use.

YIELD: 1 1/4 cups

AUTHOR'S NOTE: Rock salt is available at any good supermarket. Mirin and nam pla are available at Oriental stores.

Sources

BONIATO
Latin markets

CORNNUTS
Potato chip and snack section of
most supermarkets

CHILIES, SOUTHWESTERN AND
INDIAN PRODUCTS, CORN HUSKS
("Coyote Cocina" line of products)
Coyote Cafe General Store
132 West Water Street
Santa Fe, New Mexico 87501
800-866-HOWL (4695)

Chile Guy (wholesale)
206 Frontage Road
Rio Rancho, New Mexico 87124
800-869-9218

Chinatown or Indian markets

DRIED BEANS AND LENTILS
Dean & Deluca
560 Broadway
New York, New York 10012
800-221-7714
212-226-6800

DRIED FRUITS, NUTS,
JAMS, WILD RICE
American Spoon Foods
1668 Clarion Avenue
Petoskey, Michigan 49770
800-222-5886

Earthly Delights
4180 Keller
Holt, Michigan 48842
800-367-4709

GAME MEAT
D'Artagnan
399-419th Paul Avenue
Jersey City, New Jersey 07306
800-DARTAGN

Broadleaf Venison
11030 Randall Street
Sun Valley, CA 91352
800-336-3844

GOAT CHEESE AND YOGURT
Laura Chenel's Chevre
1550 Ridley Avenue
Santa Rosa, CA 95401
707-996-4447

The Coach Dairy Goat Farm
105 Mill Hill Road
Pine Plains, New York 12567
518-398-5325
fax 518-398-5329

HERBS AND SPICES
Penzey's Spice House
1921 Southwest Avenue
Waukesha, WI 53186
414-574-0277

MANGO PICKLE
Indian markets (recommended brand
is Bedakar)

MUSHROOMS
Earthly Delights
4180 Keller
Holt, Michigan 48842
800-367-4709

Hans Johansson's Mushrooms
and More
P.O. Box 532
Goldens Bridge, New York 10526
914-232-2113

NEEM LEAVES AND
CHICK-PEA FLOUR
Indian markets

NEW ZEALAND AND
MANILLA CLAMS
Wild Edibles
255 Elizabeth Street
New York, New York 10012
212-334-1801

ORIENTAL PRODUCTS
Katagari & Co.
224 East 59th Street
New York, New York 10021
212-755-3566

SPECIALTY PRODUCE
AND GRAINS
Earthly Delights
4180 Keller
Holt, Michigan 48842
800-367-4709

Index